THE BEATEN PATH

A true story of survival

By Emily Matthews

A novel based on the journal of Emily Matthews

This edition first printed in December 2019

Copyright © 2019 Emily Matthews

ISBN: 978 0 473 50620 9

*For my baby boy, who gave me the strength to leave,
and for my beautiful Bessie who stood beside me.*

CONTENTS

ACKNOWLEDGEMENTS

As this novel is based on the true story of my life, names, places, and some situations have been altered to protect my friends and family.

Thank you to everyone who read advanced, unedited copies of this book, and offered me valuable feedback.

To my parents, brother, and sisters (I have two of them), who have allowed me to take facets of their personality and weave them into Maddie's family, alongside numerous other friends and extended family for giving me advice, and in some places their own selves as characters in my novel, how can I ever adequately thank you?

Special thanks to my dear friend who is an author of the pen name J.C. Hart, she gave me endless assistance, and herself features in my book as Maddie's best friend, Megan. Thank you for never giving up on me.

And my enduring love and devotion to my husband Sean, our son, and twin daughters, who hold my heart forever, until the end of time.

And Bessie, she who endured alongside me, and never left me by choice.

One last note, if you spot a spelling and/or grammar error, please keep in mind I am dyslexic, and have edited this myself with the use of Grammarly. I have done my best, but seem to always miss something!

You can contact me directly by emailing:
thebeatenpath@designem.co.nz

Cover photo by Nensuria of Freepik.
Cover Design by Emily Ramsay

THE BEATEN PATH
A POEM WRITTEN BY EMILY MATTHEWS

We loved once, and we made plans
of how our life should be.
I dreamed a life, a fairy tale,
our future clear to me.

I pictured a home with girl and boy,
a happy family.
But this thing we have is torn apart,
a painful parody.

Destined to be I thought,
but failed from the start.
Now it's all been faded,
can't mend my broken heart.

And every night together,
we lay here side by side.
Separated, so far apart,
if only I hadn't lied.

Once again, I lay the blame,
solely at my feet.
How can sanity rule my head?
When it's me, you beat.

Hide my bruises, and my shame,
no one else can know.
You taint me with your hatred,
so seeds of doubt can grow.

Still, I'm strong, I will survive,
I'll mend my crippled soul.
Piece together my broken heart,
and arise feeling whole.

CHAPTER ONE

Have you ever thought about what it might be like to live with Tinnitus? It's a constant high-pitched whine in your ears that never ceases. Living with anxiety is a lot like this; it never turns off. When you are living with a human time bomb, you have to be alert, every second, of every day.

I won't bore you with how a reasonably intelligent girl from a loving and supportive family got into such a crazy situation. Needless to say, this could happen to anyone who unwittingly places their trust in the wrong person. But now I'm here I am determined to steer this wreck I call my life back on course. I created this mess after all, with lies, deceit, and a misguided notion of how my life 'should' be.

I am on sitting on the couch writing; my script is hardly legible in my haste to get it all down.

'I hate that you have deceived me. This house we have moved into has become my prison, and you are the sentence carried out against me. This is my punishment for being such a bad person.'

I startle as I hear Mal round the corner. I throw my journal under the couch cushion and freeze like a possum in the headlights. I draw in a slow, uneven breath and try to steady my nerves as my mind starts racing to come up with answers to the hypothetical questions, I am expecting from him. Frantically I try to think of the right thing to say. Only the truth is nothing I say will be correct, but if I don't at least attempt it will just make things worse.

He stands over me as I cower and look away, I know better than to attempt eye contact.

"Writing slander about me again?" he spits.

"I'm just writing …" I trail off.

"It's SLANDER!" he states loudly stalking away.

I breathe out a sigh of relief and think to myself it's not slandering if it's true.

I must do better. I can't be caught writing at home again, although he's probably already read it. This last bit of me that I have left is being taken away, but it's OK I can fix this, I tell myself. I will leave my journal at work and keep it in my locker; that's the only place I have left where my things can be safe.

I glance at the clock on the DVD player; it's getting late. There is no longer anything on television worth watching, yet I'm still rooted to the couch. I know it's stupid, but I'm waiting until he decides it's time for bed. This is another aspect of my life that has changed. I no longer have the privilege of deciding when I can go to bed, I can't even go to the toilet without him accusing me of trying to leave him, and God forbid I get up before he is ready himself.

I am surprised there isn't a permanent indentation of myself on this seat since I spend so much time sitting here. I pull my legs up and hug my knees to my chest. I rhyme words together silently in my head, using poetry as a way of expressing feelings safely, playing around with several different ways to fit the words together before settling on an arrangement I'm happy with:

'Riddled with holes, I sealed my fate. This body can't hold this insidious weight.'

I listen intently for any movement from Mal before slipping my journal from its hiding place to jot it down. The sports news is ending as I hear Mal cracking his knuckles before leaning across the keyboard to shut the computer down. As I listen to the sounds of it clicking and whirling, I shove my journal back into its hiding place waiting for him to pass me before getting up and following him meekly, like a lamb to slaughter.

I tightly fold my arms across my chest as I stand at the entrance to the bathroom, waiting for my turn to brush my teeth. I look past him at the mould that's starting to creep up the walls. We don't speak, and he doesn't wait for me to finish washing before heading to bed. I take a little longer than necessary getting myself ready, and when I finally think it might be safe enough to go to bed too, I work hard to ease myself between the sheets as gently as I can manage.

I lie quietly for a few minutes listening to his slow rhythmic breathing, but just when it seems like it will be a smooth transition to sleep, he startles me by rolling over to face my back. I hold my breath as he stretches out his arms, reaching around my waist to pull me closer. He forces my legs apart with his knee and enters me. Trapped on my side, I shuffle slightly, trying to move into a more comfortable position, but I am dry, and his thrusting feels like sandpaper. I try to think of what it would be like to still be able to refuse the advances of sex but instead, my mind is flung back to how it was at the start.

My first sexual encounter with him remained burned in my memory so vividly I could still remember what it felt like days after. Thinking about it left me with a deep longing that I had never experienced before. I honestly thought it was a spiritual connection, that I was being compelled by some higher being to become bonded to him.

What's happening between us right now is a stark contrast to our shared past, but it doesn't take long before he shudders with his climax and rolls off me, pushing me away from him. I make my escape to the edge of the bed, where I press my legs tightly together and let silent tears escape down the side of my cheek, moistening my ear.

How could things have gone so drastically wrong so fast? I don't understand what has happened because it feels like just moments ago, we were enjoying life, holding hands and making each other promises. If only I'd looked closer, in hindsight there were warning signs. I was just so determined to make it work I ignored them all, making excuses for his behaviour instead.

I think back to the first time he lost his temper with me. It wasn't long after I had met him, and he offered to help me move my stuff back to Auckland. We'd had very little sleep, so it was easy to reason that his anger was triggered by exhaustion. At the time, I couldn't understand why he was so mad at me; I had never seen him like that before.

It was close to being the wrong side of midnight and I'd just gotten my cats out of my old place and put them in the truck we had borrowed from my Dad. I was paranoid that they were going to run off and that I'd never find them again. I was relieved when I managed to pick them up so easily. But Teddy hates cars, so after I shoved him in the back, he started to freak out. He jumped up into the window and stood on the lock button.

The moment he did it, I knew what he'd done. The auto-locking mechanism kicked in, and he had managed to lock himself and Tilda in the truck, along with the keys and our cell phones. Mal was livid; he alternated between cursing at the cats and me before punching the truck.

I don't know what I was thinking, why did I have to keep pushing in this direction? I suppose that I couldn't admit to myself that our lives were not going to be the fairy tale I had planned. He was just so beautiful to me in the beginning, he was everything that I ever wanted in a lover and partner, or so I thought.

I feel like a complete and utter idiot, I was trying to make things better and just ended up making them worse. Why do I manage to screw things up in my head? Of course, he's allowed to be in a bad mood, or have a bad day, right? I hope he won't be mad at me forever. I know I am just trying to justify his behaviour, but the optimist in me really wants to be right.

He sighs heavily and violently shifts his position in his sleep, breaking me from my thoughts. Once again, I fall asleep on a pillow wet with my grief.

CHAPTER TWO

My eyes flutter open slowly to focus on the yellowish-brown wallpaper. I stare at a section that's peeling for a good five minutes before I figure out where I am. My slumber has left me with a vague sensation of safety that I don't feel right now. I glance over at Mal sleeping next to me, with his brow devoid of anger, he looks peaceful. As he begins to stir, he throws his arm out towards me. I know my cue, so shuffle closer to him. He reaches around my body and holds me close, burying his head into my neck.

This is the best part of my day. It's the part before his words twist my insides. It's the time of the day I can still pretend everything is as I imagined it would be.

I really wish I could just lie still and enjoy this moment for what it is, but I'm conflicted. After what he did to me last night, I know I should push him away, run away and never look back. But I can't, I'm stuck here. To think my life has turned into this in only five months; so much has happened. It's almost like there are two of him, this man who I love and who loves me back, and then some other being, a darker one that I can't even begin to comprehend.

I already left one lousy relationship; I don't need to be in another. But I created this; I forced this, I wanted this, I left a husband for this. I have to make it work. I swear this isn't about trying to change him, he has changed me enough already, but I have invested so much into this relationship how can I step away and say I failed?

But as I lay here, I can pretend. It's easier to think back to a few short months ago when I lay in his arms, our faces inches apart; when he was still my perfect man with a beautiful soul.

Perhaps I should have taken his words as foreshadowing, *"I never want you to be scared of me Baby Girl,"* at the time I didn't understand what he meant. I thought everyone else must have got it wrong, I believed he would NEVER do anything to hurt me, and as I lay in his arms, I felt safer than I had ever felt. I was at peace and honestly thought that I had finally found my place in the world.

A tear spills over the bridge of my nose as thoughts of the other sweet things he said rush back to me, *"You are going to be such a wonderful Mummy sweetie. I can see it in you already; together we'll make amazing parents. Our children are going to be smart and gorgeous! Everything their Mummy is."*

I loved it when he spoke about what our future together would be like; it filled the void that had been steadily growing between my husband Justin and me over the last few years. The promise of a beautiful future, with everything I had ever hoped and dreamed.

I know I'm going to be late for work again, but those moments in the morning are the best part of my day. How can I give them up to go to work?

"We should get up," Mal says as he nuzzles into my neck.

"I know." Just a few minutes more.

But he pushes me away from him and grabs his towel off the back of the bedroom door heading towards the shower.

I pull my shirt and pants on and then take the opportunity to shove some food into my bag for the day. I survey the pantry and fridge, but there's not a lot of choices. Settling on a few packets of the reduced to clear porridge Mal has taken to buying and a muesli bar I find away in the back.

I decide to wait until work to eat my breakfast, so grab my bag and perch on the arm of the couch while waiting for Mal to finish getting ready. I glance for the sixth time at the clock wondering how much longer he is going to take. I was supposed to be at work 15 minutes ago.

"Get in the car," he commands as he passes me walking so fast, I must trot to keep up.

He drives at his usual pace, yelling the occasional obscenity at other road users, and finally, I arrive to work a little over half an hour after I should have started. That's better than usual.

I rush in the front door as fast as I can, I don't want anyone to look at me as my eyes are swollen from crying. I glance in all directions and try to steer clear of the customers who are already milling around, browsing racks of beauty products and woman's clothing. I almost make it when I am spot Amy's bright blonde hair heading in my direction.

Amy works in the woman's department, and although we are friendly at work, I haven't felt brave enough to think of her as a friend.

"Maddie, are you alright?" Amy asks as she makes a beeline towards me.

"Ah, yeah, yeah, I'm fine," I blurt out, trying to reign in my anxiety.

"Are you sure, hon? Your eyes are looking pretty swollen." Concern etches her face, her gaze intense.

I can't meet her eyes; I don't want her pity. "Oh, you know allergies; someone should really trim the trees at our place." I brush my hair self-consciously. 'Allergies' is my standard reply because I can't handle her asking me if I'm OK. I already know I look like crap because my hair is uncut and unwashed. I'd tie it up, but it's great for hiding beneath.

"Well, OK then hon," Amy says as her eyebrows knit together.

I doubt she believes me; I don't even believe in myself. I need to work on my acting skills. Lucky for me a customer is approaching us, so I wave goodbye and make my escape.

I hurry as fast as I can through the rest of the store; avoiding more awkward conversations. I dash past the men's section praying I don't run into Paul then make my way up to the office as fast as humanly possible.

Once safely at my desk, I finally feel like I can relax a bit. While I jiggle the mouse to wake up the computer, I glance at the pile of post-it notes on my desk. I run through the list of people to call, records that need checking, boxes that need crossing. But instead of the work, I should be doing, I reach down and pull my journal from my bag. I click my pen a few times before I start to write.

'Mal, I have loved you like I have loved no other, and that was real. But I feel the grip I have on my own life slipping away. I can't continue to live like this; why do you have to control everything I do? I told you I was scared of you, and I meant it when said I couldn't live in fear, I shouldn't have to should I? I cry because I have nothing else, I have lost everything of myself. I cry because I have no choice. I have to do what you say. I cry because I am scared and because I am sad ...' the words trail away.

I don't know why I am writing another letter to him. I'm not going to give it to him, am I? What happened the last time I did that? That's right; he accused me of slander. He told me that I was trying to twist his words, turning it all around and making it his problem. He got right up in my face, so close his spittle landed on my skin and screamed at me to stop writing lies about him. I shut the cover and slide it under a stack of unfiled reports.

I am still sitting staring blankly at my computer monitor when Adele bustles into the office, from the look of her she has been here a good hour longer than me.

Adele is salvation in my world of madness. I feel I can trust her with my secret, even though there are so many people in my life, I can't. She has had her past with an abusive man, but it's more than that. I think maybe her soft greying hair reminds me of my Grandmother who died years ago or perhaps it's just her honest, open smile. I can't say for sure, but I trust her.

"Good Morning, my Darling, have you had a hard night? You look a tad tired." She pats me on the shoulder as she passes, the smell of her takeaway coffee filling the air.

"Oh, you know the usual." I shake my hair forward and peer at my computer monitor. "Have you seen the reports for the outgoing e?" I ask her, hoping to change the subject.

Adele hands me a wad of paper, and raises her eyebrows, "You may be able to dig it out of this mess, but Paul has been here, so who the hell knows?" She shakes her head and chuckles softly.

We all have a soft spot for the flamboyant Paul, who spends most of the workday investing more energy into inventing reasons not to be working.

Paul is the only male in my life other than my Dad and Brother who Mal has never thought to accuse me of having an affair with, perhaps that's because Mal is convinced he is Gay. He moved to New Zealand from Canada after falling in love with 'Xena: Warrior Princess' so maybe there is some truth to that.

I sigh at the mess he's managed to leave and start to sort through it when my cell phone buzzes in my pocket. It's switched to silent, but I wish it were quieter as Adele's eyes flicker in my direction. She has guessed far more than I have ever let on about what goes on when I get home, and increasingly more frequently throughout the day it seems.

I pull it out and glance at the text. 'LATE FOR FUCKING WORK AGAIN!'

I text him back 'I'm sorry.' It is easier to accept responsibility than to point out that it's not my fault. I try to refocus on work, lucky for me Adele is an old hand at this job.

Occasionally she tells me stories about her past, and how she escaped her abuser, encouraging me to be strong and leave. I can barely verbalise what keeps me in this situation with Mal, but even though I could never admit it, I value her quiet support of me.

CHAPTER THREE

I stretch my arms out above my head and roll my shoulders as the end of the workday approaches. I've been distracted, thinking about Mal and the mess my life has turned in to. I've made so many trivial mistakes I've had to redo tasks that used to come so easy.

Adele walks with me to the lunchroom so I can place my journal in my locker. I don't want to leave it here; I want it with me. I want my journal close so I can write in it. At times I think it might be the only thing keeping me sane. It used to be my safe place to vent my frustration with my life, but now it's not safe at home anymore. I must leave it here.

She hugs me goodbye, "Take care of yourself, my dear. I'll see you tomorrow."

"I will," I promise before running down the stairs and heading into the cold.

Shivering in the chilly autumn air, I pull my jacket closer around me. Waiting inside would be warmer and preferable, but if I am not standing here by the kerb, it will lead to more issues, and we have enough of them already.

I strain my ears, hoping to hear the familiar sounds of my car's engine. 'My car' I repeat to myself; I can't remember the last time I drove it. I briefly think back to when I first bought it. I saved for months on end and entered a heated debate with my Dad to buy it.

Dad wanted me to buy this crazy ugly square thing which I would have been mortified to drive. He reasoned that it was newer and would turn a profit, but I wouldn't have a bar of it. My car had looked so clean, if not new. He was nowhere near new and wore snail eye wing mirrors, and as soon as I set eyes on him, I knew that 'he' was mine.

I named him Barney and swore I'd keep him forever. Some might think this is foolish, but in my head, I have a vision of a chicken coop or even a garden sculpture for his twilight years. I let out a snort of laughter at that immature and ridiculous thought, although it's incredible I can still find amusement in anything, enjoyment in all things has been sucked from my life.

Finally, I see him coming, and he pulls up to the kerb brakes screeching slamming the car to a halt. I pull open the door and slide myself into the passenger seat, sneaking a glance at him, trying to gauge what sort of mood he's in. From the black look, he gives a passing pedestrian. I can assume he has not had a good day.

"Why the fuck was he looking at you? Do you know him?" he questions me, eyes following the man crossing the road in front of us.

"Erh no baby; I have no idea who he is." Frayed nerves turn my stomach as I silently pray 'Please God just makes him be happy tonight.'

He merges into the flow of traffic in a jerky motion, causing me to grab onto my seat belt as I'm swinging around. I hold my breath; I'm always nervous in the car with him. He personifies the term road rage, and I pity every other driver who crosses his path.

It's a brief trip home, made shorter by the fact that sticking to the speed limit seems out of his capabilities.

"So many fucking cunts on the road, does no one know how to drive in this fucking city?" he shouts while illegally undertaking. "Remind me why the fuck I moved here?"

I'm pretty safe not replying in the car; he's not directing his anger at me, so I try to calm myself by diverting my mind. I read the street signs, the advertisement on the back of a bus and silently repeat the number plates of the cars we pass. If I get bored with that, I could always count the number of swear words he uses? Fuck really is quite a versatile word.

After pulling into our street, he parks the car haphazardly on our driveway. I wait for him to get out and then follow him inside. As I climb the narrow stairs up to the lounge, my insides start to twist. I do my best to follow his lead and try to stay one step ahead of him while carefully trailing behind.

He doesn't speak to me as he goes to the fridge and throws some meat and vegetables onto the bench; I fall in behind him, helping to prepare our dinner.

If there was a fly on the wall at this point, we could resemble any couple working together to create a meal for each other, but they only have to look a little closer to observe my irregular breathing and downcast eyes. Look closer still, and you might even see me navigating an invisible minefield. Of course, it won't take long for me to set one-off, and have it explode in my face.

With dinner eaten I carefully place my knife and fork on my plate, I am sitting on the couch, and even though he is at the other end of the room I can feel the tension brewing, so in an effort to dispel some pressure I attempt to wash the dishes. I get up slowly and move towards the kitchen, walking silently behind where he is sitting at the computer. He doesn't hear me until I start to run water into the sink.

"WHAT are you doing?" he says as he swings the chair around to face me.

"I thought I'd do the dishes?" I reply in a quiet voice.

Almost hysterically he shrieks "I DON'T want you NEAR me!"

Tears start to fall as I turn off the water and back away from him. I don't understand why he won't let me wash the dishes. How on earth am I ever supposed to keep up with his mood swings?

So, I sit back down, not out of respect for his wishes, but because I'm so well programmed to obey him. I don't want him to hurt me, so I do as I'm told.

I am a smart woman; I have a degree. I was raised in a kind, caring loving family. But I sit back on the couch and leave the dishes in the sink the same way I leave the laundry on the floor and do what I'm told. Everything in my life has given way to his control. I should always wait until I am commanded to do something, and endure his anger if I get it wrong, then berate myself that I haven't had the foresight to predict what he wanted.

There is a very good part of me right now that believes that it's me that is failing him, there must be something wrong with me. I can't do anything right; everything I do is wrong. I'm glad that the computer desk is hidden out of sight from my spot on the couch, so I have a measure of privacy. I pull my knees up and start to rock, trying to hold back the tears I feel threatening. I stay like that until he moves towards the bed and once again, I follow.

CHAPTER FOUR

When Mal's not yelling and blaming every wrong decision in his life on me, I have a lot of time to think about my past. And in bed long after he's fallen asleep, images of my husband start to surface.

Justin travels a lot for work which means there were long periods when I was alone. Of course, as a couple, we had people we spent time with, but we lived far away from my family and my friends, and often I felt like I had no support at all. I can't say for sure when I fell so far apart that I no longer knew how to put myself back together, but perhaps I was born that way, broken.

Sometimes I place the blame solely on my depression, isolation and loneliness, but it's not enough to justify my betrayal. At the heart of it, I suspect that is one of the things I have had the hardest time coming to terms with, that and I hate the thought that people who I once classed friends now label me a whore. But don't worry, I'm not about to sew a scarlet A to my chest, Justin played his part in our marriage failing too.

Staring across the expanse of our bed, I study him while he sleeps. He looks angry tonight even though he's in a deep sleep. I know nightmares torment him almost as frequently as he torments me, but how is that an excuse for the way he treats me?

Tears spill from my eyes, so many of my dreams have shattered; I hold my regrets close as sleep finally claims me.

I don't have time for breakfast, so I grab an extra sachet of porridge as I rush from the house to keep up with Mal. He held me again this morning, and as he wrapped his arms around me, tears filled his eyes.

"Baby girl, this house is bad for me, there is something bad here, and it's making me do such bad things." He holds my face and stares intently into my eyes as I try to puzzle out how he wants me to reply.

"Do you think we should move?" I ask, holding my breath, waiting for his reply.

"I don't know, but there is something bad here, and it has red eyes, I see it over and over in my dreams. Can't you feel it?"

His remark sends a chill right through me, and it's that feeling of ice and goosebumps that stays with me as I sit at my desk at work.

It doesn't seem to matter how long I look at my computer I can't seem to click my brain into gear.

I don't turn at the sound of the office door being pushed open, assuming it would be Adele coming back from her lunch break, but it's Leon, our boss. His tall, slender frame stands awkwardly in the doorway as he scratches at his receding hairline. It looks a lot like he doesn't know how to handle me.

I've had plenty of practice at this charade, so I plaster on a fake smile and shove a handful of reports that need signing off in his direction.

"I'm so sorry I didn't get these to you yesterday, but things just got crazy and …"

"Madeline, look," he interrupts me. "I don't want to escalate this, but you have to make a better effort to get here on time, OK?" He doesn't look comfortable delivering this news and as bad as I feel for him, I battle to hold my tears back.

"I'm really sorry, Leon, it's just my boyfriend, he insists on driving me and …" Tears spill over in heavy drops; now I'm just trying to prevent myself from hyperventilating.

Lucky for Leon and Me, Adele breezes back in. She smiles at both of us masking her look of sympathy much better than my attempt at holding myself together.

"That's OK, my lovely; she's got it! Clock in on time." Adele sends me a quick wink and Leon rolls his eyes.

I glance up at him as he leans down to give me an awkward pat on the shoulder, so I pass him up the reports. "I'll try to do better."

"OK ladies, I'll leave you to it," he tells us and bolts out of our office like his feet are on fire.

"Are you OK, Maddie?" asks Adele, she cocks her head to one side and examines me in a knowing and sympathetic way.

I sigh as I reach to grab a new stack of paperwork to input, giving myself a moment to rearrange my face into a smile. "Yeah, I'm OK," I reply. It's all I can manage.

An hour later, I finally build up the courage to broach the subject of evil spirits with Adele.

"Do you believe in ghosts?" I ask her.

She pauses her keyboard, tapping and leans back in her chair. "Yes, I do; why do you ask?"

"Oh, well, it was something Mal said a while back, and I, well I feel a presence in our house. It feels very oppressive." I hope that I don't sound batshit crazy.

"Hmm, well I did hear that one way to remove unwanted spirits was to repeat the Lord's Prayer in the four corners of your home. That should move them on." She looks so sombre that I resist the urge to laugh, but I'm desperate enough to try it.

"The Lord's Prayer," I repeat. "Ok thanks, Adele. I'll give it a try."

The first moment I get to try it without Mal's hawk-like gaze on me, I would try it, no matter how crazy it sounded.

"You know you can talk to me, right?" She asks after a short pause.

"I know; I'm just trying to figure stuff out."

The rest of the day passes quicker than I'd like. I remember the days where I'd stare at the wall clock in the office and the hands would barely move. Mum would say I wished my life away, and maybe she was right because time has grown wings.

Before I know it, I am saying goodbye to Adele for the weekend and back standing on the kerb waiting for Mal.

CHAPTER FIVE

It's early afternoon on Sunday and Mal has allowed me to do the laundry, rather than leave it to rot in piles all over the bedroom floor. It's a beautiful day and totally out of character with the chill winds we have had over the past few weeks. The sun is shining brightly in a picture-perfect blue sky. It's the type of day that would usually make me happy. But it's also a weekend, and weekends are torturously long for me. Mondays actually might be my favourite day of the week.

I find myself staring for far too long at the way the sun filters through the star-shaped leaves of the Sweet Gum tree in our yard. Half the washing is still lying limply in the basket at my feet. My dog Bess whines momentarily, and I shift my gaze in her direction.

"I'm so sorry my baby," I utterly quietly, I know she can hear me.

Looking nervously over my shoulder, I wander over to her and pat her on the head briefly. "I'm sorry baby," indeed I am, but I'm trapped, and if I make one wrong move, he will take it out on her. I squat down to her level, checking her mouth, last week he knocked out her bottom teeth. She whines once more almost inaudibly and pushes her big head towards me.

How can one man hold so much hate for everything? I heave myself to my feet and race back to the washing line. Bess sits on her haunches and watches me silently as I bend, lift and peg the wet clothes out. I step back and look at the five sets of bright red coveralls that Mal has taken to wearing. He says it's a work thing, but I think it's probably got more to do with his jeans not fitting.

Both mine and Bessie's heads turn in the direction of the driveway when we hear a car pulling into it. I pick up the now-empty basket and attempt to calm my breathing. I strain to hear over my thumping heart, trying to ascertain who the car belongs too.

I jump as Mal throws open the back door and takes a step towards us. Bess urinates on the concrete in fear as she starts to shake; she backs away under the deck steps. 'Good girl', I think. He's got us both so well trained.

He stands there, a foot from the back door and looks at me. Not sure what to do, I stay put and wait. There is no risking movement until I know what is expected of me.

"It's your parents," his eyes burn into mine, and I resist the urge to scrunch up my face. I make a move towards the house, and he takes a further step in my direction. "WHAT are they doing here?" he asks with a heavy emphasis on the first word.

"I don't know. I haven't spoken to them in a while?" What on earth am I supposed to say, my mind races ahead but I can't think why they might be here?

We can both hear them knocking as the sound travels from the front door. Our car is parked in the driveway is a sure indication we are home, and I doubt they will go anywhere until they have seen me. My stomach turns.

"Go and open the fucking door and for God's sake, do not let them step one foot into my fucking house."

I run at his command, dropping the basket in front of the washing machine. 'Please God,' I pray, 'please'. I am not sure what I am pleading for.

I race down the stairs taking two at a time, shivering as the cold air of the stairwell hits my sun-warmed skin and open the front door. I treat it like an unexploded bomb, peeling it back and counting down the seconds until my life implodes.

I shouldn't be so scared of opening the door to my parents, should I? They are the two people in the world who love me better than anyone else. This isn't' right.

Mum and Dad fill the doorway. They are both of a similar height and a hair's breadth taller than me. Dad looks at me, and for a second, I think I see fear and worry in his eyes. I think I recognised it because I see the same look in my eyes when I look in the mirror. We both probably reflect the same amount of sadness, anger and frustration. I don't blame him for looking at me like that, but I still can't let them in. Let them into my house, or my secret.

"Hey babe we thought we'd pop over for a visit," he announces, masking the look from his eyes.

"Did you know Rosemary's new boyfriend lives on your street?" my Mother pipes up. She smooths her hair flat and swings on the backs of heels as her gaze sweeps the houses surrounding us.

Dad slides his arm around her in a very uncharacteristic display of affection and pulls her back towards my front door.

"She didn't even mention she had a boyfriend," I tell them, feeling a little put out that my baby sister hadn't told me she was dating someone.

"Oh, she's been seeing him for a few months Madeline; I'm surprised she hasn't told you. She's at the can't-stop-talking-about-him stage."

"Oh, so you're here to stalk him?" I tease.

Something about being around my parents sparks my suppressed sarcastic nature. I give them a half-smile, which is mostly not forced.

A guilty look passes across both my parents' faces, but after glancing in each other's direction, almost in unison they announce, "No, we just thought we'd come to see you."

"We haven't seen you in a while," finishes Dad, then without waiting to be invited in they both brush past me. "Well, put the kettle on Maddie, we'll all have a nice cup of tea."

Mum hums Polly put the kettle on as I shut the door quietly and with a sigh of resignation follow them up the stairs. As I pass the couch, I grab my jumper and pull it on, any warmth I had soaked up outside earlier has been sucked from my body. Just remembering to breath has become labouring.

Mal is standing between the kitchen and what passes for our office space. We don't have a dining room table, so it's as good a place as any for the computer. With his arms folded across his chest, he does not look pleased.

He is glaring at my Dad, but after I shoot him a pleading look, he wipes his face clean, "Sam, Kate," he says nodding in their direction.

Dad looks at him and replies in an even voice, "Malcolm."

Mum looks pained, and I know I am mirroring it so quickly make a move to switch on the kettle. Maybe a cup in their hands will disperse some of the tension that is building.

"So, how's the new job going, Malcolm?" Mum says.

"Yeah, it's ok," he replies. "But it doesn't pay as much as when I was in Christchurch." He sends a pointed look in my direction. It's ok, I already know it's my fault he moved here and gave up a job that he now says he loved.

The room falls thankfully silent while the kettle boils. I hover over it nervously getting the teapot from under the bench and shoving in a few of the cheap tea bags we have stuffed at the back of the pantry. My family are tea drinkers, and Mal isn't, so I know they won't find this brand palatable.

My parents remain standing next to the breakfast bar, Dad's arms loosely around Mum's back. They are about three meters from Mal, and no one looks relaxed. Mal's arms are still tightly folded against his chest. I wonder if that's because he is trying to contain or protect himself, or maybe a little of both.

As I swirl the teapot around trying to hasten the brewing process, Mum says, "Your sister and I are getting our hair done next week, you should come to Madeline."

"What day is it?" I ask. Nope, I am quite sure he won't let me have the money for something a frivolous as a haircut. But I ask anyway.

"Thursday afternoon, we are going to that new place in the Mall."

I have no idea, as I the last time I went there was before Mal moved up to Auckland. It's a workday anyhow, relief floods through me to have a genuine excuse for not being able to go.

"Umm, I'm at work on Thursdays Mum."

"Oh, well, you know you're always welcome," she says.

Mal glares at her like she just asked me to run away with her.

As he swings his gaze back in my direction, Dad asks me, "How are you finding work? We popped in last weekend for a quick look around; I needed some new socks."

"We saw that Amy, what a lovely girl," Mum tells me as I pass them their mugs of tea.

Dad looked at the chipped cup and wrinkled his nose when he smells the tea's harsh aroma.

"Yeah sorry Dad, it's not Dilmah."

"Don't worry Babe," Dad replies, but I notice he doesn't make a move to drink it. Mum is a bit braver, or perhaps conforms more to social niceties as she politely sips hers. I've made Mal a coffee and hand him his cup last. He takes it and places it on the computer table. I already know it won't get drunk; I'm just hoping it doesn't end up on the floor.

"Erh yeah, Amy is lovely," I say, trying to keep the conversation in neutral territory. "Work's ok it's keeping me busy. What about you, Dad? How's work?"

Dad is happy to talk about his job, but the longer they are here, the thicker the tension gets. Mal makes no sign of moving, and my parents don't seem to want to go anytime soon.

"Uh, you said Rosie's new boyfriend lives on this street?" The moment the words leave my lips, I regret it. I can almost feel Mal's ears zeroing in on the word 'boyfriend'.

Mum starts rattling on about him, either ignoring or not noticing the death stare Mal is giving me. "Oh, we've met him a few times; he's a lovely boy, lovely family. I think you may have gone to school with him. Thomas Whittaker? He might have been your year. He's a few years older than Rosemary."

Dads face rearranges to slightly annoyed and marginally disapproving but adds, "He 'seems' like a nice boy."

"Thomas? Umm sorry, I can't remember." I'm lying; I remember Tom. I glance at Mal. Nope. Not going to start another argument about people I went to school with.

I start tapping my foot and gulp down my remaining tea, then glance at their cups. Mum's is half empty; Dad's is on the breakfast bench untouched. I run my hands through my hair and Dad coughs.

"We've got to go out soon," Mal announces. It's the first I've heard of any outings. I shrug in Mum and Dad's direction and hope they can take a hint.

"Well we better get the food shopping done Kate," Dad said to Mum, and I let out of a sigh of relief.

Some of my tension dissolves as I follow them both down the stairs and out the front door. It's been an awkward half-hour for all of us. Mum leans towards me slightly but stops short of contact. She pats me on the arm instead and says, "Come for dinner soon."

"Bye, Babe," Dad says. "We'll see you soon, OK?"

"Bye," catches in my throat, I can't say anything else, or I might risk a sob. I watch them climb back into their car and drive away from me.

I fight the urge to burst into tears, so much has changed. I shut the front door and lean my back against it, hugging my arms tight around my body and try to hold myself together.

I take a lot more time than necessary climbing the staircase back to the living room. I'm dreading the scene that I can almost guarantee is going to happen. I around the corner and take a quick peek. He is sitting at the computer with his back to me.

Taking a few seconds to decide what I should do; I walk towards the couch. I am almost there when he jumps from his seat and yells at ear piercingly volume, "WHAT THE FUCK ARE YOU PLAYING AT!" he rushes right at me pushing me to the floor.

CHAPTER SIX

He's standing right over me; his face bent down towards mine. The volume of this voice has decreased, but there is no love in it. It has a hard edge that feels like a knife cutting through my skin.

"I said what the fuck are you playing at Madeline? I TOLD you not to let your FUCKING FATHER into MY HOUSE! Why can't you understand and obey a simple request?"

His face is inches from mine, and I can feel his stale breath on my skin. Diverting my gaze from the insane look in his eyes, I try to defend myself, "I, they just came in. He wasn't listening to me."

"Too fucking right, they don't listen to you. Who would listen to you? Look at you!" he's still in my face, and I am starting to struggle to hold down the panic I feel.

"I'm sorry, I'm sorry," I start to sob.

"Does he really think he can intimidate me? What the fuck Madeline? Do you think I am scared of him? I'm not fucking scared of him. When I was overseas, I had to KILL people. I've had to gut people, and I've been made to watch other people get gutted, and if you think for one second, I will not do the same to your precious Daddy, then you are very much mistaken."

I stare at him in shock. Did he just threaten to murder my Dad?

"And I'll make you watch. Don't test me, Madeline. You won't win."

His voice is so calm and quiet by the end of this speech, and I do not doubt in my mind that he is telling the truth. My breathing accelerates as panic has me entirely within its grip.

But as I finally spin out of control, he walks away. What the fuck did he use to do in his last job? 'What the fuck. What the fuck.' I repeat it over and over until it slides into the Lord's Prayer. There has got to be a reason this is happening, maybe he is right? Perhaps there is some evil spirit possessing his soul.

I stay on the floor, chanting the Lord's Prayer over and over to calm my mind. I am so thoroughly involved with this task I am taken by surprise when I hear the front door slam so hard that the cups on the kitchen bench rattle, followed by the sound of my car screeching down the road. So, for now, I guess I'm safe.

With Mal gone, the first thing I do is check on my dog. She exited her hovel under the deck as soon as he pulled away in the car. I think she is more finely tuned to him than I am. My big girl Bess pushes her head between my legs, and I fall to my knees, wrapping my arms around her neck. She whines and shuffles closer to me. I am failing her; she deserves so much more than what I can provide.

I sob with my arms clutched around her, and as I hold her, I realise that her collar is far too tight. I release it, but it just makes me cry harder. His jealousy has expanded to include my animals, and it's heartbreaking for me.

How on earth are you supposed to deal with such a rabid animal? And no, I'm not talking about my pets. My cats and dog make way more sense than he ever does.

Tears start to fall again, and as they do, they land on Bessie's head. My animals are my rock, so for them, I pull myself together. I feed her what little food he allows me to purchase and then refresh her water bowl. I have work to do, and I must get it done before he returns.

I only feel slightly stupid as I stand in the left-hand corner of our bedroom. I stare at the bed as I start to say, "Our Lord, who art in heaven, hallowed be thy name." Growing up in a catholic school has paid off, at least I know the Lord's Prayer, and although I can't profess to have any real faith in an all-powerful God, I am desperate enough to try.

I repeat this in every room of the house, then repeat it just for good measure. I figure I might have just enough time to start searching for the cell phone I let him borrow a few months back, at least I'll hear the car and hopefully have enough time to run upstairs. He asked to borrow it weeks ago and then replaced it with a different phone that couldn't connect to the internet, telling me that I could text him 5000 times a month with it, so it was so much better. And yes, he expects all 5000 of them sent to him. But he refused to tell me where my phone was, and I gave up asking him.

I creep down the stairwell, glad that I took the time to pull on my jumper; it's cold and damp down here in the garage. I am vaguely overwhelmed when I look at his accumulated junk; the entire downstairs space is a haphazard array of boxes full of army clothes, boots, unused bookshelves, numerous car parts and god knows what else.

My eyes are drawn to the boxes of personal stuff he had brought with him from his last home, the boxes with 'DOM' written in thick black ink. These are the ones I am most interested in, but I don't think I will find my phone there, and I don't know how much time I will have. So, I start with the draws that are pushed up against one side of the garage, but after 15 minutes of searching, all I find are stacks of paperwork and more items of army clothing.

I rock back on my heels and rub my face with my hands. He's probably broken it and thrown it away; he knew it's the last present I received from my husband. When I lent it to him, I wanted to show him how much I loved and trusted him, and now it's gone. A lot like my trust in him.

I'm starting to feel anxious about how much longer Mal will be, and I don't want to risk him coming home and finding me snooping. I try to put everything back in the same order I pulled it out and headed back upstairs.

I sit back on the couch and pull out the book I am reading; if I'm lucky, I may get a good ten minutes of escape before he returns.

The light is starting to fade as he pulls to a stop outside. I shove my novel down between the couch cushions and brace myself for him.

I can hear him slam the front door and stomp loudly up the stairs. He throws open the door and walks in. As he passes me, he belches, and I notice he is carrying two plastic bags of what appears to be parts of a car. I don't comment on them, but as he is heading towards the kitchen, I get up and follow.

"Shall I make dinner tonight?" I venture. Wow, that was brave of me.

He looks up from examining his purchase and replies, "Yeah."

If that's all I am going to get from him I suppose that's a 'Yes', so I open the fridge and stare at the contents. I pull out the chicken and throw together a salad.

I make the entire meal without talking, and he continues to give me the silent treatment as I pass him his dinner.

"You smell like that fucking dog. Wash your hands for fuck's sake!" he says as he gives the plate a cautious sniff. "Should I even be eating this?"

"I washed my hands," I protest, I don't smell Bess on me, how can he tell? Maybe it's just an educated guess.

I am totally unprepared as he hurls his plate full of food towards the kitchen. I cringe as it whistles past my head and hits the counter. The plate smashes into two pieces with parts of his dinner, falling to the floor.

"Clean it up for god's sakes and then go wash your god damn hands! How stupid are you?"

As he turns away from me, he takes my plate off the bench, and I am left blinking at his back for a few seconds trying to figure out what just happened.

Closing my eyes, I turn towards the mess he made and squat to pick up the broken plate. I dump it in the trash and return for the food. I consider eating the Chicken right off the floor, but a shard of porcelain is lodged in the side, so my dinner follows the plate into the bin.

After cleaning as well as I am able, I click on the kettle and reach into the pantry for a porridge sachet. He doesn't comment as he eats my dinner, and I make myself breakfast cereal. That's lucky I suppose, he could have just as effortlessly told me I wasn't getting any dinner. I return to my spot on the couch and turn on the TV, and after easing a look around the corner to see where his attention is focused, I pull out my book.

When I am reading, I can forget myself for a while, as long as I am careful not to get caught. Mal doesn't like me reading; I'm not entirely sure if it's because he is against such time-wasting activities or it's just another way of controlling me. But if I don't keep my brain busy, I start to panic, feeling like I am suffocating, screaming, but the sound just gets stuck at the back of my throat.

The book drops to my lap as I stare blankly at the TV. Mal clears his throat, my eyes flicker in his direction, but I can hear that the computer has his attention. It's been a long day, and I am so exhausted my eyes drop closed as I relive my past.

CHAPTER SEVEN

I remember missing Justin like crazy during his first six-month absence. I hated him being away, but I knew it was part of his job. I had just started my degree, so I just channelled all my energy into studying. I didn't have that much spare time to feel sorry for myself, and I had yet to discover the youth drinking scene. I never once even considered seeking comfort in another man's arms.

The second time he left was an entirely different story. Six months felt like a lifetime, and with little to no contact with him, it was like we were living on entirely different planets. The first time I drank so much, I lost control of any judgement I possessed is a tarnish that followed me and tempered every decision I made from that point on.

On reflection, it's easy to see how depressed and vulnerable I was. But I broke my own heart right there, at that moment. And I promised myself it would never, ever happen again. I think I thought if I could pretend it never happened, I could continue as I always had.

But the guilt chipped away at my soul, and I felt like I couldn't tell anyone what happened. If I spoke about it, it would make it real. And if it was real, then there was something very, very wrong with me.

A solitary tear escapes and travels down my cheek. I brush it away with the back of my hand and feel the same old pain rip through me. I double over and bite the back of my hand to suppress a whimper. Having Mal catch me in a weak moment would make my pity party the event of the year.

Thinking of my Husband brings memories of my best friend. It was

Megan who first suggested I speak to my doctor about the possibility of me suffering from depression. I wonder what she would think of me right now. It wasn't all that long ago she told me that she thought Mal was a positive change in my life. Megan and I had lived together and been like sisters. She's seen me through some of the darkest most challenging times of my life, but I am too ashamed to let her in now. Let her in and tell her what a terrible nightmare my life has spiralled to become.

I once found strength in her, but I can't risk letting her in, too many people I care about are already in danger. So instead of reaching out, I tuck my book back between the cushions, pull my feet up onto the couch and hug my legs close to my body, gently rocking side to side. Whether I reach out or not doesn't matter right now, I can hear he's shutting the computer down. I follow him, even though I know what he will do to me after we get into bed. But I still can't call it rape. I'd have to tell him 'No' for it to be rape, wouldn't I?

Surprisingly for a Monday morning, we have made it out of bed early enough to have breakfast before work. Mal is eating at the computer desk with his back turned to me. I'm perched at the breakfast bar as my eyes shift nervously to my cell phone as it buzzes on the kitchen counter, holding my breath I stare at Mal's back. I have to get this under control, I can't let him see me react like this, or he will become more convinced I am cheating on him.

I curse the phones 'silent mode', it's nowhere near as silent as I need it to be, please don't let him hear it. He cranes his neck to look at me; his face pulled in flat disapproval as I grab the phone to silence it.

"Who's texting you?" he asks quietly.

Quiet Mal is not a good sign, why the fuck is this stupid phone not silent when I have silent selected!

"Uh, umm," I managed to stutter. But before I can unlock it and read the text, he grabs it from my hands. Pressing my lips together, I try to contain my panic.

I'm usually fastidious about deleting messages from my family. But I can't remember if I deleted the text message, I sent to my sister asking about Tom. I really must be mental; I can't remember anything.

He smoothly enters my passcode to unlock my phone and stares at it for a few seconds. I count my breaths in and out, looking doggedly at the floor.

"I don't' know who it is," I offer timidly.

"It's your nosey fucking sister." He throws the phone towards me as he turns back to the computer. "What the fuck does she want to see you for?"

"I haven't seen her in two weeks," I say defensively.

"She practically lives on this street now she has that boyfriend," he says, putting heavy emphasis on the last word. He shakes his head and throws his hands in the air. "Your god damn family can't leave us alone!"

"I just, she misses me, and I …"

He cuts me off, "Do I need to teach her a lesson? For god's sake Madeline, what the hell do you want from me? Tell her you'll see her later."

I unsteadily drag air into my lungs and nod. A slow tear travels out of my swollen eyes.

"What?" he barks at me.

"OK," I agree.

I look down at the phone in my hands and read the text from Rosie. 'R u @ work 2 day?'

I quickly type back, 'Yes, what's up?'

Her reply is immediate. 'Just want 2 talk c u @ 9.30 xx'

I sigh, 'OK, see you then.' risking a glance at Mal I delete the last messages and shove my phone as far into my bag as it can go.

Standing amongst the lingerie at work, doing my best to hide from customers, I pull out my phone and text my sister. 'I'm standing by the knickers, hurry up!'

"MARKO!" Rosie yells from behind me, and I swear I almost have a heart attack.

She looks radiant dressed in yellow and blue. Her ash blonde hair, the opposite colour of mine is cut into a bob and quite a bit shorter than I recall. She wraps her arms around me, and I instinctively hug her back, it's very reassuring.

"I thought you were getting your hair cut with Mum?" I ask.

"I am," she says, arching an eyebrow.

"But?" I gesture towards her hair.

"Oh, I cut it like this ages ago, didn't Mum tell you?"

"I'm out of the loop." Even though it's not their fault, I feel hurt that I didn't know. I love my baby sister to the moon and back. She's been doted on her whole life by our entire family, and even though it used to annoy the heck out me as a teenager, I have to admit to a fair bit of doting myself in the past. Her presence is a balm to my soul; every fibre of my being urges me to unload onto her.

I don't, though. I'm not brave enough to let anyone in my family understand how bad things are for me.

"What's up, little sis?" I ask as I pull away.

"Just missing you Maddie, I haven't seen you in nearly two months." She reaches out and tentatively touches my arm. "Mum wants you and Mal to come for dinner on Sunday. She's going to cook a roast and apple tart and custard. Honestly, I can't remember the last time she cooked a proper Sunday dinner, and she promised the gravy would be from scratch, not that disgusting packet stuff. Do you have any idea what a momentous occasion this will be? I'm bringing my camera and taking photos; this has to be put on all my socials Facebook, Instagram and Twitter!"

Wow, the girl barely pauses for breath before she continues. I'm wondering if it's her usual 'get it all out before you forget it' manner or if she's just afraid, I am going to say no. I suspect that she's also doing my Mothers dirty work.

"Anyhow, you'll come, right? I want you to meet Tommy." Her face splits into a radiant smile as she says his name.

"I can't believe you're dating Tom! He's got to be at least five years older than you."

"Boys my age are so immature Maddie. I promise you'll like him. Please say you're going to come?"

"I'll talk to Mal; I'm not sure if he's working." I can't give her an answer until I talk to him. I glance at my watch, "I've really got to get back to work."

She's not going to let me go without extracting some measure of promise from me. "You'll try, right?" she asks.

"I'll do my best OK." I'm not entirely sure I can follow through. But I'll try. "I'll see you on Sunday. I really do have to get back to work."

"Okay then," she says, giving me a chaste hug, more fitting for our family. "See you Sunday."

I watch her prance away, recalling memories of walking her to Primary school. No matter how hard Mum tried to keep her neat, she'd end up in scruffy clothes, mismatched shoes and hair in uneven pigtails. I can't help but love her.

Not immediately racing back to my office is a stupid rooky move because a customer is heading in my direction. Oh, crap too late, they've seen me.

"Hi Love, can you tell me where I can find some nighties?" says a harmless looking elderly lady.

"Umm, I think around here somewhere," I wave vaguely at the bras probably convincing her I am the world's worse employee. "I'm one of the office staff, but I can find someone to help you." I notice Amy and wave her over with frantic arm motions. "She wants nighties?" I say, looking at the customer hopefully.

I am becoming very forgetful. Lucky for me, Amy is my total opposite and guides the customer off with ease. I shake my head to try and knock some dust-out and make my way to the staff stairs as fast as my legs will carry me. If I'm lucky, Adele will still be on a coffee run, and my absence will be undetected.

By Lunchtime, I am sitting at a table in the staff room, my journal carefully placed in front of my bowl of porridge. Thinking about Rosie and her fledgeling romance with Tom has set me off thinking about my husband again. I begged him not to go that last time. I even as went as far as to tell his employers we were having marital issues. He was so mad at me, he wanted to go, and I was making it difficult for him to leave.

They arranged for us to see a marriage counsellor, but do you think he'd go? No. I ended up attending the sessions by myself; it's very hard working on your marriage when it's like you're the only person trying to make it work.

Obviously, I can't heap all the blame on him, but his long absences and his one-track obsession with threesomes took a toll on my mental health.

When I say he was 'one tracked' on threesomes, I mean he was obsessed with the notion. It was all he could talk about, and slowly, this man who I'd once spent hours upon hours talking to, became the ringing phone I was reluctant to pick up.

To my detriment, I never tried to discourage him or tell him how this was affecting me. But I would have rather drunk battery acid than admit to him I'd cheated. I thought if I could give him this, then we would be even, and maybe some of my guilt would go away.

It was a self-fulfilling prophecy that I should fall apart again in his absence. I went back to the doctor and begged for anti-depressants, but they didn't make me feel any better. I just wanted to feel numb, so picked up a bottle of wine and didn't stop.

What would I give to feel something other than guilt and fear?

I startle at the sound of the staff room door opening. "Hey Maddie," smiles Amy, who walks through the door closely flanked by Paul.

"What are you up too?" Paul asks, flinging the nearest chair around so he can sit on it back to front and still face me.

"Lunch?" I reply puzzled. They are up to something.

Amy eyes my bowl of porridge. "Lunch?" her eyebrows raise about

2 inches. They almost look as if they will fall off the top of her head.

I slide my journal closer to me and cover it with my arm and attempt to wipe some of the pain and misery from my face to smile.

Amy must have understood how uncomfortable they were making me as she quickly follows with, "We're just off to the bakery."

"Want to come with us?" says Paul. "I'm going to get the biggest doughnut they have!"

I have no idea where he puts all the food he eats; he's as thin as a willow. My first instinct is to shout 'YES' Yes, of course, I want to come, I want to be your friend and do the normal things workmates do. But I can't.

Mal and I had only been living together for a few weeks when it happened, the first real sign of his control issues. I had left in a hurry for work and brought myself a scone and coffee for lunch. When I mentioned what I'd had for lunch, he hit the roof. He raged at me, accused me of not putting our relationship first.

I thought that if I could get him to move up and live with me, everything would magically get better. And all the anger he was exhibiting would be erased. But it didn't, and he remained angry with me.

In a desperate attempt to prove to him that he did come first, I hurtled my cash card at him and told him he could keep it. He took it from me and placed it in his wallet, and I haven't seen it since. So, with a deep sense of sadness, I say, "Oh, my break is almost over, next time, maybe?" I hold my breath, tucking my journal under my arm and placing the bowl with my remaining porridge in the sink.

"Ok Maddie next time. Come on, Amy, my doughnut a-waits!" Paul grabs Amy by the shoulders and makes for the door, but she remains rooted to the spot for a few more seconds, just staring at me. Her lip is slightly pulled down, and she looks like she is going to say something. In the end, she smiles, offers me a small wave and leaves with Paul.

Relief floods me. I don't want people to know my secret shame. I don't want anyone to know how bad things are at home. When I am sure they have descended the stairs, I retrieve the remaining porridge from the sink and make myself another coffee. My journal is still tucked under my arm, so with a glance about I open it and read the words I had just written.

For five minutes, I had the sort of life I always wanted. I was happy, in love and had a bright future. I don't know when things started to crumble. It began like black tinges forming around the edges and dissolved into the nothingness of despair.

I feel like this is my punishment for being such a terrible person. I am scared. I am so afraid of making the wrong decision. I feel like I have completely fucked everything up. Mal has changed so much; he gets angry so quickly I feel like I can't do anything right.

The truth is, if he ever hit my Dad, I would leave him, and if he hurt him, I'd want him dead. He shouldn't be trying to make me choose between my parents and him, because even though he has become part of my family too, I would never betray them. No matter what, they are the ones who will always be there for me.

If he doesn't stop threatening me, I will have to leave. This is hurting me so much. I love my Father, he is my Dad, and he loves me. He only wants what's best for us. It's time he started accepting people for who they are. Not everyone is out to get him. I wish he could see this.

It kills me that I can't be honest with him anymore. That I must keep everything inside, and that I can't even attempt to explain how I feel because I'm too scared, he will overreact and take it the wrong way. I hate feeling like this and I can't let it continue.

My break is over, so reluctantly I put the journal in my locker and return to the office. How can I continue to live like this? What on earth has happened to my life? How on earth did this happen?

CHAPTER EIGHT

After finishing dinner in relative silence for once, he lets me wash the dishes. I stand at the sink, letting the warm water soothe my frozen hands. I focus on the way the water moves over them as I slosh the dishcloth over the plates. I wish my life were as easy to wipe clean.

I know I need to raise the subject of dinner with my parents on Sunday, but I don't know how I am going to bring it up. One thing is for sure; I can't tell him Rosie asked me to come, or that her new boyfriend will be there.

Minutes tick by, and I wash and wash the same plate until I could quite possibly erase the pattern from its surface.

The washing up is dried and put away before I pluck up enough courage to attempt asking him. It's on the tip of my tongue, but I'm finding it hard figuring out the right way to phrase it.

In the end, I manage a very quiet, "Babe." He doesn't move, so assuming he didn't hear me I try again "Babe?" still nothing. I bite my nails then shift the coffee container back to its correct place, then grab the dishcloth and wipe bench again.

Taking a deep breath, I attempt one more time to rouse his attention. "Mal." That does it; he swivels in my direction.

"What do you want?" he asks.

I stand there for a few more seconds looking like the idiot I am. "Umm, Mum spoke to me again today." Mal continues to say nothing, just staring at me with a dangerously expectant expression on his face. "I, well, she umm," *'Oh God'* I think to myself *'I AM an idiot.'* I can't even phrase a simple request to see my family without making myself seem incapable of speech.

"I'm not going to sit here all night waiting for you spit it out Madeline," he says as he starts to turn back to the computer. I ask as fast as I can before I run out of courage, and I lose his attention.

"Mum wants us to come for a roast dinner on Sunday. Please say we can go?" I wait a few seconds before adding "If we go there more often, they won't turn up here." I silently repeat *please* over and over in my head, hoping for a favourable response. If I could have gotten away with it, I would have crossed my fingers behind my back.

"I am not going to sit through another whole fucking dinner with your parents Madeline. If you want to go, then go. But there is no fucking way I am going." He doesn't wait for any further comment from me swivelling the chair towards the computer and continues to browse an online auction website.

I'm relieved, though, I think that's a yes. "Umm OK, I'll ask Dad to come to get me." He doesn't reply so I walk to my couch and collapse onto it like I've just completed a marathon.

The working week flies by too quickly. It's a rinse and repeat: Get a hug, get up late, go to work, input data, eat porridge, do more work, go home, eat dinner, get yelled at, feed animals, get yelled at again, go to bed, repeat. If I am careful not to think too hard, I can pretend I am a robot. In weaker moments I think of other people who could be in the same situation as me and wonder if they feel as stunned by it as I do.

I called Dad from the office phone and asked if he could pick me up. He wanted to know why Mal wasn't coming, but I just threw in a 'he has to work'. Dad agrees to come and get me, letting me know he'll arrive at 1.30 pm on Sunday on his way home from his fishing trip with his best friend.

At quarter past one I tell Mal I'm going to wait for Dad outside, he doesn't look overly pleased I am going, but he keeps his mouth shut for a change. The weather is starting to get colder so I keep my jacket as tightly closed as I can manage. The zipper is starting to fail, and I wonder how much longer it will last before it falls apart completely.

Thankfully Dad and his best friend Phil are prompt and pull into my street at exactly 1.30 toeing Dad's shiny new fishing boat. As I move toward the car, I look back at the house to see Mal standing at the bedroom ranch slider. Arms tightly crossed against his chest, sporting a frown that I know means trouble for me later; it triggers a deep sense of foreboding. There isn't much I can do about it right now though as Phil opens the passenger side window.

"Hop in trouble," he tells me. I scramble in quickly and shift along with the seat, so I'm out of Mal's disapproving gaze.

"All right babe?" asks Dad over his left shoulder.

"Yeah, I'm ok." I pull the seat belt around me and click it in place.

"You're looking very pale Maddie," says Phil, loosening his seatbelt so he can see me.

"I'm fine," I tell him.

He stays angled in my direction appraising me, making me wonder if my parents have spoken to him and his wife Elaine about me. Who am I kidding, of course, they have.

"Did you catch any fish?" I use distraction as protection, a proven technique with most men, men who aren't Mal anyhow. Thankfully it works.

"Oh Madeline, you should see the Snapper your Dad reeled in! To listen to him, you'd think he was dragging in a Great White." Phil dissolves into fits of laughter.

"Don't listen to him Maddie he is just sulking because he didn't catch anything bigger than a sprat."

I snort and tease them both, "Ah, so you both stopped off at the supermarket on the way home to prove your hunter-gather skills?"

"We did nothing of the sort," Phil says defensively, pushing what could be a supermarket chilly bag further under his seat.

"Sure, sure," I tell them both. "But just in case, my lips are sealed."

Maybe I should have phrased that differently because they both fall silent and the fun teasing atmosphere of moments before completely evaporates. I can't think of anything else to say, so I sit and stare out the window.

I read the street name on every sign we pass; I read the bus stop posters. It's a car travel habit that is both new and familiar. It's what I do when I want to step away from how crazy my life is and stop my brain from thinking dark thoughts I can't take back.

It's not long until we arrive at my parents' house. Phil hops out to help guide Dad as he reverses the boat into the drive. I stay in the car while he does it, covertly studying his face while he concentrates on sliding the boat into the correct position without taking out Mum's car.

"Maybe Mal can go fishing with you sometime," I muse.

Oh crap, I said that out loud because Dad replies, "What's that Maddie? Mal wants to go fishing with us?"

"Umm, yeah maybe," I cover up my slip. It would be nice to have a normal boyfriend who wants to spend time with my family.

Dad pulls on the handbrake and slides up the windows before

jumping out of the car. I follow him out and walk towards the house. As I approach, Rosie throws open the front door and skips like a maniac towards me.

"Tommy is here!" she shrieks, then realising that Tom could probably hear her and clamps both hands over her mouth.

I smile at her and put my arm around her shoulder. "Come on, let's go do the meet and greet."

"Rosie," Dad says from a few steps behind us, "Go put on the kettle and make a nice cup of tea."

She grimaces and rolls her eyes in my direction. Some things never change. It's my turn to hum *Polly put the kettle on* and receive a death stare from my sister.

Elaine and Tom are sitting at the dining room table while Mum is in the kitchen frying bacon. The bacon confuses me because I thought we were having a roast, but before I can question her about it, I am fighting back a bout of nausea.

"Hey Mum, is that bacon ok? It smells a bit … off?" I ask her, burping a horrible vomit taste in my mouth. Yuck.

"No Madeline, there is nothing wrong with my bacon. I just promised your Father something very special to go with his Chicken."

"Oh, OK," I say and sit down opposite Elaine. Rosie takes the seat next to her boyfriend and leans her head on his shoulder. "Maybe you can mix it with Dad's Snapper and Phil's Sprats," I tell Mum with a glint of humour.

"His what," asks Elaine?

"His you know, fish? Sorry, I think you had to be there," I tell her.

"Oh," she replies. "How have you been Madeline? We haven't seen you in quite some time."

"I'm OK," I venture. "You know, working, keeping out of trouble."

I have known the Ferguson's for a well over a decade now. Our parents became friends while their daughter Hannah and Rosie were in Primary school together, and it didn't take long for my brother Jack and their son Theo to become firm friends.

I was that much older than them, so often spent time doing my own thing rather than family dinners and outings. But I've known them for so long, and they have become such a large part of my parent's lives they are now like family, perhaps even closer because we choose to be in each other's lives.

They were at my wedding all those years ago, both Rosie and Hannah were my bridesmaids, and in more fanciful moments when I first met Mal, I thought they'd all come to my second one.

Mum and Elaine start a conversation about cooking with seasonal vegetables, which I think is rather amusing since Mum gets most of her veg from the freezer. I sit and enjoy not having to be on high alert for a change.

Rosie is whispering in Tom's ear when he catches me looking at them and says, "I remember you from school Maddie, you were the year above me."

"Oh, OK," I say. "Sorry I have a terrible memory. People tell me I must have spent my time at school with my head in a bucket."

"Well, you know. We didn't exactly hang with the same people."

The conversation suspends for a few moments. I'm not thrilled with the prospect of having to rehash high school, so keep my mouth shut, hoping for a more favourable topic.

"Where's Mal?" Rosie asks while managing to extract herself from what I think must be a magnetic field.

"He had to work today." I'm feeling uncomfortable having to explain his absence. Fortunately, Dad and Phil come in from washing the boat.

Dad proudly slaps his 'catch' down on the kitchen bench.

"For goodness sakes don't put it there, I'm in the middle of cooking dinner!" Mum yells at him. Dad smiles while moving to the cupboard under the bench to find a container to place it in.

"Good fishing today! We got a good haul," he chuckles to himself. Even I laugh at that. We all know his trickery.

Phil walks into the room just in time to hear his boasting, covering his laugh with a strangled cough at their big 'catch'. He crosses the room to his wife Elaine and kisses her on the cheek.

He sits down at the dining table opposite Tom and Rosie and eyeballs her new beau. "So, Thomas, where are you from?"

I groan inwardly; Mal barely made it out of this tag team between Phil and Dad. Back then, I had no idea how much violence he was holding inside. It seems so long ago, but just like yesterday.

We were both sitting here at this very same table. His arms wrapped protectively around me. I felt so content and happy, confident that he fitted right into my life in a way Justin never did.

I knew he was looking for a family, one who would love him and accept him no matter what, and truthfully, he found it. It is right under his nose, but he can't even see it.

I wish he could see that my Dad doesn't hate him, or even think badly of him; all they can see is how unhappy I have been. I wish he could see how much I love him. I want him back and for us to be happy again.

I tune back into my parent's conversation about the time Jack and Theo drank a bottle of wine and Phil and Elaine had shoved them both into a cold shower. I smile at my memory of that day. I think I was happy that Mum and Dad's wrath had been focused on Jack for a change, rather than how badly I had behaved as a teenager.

Time passes, and I try to enjoy dinner. I'm not feeling all that hungry, Mum notices and asks if I am feeling alright. I tell her I'm just tired. And that's the god's honest truth; I am tired of all the pretending.

After Mum pulls out the desert, I start looking at my watch. I'm tired, but that's not the reason I am anxious to get home. I know it's only a matter of time before the texting starts. Frankly, I am surprised that it hasn't started already. Right on cue, my phone buzzes on the table in front of me.

I pick it up and look at the text from Mal. 'WHEN ARE YOU COMING HOME?'

I stare at it for a few seconds before I reply, 'Just having dessert, not sure when dad will take me.'

It doesn't take long for another text to fire through. 'I'M GOING TO BED AT 10.30 AND IF YOU'RE NOT HOME BY THEN YOU ARE LOCKED OUT.'

I am pretty sure he means it too. So, I text back that I'll be home before then and look at my Dad trying to figure out how to ask him to take me home.

I glance at the kitchen clock, its 9 pm. It should only take about 15 minutes to get home, but I want to make sure I am home before ten just in case. That gives me an hour. I stretch my arms and make loud yawning sounds, hoping to attract someone's attention, but they all seem to be pretty intent on talking to each other.

I wait a few minutes and try again when that doesn't work, I know I am going to have to ask for a ride home.

"Dad, can you take me home soon? I have work tomorrow, and I've got to get an early start." Dad breaks from his conversation with Phil to look over to me.

"Umm," he says, glancing at his watch. I bite my lip and glance anxiously back at the kitchen clock again.

"Tommy can take you home Maddie!" Rosie's exclaims brightly, and *'Oh crap'* is all I can think.

This is the last thing I need, but before I can extract myself from this predicament, Dad pounces on the fact he lives on the same street as me.

"Oh, that's a great idea, Rosie. Would you mind Thomas? I think you both live on the same street anyway."

"Sure, I can, Mr Adler. I should probably head home soon too, I've got an early start as well," explains Tom.

'*Crappity, crap, crap, crap.*' I think silently. '*Thanks, Captain Helpful.*' My stomach turns with anxiety, but I swallow it well enough to smile and thank him.

Tom leans over and kisses Rosie lightly on the cheek. "See you tomorrow Rose." She smiles, adoringly at him.

As we rise to leave, she mouths 'Thank you' to him, and I must suppress the urge to roll my eyes. I'm happy for her, she deserves to be happy, but if Mal sees me arrive home in his car, it's going to be world war three at our place.

I grab my bag, make my goodbyes to my Parents and the Fergusons and follow Rosie and Tom out to the road. I immediately recognise Tom's car. He lives two houses over from us. Our Gardens intersect at the top due to there being no fences that high up. I think he still lives with his parents, but I can't be sure. I haven't spent a lot of time 'getting to know the neighbours'.

It's an awkward 15-minute drive home. I don't have much to say to him even if my head wasn't in a spin over what Mal might say and do when I get home. I think we are going to spend the entire time in silence when he says, "You were always a cool chick at school."

Well, that is news to me, "I was?" Modesty is not the reason I am so shocked; I genuinely thought very few people at high school liked me. I certainly wouldn't have classified myself as 'cool'. I'd say more like 'alternative' or maybe even 'emo' if such a thing had existed back then, but certainly not cool.

"Yeah, you were. I always liked you."

I look at him out the corner of my eye, appraising how to handle this revelation, "Thanks."

Tom goes to pull up outside my house, but I hastily say, "Just park at your place, I can walk down." I sigh in relief when he doesn't ask why I seem so flustered and pulls into his driveway.

"Thanks for the ride home," I say, and leave him to stare at me in surprise as I practically bolt out of his car and towards my own house.

I have to take a few calming breaths before I approach the front door. I turn the handle, but it doesn't budge. I frantically pull my phone from my bag to check the time; it's only 9.45 pm so he can't have locked me out already, could he?

I stand back and look up at the windows. They are all dark apart from the kitchen light so I figure he must still be up. I walk around the back of the house, and as I pass the deck, Bess thumps her tail a few times in greeting. I chuck her a few biscuits hoping he doesn't come out and check the level in the bag and go to try the back door.

With a sinking heart, I discover it's locked too. I stand up on my tippy-toes and can see the top of his head, so I tentatively knocked. He makes me wait a full five minutes before he opens the door.

"Who brought you home?" he asks. It feels like a loaded question, the sort that doesn't have a right answer. I could risk lying and tell him Dad did, and if he weren't looking out the window, I'd probably be OK, but if he was watching and he catches me in a lie, I don't know what will happen.

"Answer the fucking question," he repeats.

"Dad did," I say on a fast exhale, imaginary fingers crossed behind my back.

He looks at me, flatly for what feels like an eternity before saying to me. "Hope you had a good time, while I was here all alone." Is he pouting because he missed me, or is mad at me for going out? I can't tell. But finally, he moves back and lets me into the house.

Thankfully he heads right back to the computer and turns it off. I guess we are having an early night.

CHAPTER NINE

When I get up in the morning, I feel like I'm hungover. Mal is still sleeping, but instead of staying put and waiting for him to want to hug me, I slide out of bed. I move slowly, trying to make as little movement as possible and lock myself in the bathroom. Rubbing the sleep from my eyes, I stare at myself in the mirror. My hair is in disarray, I'm exhausted, and right now, the last thing I want is for him to touch me. After splashing some water on my face, I pinch my cheeks in a vain attempt at making myself look a little less pallid.

Maybe Mum's cooking was dodgy because I am not feeling well. Moving slowly to the kitchen, I make myself a weak coffee and sit at the breakfast bar. The instant coffee tastes bitter in my mouth, and I am still sitting looking at my half-full cup when Mal stalks into the kitchen.

"You got up?" he accuses.

'*No shit Sherlock*' I think to myself, he should have been a police officer, he's so observant. I put a lid on the sarcasm and tell him, "I'm not feeling that great today."

He doesn't reply. Instead, he opens the fridge and helps himself to a large wedge of cheese. I try to hide my disgust, biting back the urge to suggest he have something a little healthier for breakfast.

I'm still not feeling well by the time I get to work. The trip here was blessedly silent, but he screeches a halt at the kerb outside my work and watches me enter the department store through the staff entrance. I don't wait to see him drive away but hasten to my office. On entering the store, I start to think something is up with me. I wasn't making it up when I told Mal, I was not feeling well. I should have asked Mum a few more questions about that bacon. The last thing I need right now is to be in a stuffy office, but I don't have a lot of choices.

I sit gingerly at my desk, wondering if a glass of water would make me feel better or worse. By the time Adele returns from her early morning coffee run I still haven't made up my mind and as soon as the aroma of her flat white hits my nose I fight back another wave of nausea. Adele must have noticed me change several shades of green because she shoves the wastepaper basket in my direction just in time to catch the remainder of last night's dinner and the measly amount of coffee, I managed to drink this morning. Looking into the bin, I can't quite figure out what just happened.

"I am SO sorry Adele," I say as she hands me a tissue and I wipe my face.

"Be a good girl and go get us a clean bin. I doubt anyone will notice if this one ends up in the trash." She pats me on the arm to reassure me. The strong smell of my vomit overpowering coffee prompts me to do as suggested.

I run as fast as I can down the staff stairwell in the hope no one will catch me holding a bucket of sick. It smells putrid, and after slinging it in the trash bin outside, I vomit again in a discreet corner. After my stomach is satisfied that it's completely empty, I start to feel better so head back up to the office.

On re-entering the office Adele hands, me a stick of gum and I smile at her gratefully, "Are you OK?" she asks.

"I'm not sure," I answer honestly.

It's not until a half-hour later does the penny drop. I'm looking at the scheduling calendar when it hits me. I feel like a cartoon character when one of those novelty anvils lands on top of them as I count back on my fingers trying to think what was happening the last time, I got my period. And I can't remember. I can't remember when I last got my period, and now I can't remember how to breathe.

'Oh god, get a handle on yourself Maddie.' Breathe. In, out, in, out. My hands fall instinctively to my lower belly. Could I possibly be pregnant? I know we said we'd try, but when I didn't get pregnant, I assumed Mal was right about being infertile.

He's never used a condom; I'm so stupid.

Adele stops what she is doing and swings around in her office chair to face me. She looks very concerned, so before she can ask me again if I'm OK, I almost shout, "I'm still not feeling well."

"I can take you home if you need me too?" she asks kindly.

"No, it's OK Adele; I'll try and take it easy, OK? I knew I shouldn't have eaten my Mother's bacon surprise last night. This is entirely my fault."

"Well, if you're sure, love. Let me know if you need a ride? I'm sure Leon won't mind." Adele is lovely, and the closest thing I have to a friend now.

I wish I could blurt it all out. Pour out all my shattered hopes and despair, but I'm finding it hard to hold myself together. I am overwhelmed with all the changes that have happened in such a short space of time. I don't know what I am going to do, I should do something, but I am paralysed with fear, fear that no matter what I do, I'm going to make another mistake.

I have an overwhelming desire to connect with Megan, she was my rock during Justin's long absences, and I miss her so much. Right now, I need her level-headed advice and reliable support. So impulsively I write her a quick email using my work account.

From: Madeline Adler <m.adler@mcleansdeparmentstore.com >
To: Megan Wilson <Megan-jw@mymail.com>
Subject: Hi

Hi Megan
I'm just at work, and I find myself thinking of you. I miss you, heaps.
Maddie x

I glance around nervously like I'm the kid caught with her hand stuck in the cookie jar, before deleting the sent email.

The nausea seems to have dissipated for the day, by lunchtime I am operating normally, and Adele comments that I've gained a bit of colour in my cheeks.

"I'm feeling much better," I tell her and then try to immerse myself in work, so I don't have to think about my growing certainty that a tiny human is forming inside my body.

It's the end of the day when the computer pings its message alert for the final time. I've been flicking back to Outlook over and over all afternoon eagerly waiting to see if Megan has replied. Thank god she does before I have to go for the day.

From: Megan Wilson <megan-jw@mymail.com>
To: Madeline Adler <m.adler@mcleansdeparmentstore.com>
Subject: RE: Hi

Hey you!

Where have you been? It's like you have dropped off the planet. I even rang your folk's place, but they said they hadn't seen you in ages. What's going on?

Megan xxooooxxxooxoxoxox

P.S. Write back soon!

I stare at her message for a bit, wondering what I can tell her that won't lead her into a full-scale panic attack.

From: Madeline Adler <m.adler@mcleansdeparmentstore.com>
To: Megan Wilson < megan-jw@mymail.com>
Subject: RE: Hi

Hey, you back Megan,

I'm OK, mostly. I'm just really busy with work, you know. I just wanted to say hi and that I'm thinking of you. I wish you weren't so far away right now. :(

Anyhow, it's home time. If you email me back, I'll reply after I get to work tomorrow.

Maddie x

Adele is leaving the office by the time I hit send. I'll have to run if I am to reach the kerb before Mal arrives. I grab my bag and run to my locker. Throwing my Journal into the back, I grab my Jacket before clocking out and running full tilt down the staff stairs. I arrive out of breath with minutes to spare.

I need not have worried. I'm still standing here 15 minutes later. I pull my cell phone out from my back pocket to check his last message. He told me to be ready by 5.30 pm, and I'm here. Maybe he waited and went before I got here?

Just as I get ready to send him a text message, I see my car screech around the corner. I can see from this distance there is a new dent in the front bumper. The insurance has lapsed, so I have no idea how I am going to fix it. Not that I am worried now, he's crashed it so many times in the last six months it hardly matters.

I get in and pull the door closed. "What happened?" I ask him. "Are you OK?"

"Do you have any idea at all how much I fucking hate this piss hell city? No one knows how the fuck to drive!"

If he were any madder steam would pour out of his ears and nose, he's turning purple with his rage. I don't comment; instead, silently, I wait for him to continue.

"This wouldn't have happened if you had just moved to Christchurch as I asked you." He shifts his whole body in the driver's seat and looks at me accusingly.

He carries on with his rant about all the bad drivers on Auckland roads and how I am the root cause of all his unhappiness. I start to tune him out, and my mind turns back to the pregnancy. I am sure we have begun. I glance in his direction, wondering when or how I am going to tell him, or if I am going to say to him. He's way too volatile right now, and I don't want to tell him in the car. He's erratic enough with his driving right now as it is.

After getting home, Mal seems to have calmed down a bit. He jumps out to examine the damage. After pushing the bumper back up, it doesn't seem as bad.

"That stupid bitch thought I was going to *pay* for the damage to her car, can you believe that?" he asks while still staring at the bumper.

"Oh, what did you say?" I ask.

"I told her to fuck right off, this was her fault, and I am not going to be fucking paying for it." He kicks at the bumper, then once again more forcefully making it drop back down. I cringe inwardly, dutifully waiting for him to open the front door.

Before he has a chance to pull out his key, Tom walks past our drive with a small white fluffy dog.

Stopping at the end of our driveway, he calls to me, "Hey Maddie!"

Turning in his direction, I make a small waving motion, "Umm, Hi," I say, but don't offer anything else. I'm just hoping he keeps on walking before Mal starts to get suspicious.

"Car alright?" he asks, in an obvious attempt at small talk. Mal stops the ministration to the bumper and gives Tom the death stare.

"Umm, it's OK," I say, silently hoping he will keep walking.

"My Dad's a panel beater, so if you need a hand I can help," he says helpfully as my insides start turning over, my nausea from earlier today returning.

"Thanks, bye," I say praying that this ends the awkward conversation.

"Well, if you change your mind, send a text, and I'll come over. Bye," says Tom staring at the both of us for a while longer before continuing to his house. I am quite sure I'll hear from Rosie after this gets back to her.

I jump as Mal exclaims loudly, "Who the fuck is that?"

"Erh, that's Rosie's boyfriend," I tell him as I back closer to the front door.

"What's he doing here and why do you have his phone number?" His eyes narrow, and he looks at me closely. It's like he thinks I have been keeping a secret from him. Of course, I have, he overreacts so much how can I tell him the truth about anything?

"He lives on this street," I tell him. "Don't you remember Mum telling us a few weeks ago?" He continues to stare at me, his eyebrows drawn together, silently appraising me. "Umm not sure what house though." I glance nervously in the direction Tom walked, and Mal follows my gaze.

"And why do you have his phone number?" He prompts.

"I don't have his number. I guess he figured Rosie would give it to us?"

He looks back at me, and I shrug in a manner I hope conveys that I don't care about Tom, or where he lives. He pushes past me, opening the front door, so I follow him up the stairs, heading down to the bedroom to change out of my work clothes. I am convinced I can still smell vomit.

He leans past me, throwing his jacket onto the bed and turns to face me. His face is flushed red, and the glint in his eyes frightens me. Like a volcano, he erupts so violently I don't have a chance to defend myself.

CHAPTER TEN

Using both hands, he shoves me, and I skittle across the floor, slamming into the ground. I stare at him wide-eyed. The words I can deal with, but this, this is the first time he has been physical with me.

Mal stalks across the bedroom and crouches down, leaning right over me as I lay on a pile of unwashed clothes.

"What are you trying to hide from me?" He accuses, his eyes searching my own.

I'm so petrified I can't think straight. Tears start to fall down my shocked face, and my breath escapes in ragged gasps. This is a turning point; on some level, I know that. In a moment that stretches between being contacted by his rage and him regaining some control over his own emotions, our relationship could go either way.

I'm not stupid, I, just like millions of other women, tell myself if I was ever in this position I would leave, right? Right, not so clear cut is it. Because there is now something other than my guilt tethering me to him and its cells are rapidly dividing and growing its way into a whole new human being.

In the fraction of a second, before he starts to talk again, my mind flickers back five short months ago when in the thrill of passion, we decided why wait to make a baby? It's what we both want, so I stop taking my contraceptive pill, and in effect, sealed my fate right then.

He told me it was a long shot, and that he was told he could be infertile, but I was thrilled. He could give me what my husband was unwilling to, and even the chance that it could happen made me so happy, happy enough I was willing to risk everything for it.

He turns away from me, pacing up and down, muttering under his breath. It seems like he is reliving his past, fighting with his demons. I stay on the floor where he's left me, not sure what I should do. After a while, he comes to me. He picks me up and puts his arms around me and sobs into my hair.

"I'm so sorry Baby; I don't know what came over me. I'm so, so sorry."

His anguish renews my sobbing, wrapping my arms around his neck I bury my head into his shoulder.

"I was just so angry with you," he continues, "I didn't know what to think when that guy spoke to you. You don't tell me anything, how can I trust you if you don't tell me the truth?"

My sobs start to get louder as I apologise, "I'm sorry; he's just Rosie's boyfriend, he's nobody."

He moves away from me slightly and looks at me with such disappointment that my heart breaks again. "Mal, you're my light, I have never loved as much as or as completely as I love you. I don't want to lose you because it would be like losing me." I wait for some response from him, but he holds his silence. I try again, "You're right to be angry. I'm so sorry I didn't tell you that I'd met Tom and spoke to him before. It's a terrible and destructive habit, and I promise I'll never keep anything from you again."

"What am I supposed to think Madeline, when you don't tell me the truth?"

"Please don't be angry with me, I love you," I say and lean my head against his chest.

He reaches his arms around my back, and for a while, I try to find a moment of peace within his arms. I can still feel the tension in his shoulders, I don't know if this is the right time to tell him about the baby, but at the very least it might distract him from his misery.

"Mal, I think I might be pregnant."

He pushes away from me, rocking back on his heels as he studies my face. "Are you sure?" he asks.

"I'm pretty sure." I wipe my arm across my face trying to clear tears from my eyes. "I missed my period, and I've been feeling a bit sick. I should probably go see a doctor."

"Yeah," he says slowly. "That's probably a good idea." He pulls me up with him as he stands. "Maddie baby, we are going to have a little bubba of our own!"

His face lights up like Christmas, and I can't help but smile back and feel hopeful.

I'm too hot, I can't breathe, I try to move my arms and legs, but I can't. *Can you hear my heart whispering to you?* I whimper once in my sleep and try to turn over, but the blankets are wrapped tightly around me. *My thoughts are with you every moment.*

I don't know it yet, but my nightmare life is overlapping into my dreams. *You make me happy beyond words and completely excited about my life and our future.* I am trapped and haunted by words I had written of what my life was supposed to be.

Awaking startled I sit bolt upright, struggling to get my breathing under control. I glance instinctively towards Mal, looking past him to the alarm clock. It's still dark outside, 3.42 am to be exact.

I need to pee, so I ease myself out of bed and walk silently to the bathroom. I can't help but think about how stupid I have been. I filled page after page in my old journals with love poems and letters to Mal before I'd even ended my marriage to Justin.

I thought I knew Mal, knew him better than anyone else, and that I could see into his very soul. Nothing he had done before mattered, only our future.

Sitting on the toilet, I rub my sore shoulder as the oversized tee-shirt I am wearing slips slightly, revealing a sizeable angry purple bruise. It hurts more than I had expected it too, it must have coloured up after I went to bed. I drag the collar up to hide the discolouration on my skin. I don't want to think about that, or what it might mean for me, and the baby inside me.

I don't think I am going to be able to sleep again tonight, and the thought of lying so close to Mal sends a cold shiver down my spine. I grab the blanket off the spare bed and huddle on the couch.

Pulling the blanket tighter around me, and I am transported back to the first time, I ever laid eyes on him.

It was late November, and my husband was still overseas. I had travelled back up to Auckland with some friends to attend a wedding Justin and I were supposed to go to together. I tingled with excitement and apprehension while sitting across from Justin's friend Brad. But it wasn't because I was visiting my old home, spending time with my family or seeing old friends. I could hardly keep still, trying to plan the best way to disengage myself from the wedding party and rendezvous with Mal without attracting too much negative attention.

Fortunately, 'luck' seemed to work in my favour and an opportunity presented itself in the form of a party with the groom's cousin. The wedding seemed to drag on forever, and while I made small talk with people, I pretended to like I tried to focus on what I thought was important, meeting Mal for the first time.

I first 'met' Mal on the computer in a random chat room, when there was such a thing, during the first time Justin went away. But I'd not spoken to him for years, so it was a surprise when he popped up on my chat messenger and said 'Hi'.

He paid attention to me, he wanted to talk to me, and he seemed fascinated with everything I had to say. So, for months now we'd been exchanging letters and talking on the phone.

I swallowed my anxiety when it was time to leave for the party, and I reassured Brad that I'd be able to find my way back to my parent's house.

He took the role of his best friend's wife's protector very seriously, and I had to wonder if he'd call to tell Justin that'd gone off to a party instead of getting a ride with him like he assumed I would.

The party was in the student area of town. The houses on the street clocked at least 100 years each, multileveled giants who held dozens of student flatters.

The house we were going to was packed and thick with smoke, both legal and otherwise. I began to feel excited when I passed the first room where a live band was set up, scantily dressed bodies pressing against each other swaying in time to the music.

Someone offers me a joint, but I smile and wave them on. I've had more than enough wine, and I want to stay as clear-headed as possible tonight.

I pull my phone out and send Mal a text. 'I've extracted myself from wedding duty. Let me know when you're close. I can't wait to see you!!! xoxo drive safe.'

I don't wait for a reply I just put my phone back in my bag, he let me know earlier he was driving so I didn't expect the almost immediate response.

'BABY GIRL … I CAN'T WAIT! SEE YOU SOON SWEETIE XXX'

I text back a smiley face and smile broadly.

Doug, the groom's cousin, surprises me from behind and asks if I'd like to go outside with him. They are lighting a bonfire and have fired up the BBQ.

This is possibly the most amazing party I've ever been too, but I don't seem to be able to enjoy it because my brain is too full up with meeting Mal for the first time.

I stand for what seems like hours next to the raging bonfire, feeling the heat against my skin and watching the flames dance. I feel like I am among them, catching alight, burning with passion and playing with fire.

It was nearing 2 am when finally, my phone begins to ring. I snatched at it as fast as I can and breathlessly answer, "Yes!"

Mal laughs "So eager Baby Girl? I'm almost there. Where do you want me to meet you?"

I glance at all the people around the fire; I doubt they'll miss me at all. "I'll meet you at the end of the street?" I don't want to risk Doug seeing me meeting up with a strange man.

I make my way down the street towards where I said I'd meet him. Now I've moved away from the fire its cold and my jacket not warm enough to keep the chill at bay. Butterflies are making my stomach summersault, and my heart is literally in my mouth as I see him pulling up in a beaten-up old work truck.

The sight of him stepping out of that truck is forever burned into my memory. I drink up my very first sight of him standing there wearing a white army snow jacket, paired with blue jeans and black boots. He has his beige baseball cap pulled down low over his eyes, dark skin and a smart goatee.

The biggest smile stretches my face as we are drawn together like magnets. His arms wrapped around me like we were moulded to fit together. I notice how he is only a head taller than me, his cheek resting comfortably against my forehead.

I don't think I was planning on anything untoward happening, but with several glasses of wine still swimming in my blood, tempering my urges was becoming difficult. I couldn't believe he was here, in my arms. I just wanted to look at him and memorise every curve and turn of his face.

"Look at me Mal, let me see you." He seemed shyer than I imagined him to be, almost like he was trying to avoid my gaze.

"Oh, I'm not so good to look at," he tells me.

But he was. He was absolutely beautiful to me. Not exactly what I was expecting, he certainly hadn't told me he was Maori, but still to me he was perfect.

"What's this?" I ask him, as I tug gently on his facial hair.

He smiled down at me and said, "I've missed you. I'll shave it off if you don't like it."

I shrug in what I hope seems like indifference and poke my tongue out at him, it was this moment he crosses the short distance to my face and crushes his lips against mine.

As he deepened the kiss, every part of my body melted. From that moment on, it was like he owned me in my entirety. He pushes me up harder against the brick wall we are leaning on and slides his hand up my leg and under my skirt. I let out a small gasp as November rain starts falling softly about us, but as cold as it was, I'd never felt warmer.

Looking back, I did feel a little awkward that even though he knew I was married and that I was fragile with conflicted emotions, he was still so keen to kiss me, and put his hands on me claiming me as his. In my inexperience, I missed these warning signs, and instead, I read them as passion.

He took me back to his hotel room and begged me to stay. Any resolve I had before passing myself into his hands was long forgotten, and we made love with wild abandon, wrapping our bodies about each other, hungrily demanding more. When was the last time I had felt this? Had I ever felt so complete? I think not. He took me with command, touching me with a practised hand, I had nothing in my head except that moment in time with him, no words were uttered save for our small gasps of pleasure.

But after the passion subsided, and I was once again in control of myself the realisation of what I had done set in. Before I had a chance to process all the emotions flooding my body, I wept.

"Baby girl are you OK?" he asked me and pulled my naked body closer.

I laid my head on his shoulder and sobbed, "Oh god, how can I do this? I shouldn't even be here, I, I, oh god." Losing control for the second time that day, I broke down.

"Baby Girl, Maddie, it's OK." He pulled my chin up, so I am forced to meet his gaze. "Let it all out; I'd rather you cry here with me than later on your own. You know I love you."

As the tears start to subside, I reply, "I love you too."

"Don't be sad; something this good can't be wrong. I shall treasure this moment forever," and he kissed me again.

This one beautiful moment with him, could it last me to the end of my life? How could I go back to my husband with this in my heart and still feel whole?

Birds are chirping before I drag myself back to my current reality, I look at the clock on the DVD player; I still have an hour before Mal will wake up, so I return the blanket to the spare room and ease myself back onto my side of the bed.

CHAPTER ELEVEN

The first thing I do after getting to work is a search for the number of the family planning clinic. Holding my breath, I dial and hope I can make an appointment before Adele gets back from her morning coffee run.

Five minutes later, she returns coffee in hand, and I have an appointment for tomorrow morning 40 minutes after I am supposed to be at work. Well, everyone is so used to me being late. I doubt it will cause much of a stir, but I still nervously clear my throat before asking Adele if she minded covering from me.

"Is your tummy still bothering you?" she asks.

"Yeah, I've been feeling a little under the weather."

Adele smiles in sympathy at me. "Not just your Mum's cooking then, she'll be pleased. Of course, I'll cover for you, sweetheart."

I'm so lucky to have her support because I feel like I'm falling apart. At least my tummy seems a little more comfortable with the aroma of coffee than it did yesterday, but I'm dreading sitting in the lunchroom while everyone is eating. I don't want a repeat of yesterday; people will talk for sure if I must make any more mad dashes to the lady's room.

I spend an unreasonable amount pof time composing an email to Megan because I'm far too distracted to get any real work done. After having written and deleted the first line a dozen times, I end just staring blankly at the blinking cursor.

What am I going to tell her? If I let her know how awful things have gotten, how will she react? It's hard to explain why I didn't just leave Mal last night. It kills me that I can't be honest with him anymore, epically because I used to think I could tell him anything.

After keeping so many secrets from my husband I wanted to lance all lies from my life, but it's like I've come full circle and here I am trying to protect myself, armouring my body with secrets again.

I am keeping the truth from so many people I've lost count of the lies I've told. I have to keep so much bottled up I feel like I'm going to explode. I can't tell Mal anything anymore. I'm too scared he will overreact and take it the wrong way.

I hate feeling like this, so how can I let it continue? I feel like I'm being poisoned. He's so controlling I have to repeatedly change myself to fit in with him; I'm exhausting myself in a futile effort to keep up with his temper. Maybe I need to learn how to keep my mouth shut.

Asking permission to spend my own money is crippling me, and I feel guilty on those occasions when he says yes. I hate when he completely blows up, it scares me so much, and he told me never to be afraid of him.

As my eyes refocus on the screen, I see I've not written an email to Megan at all; I've been writing a letter to myself. I'm not sure I am ready to read it yet, so I push and hold my finger on the backspace key and watch the cursor gobble my words as if they never existed.

I'm so tired I'm almost too drowsy to keep my eyes open. I am lying on the couch, eyelids heavy. I lean my head down against the cushions and tuck my legs under me. I have the TV volume turned down so low it's barely audible. I don't mean to sleep, but I am fast losing the battle, I've been so tired these last few days I wonder if I will start to get a bit more energy back as the pregnancy progresses.

Mal wasn't happy about the timing of my doctor's appointment. He can't take the day off on such short notice, but perhaps that's part of the reason I got one for tomorrow rather than making it for a time I knew he could make.

I still haven't decided what I'm going to tell the doctor, the bruise on my shoulder has faded slightly but still visible. I sigh deeply to myself and place my hands on my abdomen.

'*What are we going to do?*' I silently ask my little invader.

Contemplating my future always seems to conjure thoughts of the past, and as I drift into a fitful slumber, I think back to when I told my husband I was leaving him.

I didn't expect for Justin to cry, how could I? He claimed he didn't feel emotions; he had even confided that the last time he cried was when his childhood dog was hit by a car over twenty years ago. I knew I was a coward telling him before he came home, but I just wanted to get it over and done with before he returned. I knew I wouldn't be strong enough once he was back.

But I'd made more mistakes than I ever had a hope of fixing, and the thought of being honest with him petrified me. Then I'd have, to be honest with myself, and that was something I wasn't prepared to do.

"Don't do this Maddie," he choked out between sobs. "Please, I love you. I can change it. I can do better." But it was me who had changed, and even though it was incredibly painful, I couldn't see another way out.

"I'm not going to change my mind, Justin," I tell him through my sobs. "It's too late."

"But everything I do is for you! Everything I buy, it's for you."

I have no reply. I've heard this before and didn't believe it then either.

"Maddie, is there someone else?"

My heart froze in my chest; I was sure he'd hear the lie in my silence. "There is no one else; I'm not happy. I can't do this anymore."

"Just stay until I'm home. I'll be home in a month; please stay."

His voice was so wretched I agreed to stay until he got home so that we could sort through things together. I was so sure that it wouldn't matter what he might say or do, I wasn't going to change my mind. I couldn't change my mind, not after setting this in motion.

God, it hurt so badly, and I hurt myself as much as him. I was ripping through our marital ties as freshly as when I laid with another man. I was so torn, I was changing my entire life, but I thought the risk was worth it for the chance at something special, something we hadn't been in a long time.

Justin had never shown me anything close to this kind of feeling before, which made believing that he loved me difficult.

It's tough to believe in yourself when someone seems to get enjoyment out of tormenting you for amusement. He was never physically abusive, certainly not how Mal has been to me, but he did seem to enjoy pushing my buttons and winding me up.

Tears roll freely across my cheek as I think of all the times Justin would drive me to distraction. Push me so far, I'd shriek at him and hurtle a couch cushion in his direction. Then he would fall down laughing, and I'd instantly forgive him.

I think he felt like he'd be able to save us if I just stayed until he got home. He even rang Annette, the wife of one of his co-workers, which was unheard of before. Justin reaching out and asking for someone else's help or advice was just beyond my comprehension.

Annette called me the next day and told me he 'knew what the problems were and thought he could fix them.' I suppose the fact that he said he could change meant he recognised we had significant problems to start with, but it was just too late. I'd made too many mistakes to put us back together.

It didn't matter what he said to me, or what he told other people, I just pushed it all aside, and focused squarely on what I wanted for my future. Justifying my actions but reassuring myself that despite the fact he was sad at the time, he would be happier in the future and at some point, realise that what I did was best for both of us.

Annette told me that she could see how unhappy I was a month after first meeting me, I didn't realise it was that easy for people to see my pain and I hope I have become a better actress.

Back then, I thought Mal would be the balm to heal all my wounds. That being near him would make things so much easier. After ending my marriage to Justin, I told him six months, that in six months we can be together, but I desperately wished for him to fix everything immediately.

I told Mal then we shouldn't rush into anything, that I loved him so much but didn't want to risk building our relationship on unsteady ground. I had zero confidence in myself, and I was still carrying the guilt of my betrayal with me.

Talk about your self-fulfilling prophecies, I wonder now why I didn't stick firmer to the six-month rule, but Mal has always been on the pushy side.

In the beginning, I thought it was him showing his passion for me, and his insistence on starting our life together as soon as possible genuine. Now, however, I know it's because of his overwhelming need to control absolutely everything.

I know wallowing in my past mistakes will not make things better for me, but right now, I am at a loss to understand how to fix things between Mal and myself.

He seemed so happy about having a baby with me. It was all we could talk about in our first weeks together, this should be the happiest time of my life, but it just feels like his grip on me is tightening.

The couch beneath me is damp with my tears as I surrender to sleep; I hope my dreams are gentler than my reality.

CHAPTER TWELVE

As I turn and stretch in my sleep, I shudder from the cold. Reaching for the blankets, I realise I am still on the couch. The television is trying to convince me to buy a miracle chopper.

All the lights have been turned off; the DVD player tells me it's nearing 3 am, and I am quite sure that Mal has just decided to go to bed without rousing me. Sitting up, I rub my arms briskly, trying to warm up and carefully make my way to bed.

He is lying diagonally; his arm flung out across my pillow with the entire duvet tucked up around him. He murmurs under his breath, and I move closer straining to hear what it was. I can make out him repeating 'red eyes' under his breath.

I swear the temperature has just dropped 10 degrees and I don't waste time sliding into place on the edge of the bed. I ease as much of the duvet over myself as I can without waking him. Squeezing my eyes tight shut, I fall back to sleep silently rocking myself.

The next morning brings a new dilemma. Adele has given me the all-clear for my doctor's appointment, but it's at least half an hour walk from the surgery to work and to glance out the lounge window the clouds are starting to look a bit ominous.

I glance at Mal from the corner of my eye and try to judge his mood. He's wrestling with the laces on his boots. Even sitting on the edge of the computer chair crouched over the keyboard, he manages to emit a hostile vibe. Sighing inwardly, I cross the lounge and wait by the stairwell for him to finally be ready to leave.

We sit in silence as he drives us towards the Family Planning Clinic, he crunches the gears as he rounds a corner, and I wince in sympathy with my poor car.

"Make sure you get an appointment for an ultrasound," he says as we are nearly there.

I'm pretty sure I'm quite early in the pregnancy, and I have a feeling that they don't usually do scans until a bit further along but since there is no point antagonising, I let him know I will.

As I push open the car door and step out onto the street, the rain starts to fall. I look up and then back to Mal.

"See you later, sweetie," he tells me. I'm shocked as he rarely uses those endearments anymore.

"OK, bye," I reply. The sense of relief I feel as he drives away is indescribable and almost makes up for how wet the rain is making me. Pulling my jacket tighter around me, I hoist my bag up further on my shoulder and head in the direction of the clinic.

This is the same clinic I've been going to since I was a teenager and I've always felt the same level of awkwardness climbing these stairs. I would imagine that everyone thought I either had a sexually transmitted disease or that I was a wanton sex addict there to get an abundant supply of condoms. Only this time I think all the eyes on me are thinking pregnant whore.

I shiver as part of me contemplates changing direction and fleeing, only I am not stupid enough to think I can outrun a baby. I must do this so I march up the second flight as fast as my legs can carry me and crash through the door. As I enter the reception area just being back in a place, I am familiar with starts to calm me. All the judgemental eyes are on the outside of this room, and here, for now, I am safe.

The receptionist looks up at my sudden appearance in the doorway and smiles politely in my direction. "Good morning, can I help you?"

"Umm," I stumble over my words, but she patiently waits for me to continue. "I have an appointment for ten past nine?"

She glances at the clock over her right shoulder, it reads 9:20, but she doesn't comment on that, and instead tells me to take a seat.

I take a seat opposite the muted TV and pull one of the dog-eared magazines onto my lap. I try to concentrate on the words as I flip the pages, but my stomach is in knots, and I'm beyond any hope of stilling my brain.

I'm at maximum capacity as a nurse appears in the waiting room and calls my name. "Maddie? Come with me love," she says to me as I get up and follow her. "We've just got to get your weight and blood pressure before you pop through for your doctor's appointment."

She points to the chair adjacent to the desk as I roll up the sleeve on my jumper. I cringe a bit as she slides the cold blood pressure cuff up my arm and tightens the Velcro strap.

She slips a stethoscope into the nook of my elbow and watches the line on the gauge decrease as she releases the pressure. She frowns slightly but a moment later smiles in my direction and tells me I can go for my visit with the doctor. Doing my best to return her smile, I go towards the open door she is gesturing towards.

The wooden louvred doors are the same as they have always looked, even if the faces have changed. It feels a bit like I've grown up within these walls, having the different stages of my adolescence chronicled in their medical files. It's that same medical file that is open in front of the Doctor.

She looks up as I enter, "Hi Maddie, I'm Doctor Sand. What can I do for you today?" I am still not sure what to say so continue to stand in the doorway, so she adds, "You can take a seat if you like."

I take a deep breath and do as I'm told. "I think I'm pregnant," I blurt.

"OK then, we had best get you to take a test." She pulls a wrapped foil package out from a cupboard above her head and places it on the desk, reaching for a plastic urine collection container she shows me the way to the toilet. She needn't have bothered, after ten years of coming here I know the drill.

Now I am sitting on the toilet. I find it next to impossible to empty my bladder. I can barely manage a few drops before the full realisation of what is happening starts to sink in.

"I'm pregnant," I say to myself as if repeating it will make it seem less surreal. Looking at my tiny container of pee, I know there is only one way to know for sure. I tip it into the plastic tub and screw the lid on tight. After washing my hands more thoroughly than would usually be warranted, I return to the doctor.

Doctor Sand takes my jar of pee like it's the most normal thing in the world, and I sit down slowly, eyes resolutely looking at my feet. She pulls on latex gloves and rips open the pregnancy test and dips it in my pee. I'm glad the test only needs a few drops since I was too nervous to squeeze out more. Now the test has been activated I sit and stare at it, waiting for the final verdict on my future.

"We just have to wait a few minutes," she reassures me.

I burst into tears. Not the silent tears I've gotten so good at hiding, but loud heaving uncontrollable sobs. She waits until I get myself back under control and passes me a box of tissues.

"It's OK; many women feel tearful at this point. It's totally normal."

"Nothing about this is normal," I tell her, exhaling sharply.

"You know you can talk to me, right?"

I struggle to maintain some of my self-control but tears well in my eyes again and my bottom lip trembles. "My partner, he's difficult," I tell her, eyes downcast, I slide my hands between my thighs and continue. "I don't know if we are going to last the week as a couple, how can we raise a child together?"

I've been keeping this thought inside so tightly it's almost a relief to tell someone else, and once I started, I can't stop.

It's pouring out of me in waves, and once I've talked myself around in a full circle, the doctor tells me, "It's a positive test."

I stare at her while I let this news sink in, she's confirmed what I already knew. I'm pregnant with Mal's baby.

"I can't do this, I can't have his baby," I start to cry again. What kind of person am I to suggest murdering my baby?

I'm still trying to assimilate the fact that I am indeed pregnant, while Doctor Sand calmly talks me through my 'options'. I tune back in as she says, "You don't have to continue with this pregnancy Madeline, we can do a scan to confirm your dates, but from all indication, you should be well within the time frame for a termination if that's what you decide. You have plenty of time to consider your options."

This word 'options' keeps repeating in my head. I don't feel like I have any at all. A termination, though, ending this new life that we have created? Could I do this? I'm not so sure. I stare at her blankly and shake my head.

"I don't know; I don't know. How can I bring a baby into this mess?"

"Well, you don't have to decide anything today. Let's schedule an ultrasound and take it from there."

As I glance back up at Dr Sand, she smiles and pats my arm. "Your blood pressure is a bit higher than I'd like, so how about we to send you for some routine blood work, and I'll write you a script for some folic acid. This will help the foetus develop."

After typing on her computer, the doctor's printer spits out three pieces of paper. One is for the ultrasound to confirm dates, I look closer and see TERMINATION DATING highlighted, the second is for the blood work and the last a script for folic acid.

"I have to get to work," I tell her looking at my watch; I already know I'll be cutting it fine. She shows me back to reception and reminds me to make another appointment after my scan results.

I walk back down the stairs without feeling as self-conscience as when I arrived. All I can think of is the baby growing inside me. The overwhelming feeling of every single thing in my life spiralling out of control beings to envelop me. I have to pull myself together before I get back to work. I fasten my jacket and bend my head to the wind. The rain has eased off, but the sky doesn't look that much lighter than when I arrived. Knowing my luck, it will probably start to hail. I pick up my pace, and my heart thumps in response. I can block some of it out just by focusing on my breathing and moving my legs.

Before I'm halfway to work, the rain starts to come down harder, mirroring my misery. By the time I make it back to work I look like I've swum there.

CHAPTER THIRTEEN

I bump into Paul in the stairwell, "Good God woman, what on earth have you been doing? You look like you fell in a puddle?" He reaches towards me and pulls a lank wet strand of hair from my eyes.

"I had to walk from the Doctor's office," I tell him, scrunching up my face as a stray raindrop trickles down my forehead.

"You should have told me! I would have come and got you!"

"Thanks, Paul," I tell him, his concern is touching.

He pulls out a scrap of paper from his pocket and scribbles his number on it. He hands it to me scolding, "Next time Missy, you call. Crikey if you come down with a cold this whole place will collapse."

"I highly doubt that, but I appreciate the sentiment,"

Paul smiles and continues down the stairs. I stuff his number in the back pocket of my pants and leave a trail of wet footprints in my wake.

I enter the office 15 minutes later, after hanging my head upside down under the hand drier in the woman's bathroom. I now resemble a disgruntled porcupine, but at least I'm not quite so wet.

"Hello Dear, you look at bit damp," says Adele. "Everything went OK at the Doctors?"

"Yeah, I had to walk here in the rain. The Doctor says it's viral," I shrug in her direction, avoiding her gaze.

"Walking in the rain is not ideal when you're sick Maddie. If you need to take a few days off, you go right ahead; I can hold the fort. How about I go get you a nice cup of something hot?"

I gratefully grin, and I see a measure of relief in Adele's face that she can do something to help me.

Its dark before Mal approaches the kerb, I have had plenty of time to consider my situation while waiting for him, but all I've managed to do is tie my stomach up in knots. It feels like I am bleeding on the inside, everything that makes me, me, is seeping out. I don't think he grasps how much he is hurting me. He is far too busy with his depression to see how I am dying on the inside.

"Well, what did the Doctor say?" he asks as I ease myself into the passenger seat. "Are you, or aren't you?"

"Yes. You're going to be a Daddy," I smile at him.

He looks at me, and it's like it's the first time he's seen me in months.

"Yeah," he says with a half-smile. "I guess I am."

I reach over to touch his hand resting on the gear stick, and to my surprise, he rubs his thumb against mine.

"Did you get a scan booked?" he asks expectantly.

My tummy clenches as I recall the termination query, but I try to keep my tone light as I reply, "Oh yes, next Thursday," gesturing towards my handbag I add, "She gave me a script for some folic acid."

"Is that free?" he asks?

I shrug my shoulders, "I don't know."

"Hmm let's get you home and feed Mummy Bear," he says with enthusiasm.

This time, he does get a smile from me; maybe this baby is our salvation.

The lull lasts us throughout dinner. He seems upbeat as he tosses a chicken breast around in the frying pan. I stand next to him at the kitchen bench and bask in this relative calm. I shall refuse to examine this too carefully and focus on chopping a tomato.

"Do you remember the first time we cooked together?" he asks.

"Hmm? Sure, you made me chicken." I look at the chicken he is currently cooking. How much has changed since that night?

"You looked sexy as hell in those shorts." He turns from the stove and in one short step, he is standing right next to me. I freeze and stare at him, my hand still resting on the knife.

He pulls me closer, spinning me to face him, sliding his hand around my waist, kissing me firmly on the lips. As his tongue invades my mouth, I'm reminded of the passion we felt at the beginning.

He's never been a gentle lover, and the last months he's been nothing but a brute, but my hand loses the knife and settles on his hip. I hope fervently that this is a positive turning point for us.

He drops his hand to my butt, and after giving it, a sharp squeeze slips his fingers into my rear pocket. Such an innocent gesture in another world and a different time, but I freeze as he withdraws Paul's scrap of paper with his hastily drawn phone number.

"What the fuck Madeline? What the actual fuck?" He thrusts Paul's phone number towards me until it's only centimetres from my eyes.

Leaning back, I stutter trying to apologise and appease him as quickly as possible. "It's Paul's number, you know, from work? He told me I could have called him to get me from the Doctors."

"That scrawny fag you work with?" His body looms towards mine, his eyes wide. "What the fuck, you better not tell that cunt you're pregnant, this is MY baby!"

"I didn't," I start to protest.

"I pick you up. You don't go in anyone's car but mine. If he touches you, I'm going to fucking kill him."

The house of cards I had built my new hope in is destroyed, and I chew on my lip.

"Now look what you've made me do," he shouts at me as he turns back to the chicken that's starting to burn. "Why do you have to ruin everything, Madeline?"

He slides the chicken on top of the salad on my plate and thrusts his on the other. Grabbing the sauce from the fridge behind me, he turns away and throws himself into the office chair.

With little else to do, I retrieve my own burned dinner and retreat to my spot on the couch, the dinner plate resting on my knees. Mal is angrily pushing food around his plate. The sound of his fork scraping is sending lightning bolts through my nervous system.

I hack at a bit of the charred chicken, stabbing it with my fork. I raise it to my mouth where it pauses while I envision how a bit of blackened chicken has become a metaphor for my entire life.

It's way past 11 pm, and Mal has been in the bathroom for the better part of an hour. Do I stay here on the couch and wait for him to finish or get myself ready for bed? In the end, my indecision leaves me on the couch for another 20 minutes, but the early stages of pregnancy are starting to weigh on me. I'm so tired I am struggling to keep my eyes open.

As I make my way down the hall, I hear the toilet flush. I've made it to the bedroom door, so I stay where I am and wait for him. He walks past me, barely looking in my direction. Before I have a chance to make for the bathroom myself, quicker than I could ever anticipate he grabs my throat and hauls me up onto my toes. I have no choice but to look directly into his eyes.

"Were you going to call him?" he asks softly, dangerously.

"What?" I answer dumbly.

He flings me across the bedroom where I land haphazardly on the bed.

"You know who the fuck I'm talking about slut! How the fuck am I supposed to trust you if all you do is lie to me? How am I supposed to know if this baby is even mine?"

Far too scared to answer, I look at him dumbfounded as he thumps me with force in the left shoulder and pins me to the bed.

Through ragged breaths, I beg him, "Please, I haven't cheated on you," but he doesn't listen. Instead, he yanks down my pants and jams a finger into my anus. He thrusts his face towards me until he's inches from mine threatening me, "Fucking slut, get the fuck out of here." But I can't.

I can't breathe or move, and I am shaking uncontrollably. I'm pretty sure urine may have leaked out as he jammed his fingers into me.

For the first time, I think he has lost it, and I can't help thinking of the day he told me he never wanted me to be scared of him. The Mal I fell in love with would never have done this to me. He would never have scared me like this.

I can't get the vision of him poking his finger into me out of my head. I have never felt so helpless. I feel betrayed and dirty. The image plays over and over in my head, and I start to become hysterical. The volume of my sobs increases, I usually hide my tears, but I don't have the strength to protect myself like that in this moment.

Mal stands next to the bed, staring at me until my sobs subside, then kneels next to me and scoops me into his arms.

"Please stop crying, Madeline. If you didn't lie to me, I wouldn't get so angry with you."

I don't know what to say to him, so I close my eyes. It's not long before exhaustion and grief pulls me under and gives me the illusion of a few hours of peace.

CHAPTER FOURTEEN

The morning comes all too soon, but at least I wake up in his arms. He reaches around me to caress my belly, so I sink into his embrace, soaking up his warmth and affection because it's sucked away all too soon. Before I know it, I am looking at my swollen-eyed reflection in the bathroom mirror, trying to decide on the best way to cover the bruise that extends from one side of my jaw to the other.

Taking care not to overextend my similarly bruised shoulder, I settle on some hastily applied concealer and a black silk scarf.

I hold back a manic giggle at the insanity of what I am doing. I look like I've offered myself to a vampire.

The first thing I do after arriving to work is retrieved my journal from my locker. I retreat with it to the lady's room closing the toilet lid so I can sit on it, then rest the journal gently on my knees. I take a few deep breaths to steady my nerves and pull out my pen.

I don't know what I'm going to say, but I know something must be said, and it can't just be me who knows, can it?

Mal

I don't think I'm the bitch you say I am. I told you if this happened again, you would lose me for good. Mal baby, you need help, and I don't know if I can be the one to do it. I am willing to go to counselling with you, but the violence has to stop … I can't trust you right now and live in fear is so so bad for our baby. I'm scared Mal; I'm so scared of you. Once you said, you never wanted me to be scared of you, once you said I should never be afraid of anyone. Last night wasn't an act. I was so afraid I almost wet myself.

It kills me that I can't be honest with you anymore, that I have to keep so much inside, that I can't even attempt to explain how I feel because I'm too scared you will overreact or take it the wrong way. I hate feeling like this and I can't let it continue...

I hear the restroom door open; my solitary retreat has been breached. My head drops down, and I rest my forehead in my hands, taking a few more breaths to fortify myself before easing myself up. I flush the unused toilet and washing my hands before heading back to my desk. I don't know who is sharing the bathroom with me, but I don't want them to know I was in here writing.

I don't know why I am bothering to write to Mal at all; there's no point. Nothing I say makes a blind bit of difference, but at least I could perhaps suggest couples counselling? Maybe, but I am starting to believe part of this is my fault.

It doesn't take long for the week to pass, and things at home seem to settle down. Mal doesn't bring up me having Paul's number again; I assume this is because he is so confident, he's gay. I'm still not sure why he thought me having his number was anything other than innocent. I've never given him any reason to doubt my fidelity.

I'm nervous about the dating scan. I pull the sheet out at intervals and stare at the highlighted query of termination. I have no idea what to expect, but on the morning of my appointment, Mal pulls out a recordable DVD.

"What's that for?" I ask him.

"Well, when my Ex had her first scan, we had to bring one with us so we could get a recording of it."

"Umm, what?" I reply, stunned. He told me that he didn't even think he could have kids.

"The fucking whore cheated on me, but it doesn't mean I didn't think that baby was mine." He looks up at me and tears start to well in his eyes. "I wanted it to be mine, but it just wasn't."

Leaning towards him, I pull him into an awkward hug, his arms rigid by his side. "I'm so sorry, Mal. That must have been so hard."

"This is a fresh start, Maddie," he says, rubbing his knuckles against my belly. "We are going to be so happy with baby bear."

I grab my jacket as we head out to the car, and I chew on my lip. I have a terrible feeling about this. I still don't know what I'm going to decide; I was banking on him not being able to make it today. He's going to see his baby for the first time, and he's so happy he's even humming under his breath I wish I could enjoy it as much as he seems to be.

The trip there is uneventful; he doesn't curse at the elderly lady who almost cuts us off as we enter the carpark, and he even holds my hand as we enter the New Horizons Radiology building.

I hand my paperwork to the bubbly young blonde at the reception, and I almost feel like I can get through this without Mal finding out what this appointment was made. While sitting in the waiting room he idly plays with my fingers as I pretend, I am watching the *Dr Phil* rerun on the television.

"Madeline Adler?" calls a nurse wearing scrubs. I stand and walk towards her with Mal following closely behind. She moves aside after opening the door to a darkened room, housing a seat that looks a lot like a dentist chair, and what I can only assume is the Ultrasound.

A man is sitting at the desk with a computer monitor on his right, and he looks up and smiles as we enter. "Good morning Miss Adler, I'm Graham. If you'd like to sit here in this chair, we'll get started."

Mal thrusts the disc towards Graham who looks at him puzzled.

"We'd like to have it recorded?" Mal prompts.

"Reordered?" Graham repeats. "I thought this was a termination dating scan?" He picks up the document on his desk, scanning the back, making sure he wasn't mistaken.

Mal stares at me with disgust. "We are not here to murder our child," he tells graham without taking his eyes off me.

"Umm OK, well, Madeline just lay down here please and we'll get started." He stands and gestures to the chair again, I swallow audibly and do as I'm told.

"I can't record using this machine," he tells us apologetically. "If you can open the front of your jeans and slide your top-up, we can get started."

I expose my stomach and Graham gives me a warning before applying the cold gel to my lower abdomen. I try to stay as still as possible while he slides the wand over my skin.

My eyes are transfixed on the monitor as I start to make sense of the grainy image. Graham starts to talk us through what we are seeing, but he need not have bothered. I can see my tiny little invader, a tiny little tadpole with a fast blipping heart.

A tear slides down my cheek, closely followed by a second, and I know for sure I could never go through with a termination. For better or worse, I am going to be a Mother.

As we stand to leave Graham prints a small and grainy image and I hold it close to my heart as Mal grabs me roughly by the arm and tosses me towards the exit.

"And when were you going to tell me about that little stunt?" he asks me. He is still holding my arm as he opens the car door and pushes me into the passenger seat.

Walking to the driver's side he snorts and growls, "I guess it was too much to expect one little thing to go right? When were you going to tell me you were going to murder my baby? Or is it *even* my baby? Is that what this is about?"

"I wasn't!" I almost yell at him. "It's just they don't scan this early," I trail off and hope that he buys it.

"Stop acting like I've never done this before." He stares resolutely at the road getting me to work in record time.

He's still grabbing the wheel tightly as he parks half on the kerb closest to the staff entrance. His breathing starts to become more rapid as he leans towards me. His voice hateful and his eyes bore holes into my head. "Is it that easy for you to get rid of our baby?" He stares dramatically at me before continuing. "Have you got any idea how easy it would be for me to get rid of you?"

Blood drains from my face, and I hug myself tightly. I feel a rush of air as he elbows the driver's side window. The glass shatters into thousands of pieces, landing all over the place. Before the last part falls, he grabs me. As he pulls me towards him, I panic, opening the car door, I fling myself back onto the pavement. My eyes fly in all directions at once, hoping no one is watching, thankfully no one is in sight.

Mal gets out of the car and rushes towards me, and I cringe preparing for another strike. "Are you OK?" he surprises me.

"You smashed the window?" I say dumbly. He reaches towards me in an attempt to hold me.

"I just love you so much, Maddie."

He tries to hold me tighter, but I pull away. I love him too, maybe. I'm not sure anymore. He has lost it. I just have to see my dog shake in fear to know. I feel so bad about abandoning him, but what else can I do?

He is looking at me with such loss that it propels me towards him. Before I know it, I am holding him, comforting him as if this were my fault, it happened.

Well if I'd just been honest with him from the start, this wouldn't have happened.

"Do you have to go in today? Let's go home okay," he says into my hair.

"OK," I reply. I don't much feel like facing people either.

I pull out my phone and send a text to Adele. 'Sorry Adele, I've got a migraine. Can you let Leon know I won't be in?'

'Rest up. I'll take care of the boss.' she replies.

I sit back in the passenger seat, pulling my jacket tighter around me. Air blowing around the car whips my hair into my face, and I realise we will need to take care of this quickly.

It appears Mal is reading my mind as he pulls off the main road and heads towards the wrecker's yard. "I'll get a new window."

"OK," I reply. I don't much feel like talking to him.

The following day Mal refuses to go to work. He calls his boss early in the morning and tells him he has a splitting headache. After that, he refuses to leave the house, so if I am to make it work, I'll have to walk.

He fiddles with my hair and nuzzles my neck. "Stay home with me today, and we can play hooky together."

"I really should go in Mal," I try to protest; my job position is precarious at best with my current track record.

"Please don't leave me," he begs, making it impossible for me to say no to him. I send Adele another text saying I'm still under the weather. I am lucky she is good at covering for me.

CHAPTER FIFTEEN

After the weekend, Mal thankfully seems to have run out reasons to stay home. He's actually been terrific, but I am struggling to be anything but indifferent towards him. By Monday I am exhausted, and when I finally arrive to work, I gratefully sink into my chair. Adele hands me a hot tea, and I thank her profusely.

"Madeline darling, your parents came by on Friday and wondered where you were?"

"Oh?" I reply noncommittally.

"Look, Hun. I don't want to blindside you. I told them I'm worried about you." She drags her chair, nearer to me and looks me in the eyes. "Are you OK?"

I take a sip from the cup in my hands. The warmth seeping through my body does nothing to defrost my heart. I take a deep breath. "Not really, Adele. I'm pregnant."

Adele's shoulders sag noticeably, and I feel like I've disappointed her somehow.

"Oh Maddie," she exhales. "No wonder you've been so tired and ill. How far along are you?"

"Eight Weeks, I had a scan last Thursday."

"And how has Mal taken the news?" she ventures.

"He's over the moon when he's not accusing me of carrying another man's baby," I cover my face with my hands and grown loudly. "I don't know what the hell I'm doing."

Adele gently pats my shoulder, "You have to let your Parents in Maddie. You're going to need their support now more than ever."

"Please don't tell them! I just need some time to work this out."

Adele squeezes my arm again; she looks at me with resignation and trundles her way back to her desk. "It's not my place to say anything; I already feel like I've overstepped the mark. But this isn't just about you anymore is it dear."

No, it's not just about me. I feel like I've got everyone else's feeling and safety to consider, and now I've got a baby to think about too. There are far too many balls in the air, and they are dropping to the ground all around me.

"I know. I just need some time to assimilate this," I hang my head.

"I'm here for you Maddie. But it's going to be your parents you are going to need the most."

I try to focus on work, but it's pointless, there is just too much taking up space in my head. I stare at the calendar on the wall, focusing on the date. It's Justin's birthday today, and I didn't even realise it. Today would have marked the seventh year since I met him. I'll never forget the first moment I laid eyes on him. I was so sure he was my soul mate, not that I believe in that anymore. I don't think I believe in love anymore.

After Adele leaves for her morning break, I succumb to my impulse to call him and grab the phone. Without pausing to think, I dial his number. I don't know what I'm doing, I don't even expect him to answer his phone at work, but he does.

"Hello?" he says. Oh god, it's so good to hear his voice, but I'm frozen, and I can't reply. "Hello, is there anyone there?" he repeats, drawing out the syllables.

"Hey," I say quietly.

"Maddie, Is that you?"

"Yeah, I just wanted to say Happy Birthday."

He is silent for a long time before he replies. "Thanks."

"I miss you," I blurt.

"Then come home Maddie," he tells me.

I wish I could; I wish I could take it all back and fling myself into his arms and have him make everything OK. "I can't," I begin to cry.

"Yeah, I know. How's Bess?"

We switch to a more comfortable topic glossing over the hard stuff, "She misses you."

"I'd love to see her."

"Well, when you're next in Auckland let me know. I'm sure we can manage something," I say with another empty promise. "I've got to get back to work."

"Yeah me too, take care, Maddie."

I cry for a few minutes after he ends the call. Then place the handset back into its cradle.

I wish I weren't pregnant; I can't have his child. A baby isn't the only thing growing inside me. There is also humiliation and hatred. I pull the small picture of my baby from my wallet and stare at the grainy image of my tiny invader.

I wish this were easy. I wish I knew he would be OK, but something in my heart makes me believe he'd try and kill himself if I left. How can I carry the guilt of that with me too? What would I tell my child?

My life truly sucks.

Feeling melancholy, I push a stack of invoices to one side and call up the work email programme.

From: Madeline Adler <m.adler@mcleansdeparmentstore.com>
To: Megan Wilson < megan-jw@mymail.com>

Hi Megan
I really need to speak to you.
Maddie x

Before I've had a chance to turn back to my invoice pile, another email pops up.

From: Megan Wilson < megan-jw@mymail.com>
To: Madeline Adler m.adler@mcleansdeparmentstore.com

Maddie!!!
What's wrong?
Megan xx

From: Madeline Adler <m.adler@mcleansdeparmentstore.com>
To: Megan Wilson < megan-jw@mymail.com>

Megan
I've made such a mess of everything. I'm pregnant. I don't know what the hell to do. I wish you didn't live so far away.
Maddie :(

This time, it takes longer for her to reply, but when she does, it gives me plenty to consider.

From: Megan Wilson megan-jw@mymail.com
To: Madeline Adler m.adler@mcleansdeparmentstore.com

Maddie, my darling girl.
You are going to be an amazing Mother. I know you'll wear this new cap so well. But that man is bad news; he's bad for you. If you want to leave, please come here. Raise your baby here; we can help you, support you and keep you both safe.
Megan xxx

Megan has belief in me; she believes in me. Could I move in with her? I don't know. I doubt it, but it's a comforting thought and the only thing that consoles me during another long night of sitting on my couch and lying silently beside Mal at night.

CHAPTER SIXTEEN

There isn't much variation in our morning routine. Mal pulls me closer to him and snuggles his face into my hair. Rather than feeling affection, it just reminds me that it's lank and greasy and I should probably wash it before leaving for work.

But as usual, I am reluctant to leave the circle of his arms and the absence of his anger. I'd stay here all day if I could, I'd pee in a jar if it meant I could keep 'My Malcolm' with me, the one I fell so completely in love with.

Life has made sure to teach me all good things come to an end, and with a grunt, he shifts himself to sit on the side of the bed. I see him sigh heavily and run his hands across his face and over his hair. I cringe as he cracks his neck both right and left, then pop's each knuckle.

He pivots and looks at me, he says nothing but leans in to rub my belly.

"Good morning Baby Bear."

"Good morning Daddy Bear," I dutifully reply.

There isn't a lot of talking this morning; we shuffle around each other, I grab a couple of porridge sachets, which seems to be pretty much the only food source I can take out of the house and shove them in my work bag.

"Are you ready to go?" Mal asks.

"Yeah," I tell him. It's been an uneventful morning and gives me a small glimmer of hope that perhaps the rest of the day will be equally blissful.

The workday is usually a solace for me apart from the constant barrage of text messages I get from Mal. So, I am horrified when I look up from my stack of paperwork to see my parents standing in the doorway.

Oh, crap. I love my parents, but they are the last people I want to see right now. Adele stands sheepishly behind them.

As they move aside for her to enter the office Dad says, "We've come to take you out for lunch." Mum backs him up with a smile that appears too forced to be natural.

This feels like an ambush, but before I have a chance to protest Adele chimes in with, "Go on girl, I'll hold down the fort."

Briefly checking my watch I grab my bag and follow my parents.

Shuffling down the stairs my Mother natters inanely about the weather, about Rosie's boyfriend, about what the senile neighbour was doing with her breakfast, anything to fill my silence I guess. Dad stares resolutely ahead as if I need another clue that they are planning an intervention.

"Shall we head to AJ's?" asks Mum. It's the café that's relatively nearby work but not so close that my fellow employees will be there, so I agree, and we set off in the car.

It doesn't take long before I'm sitting opposite my parents in a small booth. Thankfully my parents head towards the till first and ask me what I'd like for lunch. I'm relieved because I don't want them to find out I don't have any money to buy my own. My stomach growls appreciatively as I order poached eggs on toast with a fruit salad. I knew it wouldn't be long before they spit out why they came here, so I hope I get to enjoy some of my lunch before that happens.

For a while we sit looking at each other, pretending to wait for our food. I twist the number six around on its metal stand, finding the whirling motion somewhat comforting.

"Madeline Darling," Mum starts. "We came in a few days ago to see you and Adele told us you had called in sick?"

I suck my bottom lip in my mouth and start twisting the napkin in my fingers instead, winding it into a tight cord. When I don't make any effort to explain my absence Dad prompts, "Are you feeling OK? We can take you to see a doctor?"

"Oh, I'm fine, Dad. I just had a migraine," I keep it vague.

"You were away yesterday too?" says Mum.

Damn it. I bite my bottom lip harder.

"Look," Dad replies more firmly. "We spoke to Adele, and she said she's worried about you."

I stare at him as my mouth falls open. I want so badly to fling myself into his arms and ask him to make everything all right, but the vision of Mal telling me in minute detail how he would murder and gut him while making me watch flashes in my mind.

"I know it's your choice, but you're my baby girl. Why don't you tell him it's over and move back home with us?"

"Dad, I wish it were that easy," I take a breath and prepare to begin trying to put them off this line of questioning.

Before I can phrase a coherent sentence, Mum speaks. "It's up to you, but we still have your room set up. It's ok to say it didn't work out."

I sigh, sucking up all the warring emotions in my heart and tell them both. "I want too, but I just can't give up on him yet."

"It's your choice," Dad repeats, but I can see the hurt in his eyes. I can read his body language as well as Mal's. I know that he just wants to make everything all right in my world. I resist the urge to rub my belly and hold back the tears that are threatening to overflow. I have no idea how they would react to the news of a baby; I have barely been able to process it myself.

I consider for a few seconds just blurting it out, but I can't.

"I'll give him eight weeks. I'm going to ask him to go to counselling with me. I owe to us to try and work things out, but I'll end it if I have too," I trail off, this last bit of bravado sounding weak even to my ears.

Suddenly the idea of going to counselling with Mal doesn't seem like such an unrealistic idea. I mean OK, so I failed at getting Justin to go with me to save our marriage, but Mal and I are expecting a baby, one he desperately wants. That has to change things, right?

I cling to that hope all the way back to work, where I promptly return my lunch into the toilet. Thanks, baby bear, that's all I need.

Adele looks up as I enter the office. I think she is pretty good at reading my face because I see her lips pressed into a tight line.

"Maddie, I'm not sorry I spoke to your parents," she says defensively.

"It's just made everything so much harder!" I almost yell at her.

Instead of yelling back as I expect, she gets up and walks over to me, wrapping her arms around me to rub my back.

She holds me closer as I try to pull away, and tears spill unbidden from my eyes. Before I know it, I am sobbing.

"I just have to try, I have too," I beg her.

"I know you do. I take it you didn't tell them about the baby?"

"How could I? I don't even know how I feel about it, and Mal is, well Mal."

Deflated I pull away from her and fall in my office chair. I don't want to talk about this anymore. Dragging in a deep breath, I try to push my worries from my mind and grab a stack of whatever paperwork is in my in-tray.

Adele sighs audibly as she picks up her handbag; I can hear her rummaging in her large canvas bag. She sides an A4 piece of paper onto the desk in front of me. At the top are the words 'The Power and Control Wheel'.

"Take some time to look at this dear, really look at it. And know I am here for you."

Adele rubs my shoulder one last time before heading out for her lunch. I pick up the paper in front of me and lean back in my chair.

Power and control, I have neither of these. I look at the subtitles around the circle. Coercion and threats, intimidation, emotional abuse, isolation, minimising, denying and blaming, using children, using male privilege, using economic abuse. Every single thing on this list Mal does to me. I recognise that he is abusing me; I know this is wrong. So why can't I leave him?

The computer chimes alerting me to a new email, shoving the paper into a draw I flick across screens, and it fills my heart with joy that instead of another invoice it's from Megan.

From: Megan Wilson <megan-jw@mymail.com>
To: Madeline Adler <m.adler@mcleansdeparmentstore.com>
Maddie,
How are you feeling? I just thought I'd drop you a quick message to let you know I'm thinking of you. I saw Justin at the weekend. I think he regrets a lot of the bad mistakes he made too.
Much love,
Megan x

My heart lurches, she's spoken to Justin. It hurts to think about him, but as I cast my mind back to the last time, he held me, I also feel a sense of comfort. Of their violation, my hands call up a blank email, but it's not Megan who I am desperate to speak with.

From: Madeline Adler <m.adler@mcleansdeparmentstore.com>
To: Justin Robinson <justin.robinson@mymail.com>
Hey Justin,
Thought I'd check-in, how are you?
Maddie.

WOW, did I do that? First, a phone call and now an email, Mal would hit the roof if he ever found out. I take a minute for my breathing to return to normal but then nearly jump out of my skin as the office phone rings. I stare at the caller id; it's Justin.

Gingerly I pick up the phone. "Hi," I say rather than the usual welcome statement I am supposed to answer all work calls.

"Hey," he replies. "So, you're working in a department store?"

"Oh yeah, for now anyhow," I tell him.

"How are you?"

It feels like a loaded question, so I carefully answer, "I'm ok, Bess misses you." I know it's a repeat of our earlier conversation, but diversion is always a good tactic; even if we only just spoke about her.

"I miss Bessie too."

Do I hear more in those words than just missing our dog, or am I just so desperate to reconnect with him I am making things up?

"You know you can come home, right?" he tells me again.

"I wish it were that easy Justin." I stare at Adele's empty chair; she's not back from lunch yet. "I can't talk for long; can you email me?" I don't want to hang up, but I'm not sure I can talk to him for much longer without crying again.

He sighs heavily, "Is there someone else, Maddie?"

"No, it's not that. Me leaving, it had nothing to do with that." I can't talk to him anymore; my voice is breaking. "I have to go." Before he has a chance to reply, I softly replace the phone into its cradle.

With a heavy heart, I return home. I replied to Megan's email, letting her know that I'm ok, the baby is ok. Justin called me and that it made me feel both sick and sad. I still despise myself for what I did to him. I feel like it will be one of my life's biggest mistakes. I desperately wish I could do what he asked, move back to him, slot back into his life and pretend none of this happened. But my little invader has made sure that there will be no fresh starts for Justin and me.

I think Mal must have a sixth sense as he immediately asks what's wrong the moment I step into the car. It's been an emotionally draining day, with my parents turning up, and then the stupid impulse to reach out to Justin again. I need some calm in my life.

"I'm just tired," I tell Mal. "You know. I think it's just baby growing stuff."

He smiles a rare smile at me, "Dinner and early bed then!" he says.

"Yeah," I agree. There is no point arguing with him.

CHAPTER SEVENTEEN

The next day I have two more non-work-related emails in my inbox. The first is from Megan, the second from Justin telling me he hit his finger while trying to fix the loose planking on the deck. I smile at the thought of Justin wielding a hammer. He does need constant supervision when attempting home improvements; because now he has to take a week off work while he recovers.

When we brought the house, it was a blank canvas, and I was so excited to get stuck into making it truly our home. But he made so many false starts on home improvements and left so many projects unfinished I just gave up trying to make it something special.

It's taken years for me to smile about the time he decided to rip all the Gib off the walls and ceiling. It was supposed to be easier than taking off the old wallpaper and plastering. It's probably still unfinished, while he moves from project to project.

I am not sure what I want from him, reconnecting like this is dangerous and stupid for both of us, but I can't help replying to him.

From: Madeline Adler m.adler@mcleansdeparmentstore.com
To: Justin Robinson <Justin. Robinson @mymail.com>

Justin,
OUCH, you really should be more careful! Why don't you get one of your mates over to help you? I'd kiss it better if I thought it would

help. Take better care of yourself.

Maddie

I hit send before I can second guess what I've written, but I have that gnawing sensation in the pit of my stomach. I feel like I am flirting with disaster. To shake this feeling of unease, I send a quick reply to Megan, too and try to get some work done. I only pause as Adele passes me a coffee.

"It's OK to take a break, Maddie. We can't have you making the rest of us look bad," she says with a touch of humour in her voice, but I can tell she is trying to mend yesterday's rift. She is one of the only people I can trust; I can't afford to lose her support.

I take the coffee and pat her hand, "Thanks, I'm ok. I want to get these out of the way before the weekend." I shrug and try to convey an aura of a person with not nearly as many problems as I have. She doesn't believe me, but to her credit, she lets it go this time.

It's a long slog to the afternoon; my back is killing me. I'm at a point where I'm even considering finding Paul for a distraction when my computer alerts me to another email.

It's Megan again; I've told her how I think I've ruined my whole life. That leaving Justin was the dumbest decision I've ever made, and I will regret it for the rest of my life.

'Maddie,' she tells me in another email. 'Justin is one of the most selfish, self-absorbed men I've ever met; he probably only noticed you were gone when he wasn't fed regularly.' I know logically she is right, but it's hard to believe while I am wearing rose coloured glasses.

Just because my life isn't what I had planned doesn't mean I should rebound back to my ex. It's sage advice. It's a measure of comfort, having her tell me that I deserve better and that I can successfully raise my child on my own. It all sounds so logical, so why is it so hard to accept?

Later that night, as I lean back on the couch and lightly settle my hand on my tummy, I wonder how long it will be until I feel pregnant. I'm 12 weeks according to the ultrasound, but I don't look any different. I slide my top up and examine the expanse of white flesh. Idly I wonder if I'll have to take my belly piercing out. I don't want too, Mal told me a few months ago he thought they looked cheap so out of spite I am reluctant to remove it.

He's already put a stop to me wearing make-up. The last time I applied some before work, he asked me if I was trying to attract someone better. He is incapable of realising that any make-up I wear is to make myself feel better.

Attractive is the last thing I feel. I feel old and tired, and when it comes down to it, I feel angry.

I'm startled out of my thoughts as Mal screams my name. I run to where he is standing by the back door.

"WHAT THE FUCK MADELINE! Your fucking dog has shit under the washing line again! She's fucking up my clothes! Is your useless fucking dog more important than my stuff? Why was she not tied up?"

He yanks my cowering dog by her scruff, manhandling her to her rudimentary kennel. Holding her still with one arm, he shortens the line by a meter and attaches it to her collar. He looks at me in defiance, daring me to challenge him.

I am trying hard to control my shaking. One wrong move and he will take it out on Bess again.

"I don't want her near my stuff Madeline, is that too fucking hard for you to understand?"

My dog whines and cowers from him, but the leash isn't long enough for her to get fully undercover. "The rope is too short, she can't reach her water," I try to reason with him.

He responds by kicking her so hard it shunts her to the full extension of the rope, making it almost impossible for her to breath.

"She can reach," he says with triumph, his eyes gleaming with a pleasure far beyond my comprehension. He pushes me into the door frame as he strolls past me, slamming the back door closed behind him.

Bessie cries quietly begging me with her big sad brown eyes, and I rush to her side to see blood trickling from her mouth. Tears spring to my eyes and my chest heaves in with repressed sobs. Quivering as I try to maintain control of myself, first I let him do this to me, and now my poor defenceless animal has been dragged into this. I'm an echo of who I once was. I live in abject fear of him.

I wrap my arms around her; I hate that he hurts Bessie, and I hate myself for not being able to protect her. He wants me to talk to him, but he's not interested in how I feel. He always makes me out to be the bad person in his head. He thinks I'm playing games, but he cannot see how much he is hurting me. The very last thing I'd be willing to do is to play games with him.

I'm 12 weeks pregnant, I'm lonely, and I'm so scared. Bessie pushes herself further onto my lap if she were a smaller dog; she would be sitting on top of me. Her large head pushes under my chin and her soft wet nose pressed against my face. I hug her tighter and sob into her smelly unwashed coat.

"I'm so sorry Bessie, I am so, so sorry. I can't protect you. I don't even know how to protect myself. I'm so selfish. I should call your Daddy; he'd take you back in a heartbeat."

I don't know how long we stay like that, drawing comfort from each other. Both Teddy and Tilda wander over silently to us to rub up against my legs, lending me their strength also.

I am selfish, I should be getting them out of this hell hole, but I need them.

CHAPTER EIGHTEEN

The next day I am tightly wound with tension. Mal is home, a self-declared day off. He tried to get me to stay home from work, but I've already taken so much time off recently, I am not sure that Leon would wear another sick day. I can't focus on anything for more than five minutes straight, so. Instead, I write in my Journal.

I think of my poor beautiful dog. All the harsh words and slaps on the back are going to wear her down, and she has such a beautiful nature. I am scared it is slowly being destroyed. I don't agree with the way he treats her; I am sure it would be the same with any dog with him, but she isn't just any dog, she is mine, and I love her. This is not the way I treat dogs; this is not the way I treat my animals.

If he read my diary, he would get so mad at me. Will, I ever learn to keep my mouth shut, or will he kill me first?

I can't handle his anger; all the rage he builds up inside of him. It eats away at me, and I don't know if I will ever love him as much as I did. I don't know if I'll ever trust him again. I don't see the bright side, there is no light.

I HATE HIM FOR WHAT HE HAS DONE TO ME. I HATE HIM I HATE HIM I HATE HIM. I find myself stabbing those worlds harshly into my journal, so hard that my pen tears the paper.

I run out of steam after that. So, I take turns staring at the blank email inbox and swinging my office chair around until Adele tells me to go for a break before she ties me up. I can't help but think of Bess, tied up and alone at home with him. Walking isn't going to alleviate the tension, but at least I can stop irritating my friend.

I take the long route to the staff room and sit down with a coffee. There are a few other people seated sporadically around the room. Usually, I manage to pick times that avoid company.

Amy is chatting amicably to a young sales assistant named Todd about the upcoming work quiz night. There is some discussion over who the smartest people to team up with are.

They look up as I enter and Amy's face lights up. "How smart are you Maddie? You know stuff, right?"

"Uh, I know some things. My sister is the smart one in our family."

"Oh yeah?" she pauses while she ponders this titbit. "Is your sister any good under pressure? How much does she know?"

"HAH," I bark out a laugh surprising myself with the sound. "Rosie is the queen of all useless information, if I were going on a quiz night, I'd want her with me."

"Oh, you guys have got to come," Todd urges. "I must have you on my team!"

"You just want her brainy sister on your team Todd," Amy retorts as she playfully shunts him under the table.

"I don't think I'll be able to make it sorry," I say. I don't need any more drama at home.

"Come on, Maddie! You never come to any of our team building activities," Amy begs.

"I don't know. Can I let you know?" I finally relent.

Before I have a chance to protest, Todd jumps up and shouts, "BAGS!" and races Amy towards the signup sheet on the notice board.

"For God's sake, you two," I exclaim as they collide and wrestle over the pen.

I am impressed by Amy's defence manoeuvrability as she successfully relieves Todd of the pen and triumphantly scrawls my name and Rosie's next to her team.

"You have to come now. Otherwise, you'll be letting the whole team down," she pouts hands on hips.

I laugh and cave, "Okay. If it means that much to you, I'll do it. But I hope there is going to be more than us three on your team or we're screwed." I write the date into my diary; I'll figure out a way to convince Mal I need to go later. Maybe I should tell him it's compulsory.

"We have just over a month to prepare, so I'm going to bring *Trivial Pursuit* tomorrow, and we can start studying!" she tells me joyously.

I stare at Amy as if she has gone insane and Todd laughs.

"You should have joined my team," he winks at me.

I'm glad I have at least four weeks to figure out how to get Mal to let me go or much more likely, a way to let Amy down. I yank my mobile from my pocket and text my sister if I have to pull out then I can at least leave Amy with Rosie.

'What are you up to in 4 weeks? Want to go to my work quiz night?'

Her reply is almost immediate. I wonder if her phone is superglued to her hand, I never have to wait long for her response.

'Just let me know when k :)'

I knew I could rely on her, even if texting with proper grammar is beyond her.

I sigh deeply while doodling a few more lines in my journal while taking the last few swigs of my now mostly cold coffee. I've been sitting here for far too long. Even Amy and Todd have gone back to work, and I should do the same.

I just wish I could figure out where I put my motivation, it's like all my ambition has been sucked out of me since moving in with Mal. But I head back to the office, carrying a peace offering coffee for Adele with me. I know she usually buys hers, but I suspect she will appreciate the sentiment.

"Oh love, you didn't have to fetch me coffee," Adele says as I hand her the mug. "Are you feeling any better?"

"Well, Amy just steamrolled me into joining her team for the quiz night."

"Well done!" Adele beams. "Getting out of the house is just what you need."

"My sister is going to come with me," I add. I feel a need to reassure her that I'm OK, despite everything I've offloaded on her.

"Even better," She smiles, although I am not sure it is. I am dreading asking Mal for permission to go, I am sure he will say no.

The afternoon settles into a lazy routine, I even manage to get through a stack of sorting and filing. I have no idea why I thought being an Office Administrator used to be interesting. The endless piles of paperwork seem to dull my mind, not that I have any idea what I'd rather be doing.

Maybe I could run away and join a circus? I could star as an incredibly stupid woman.

The ping of an email notification draws my attention as I flick between screens. Justin has messaged me again, he just wants me to know that he misses me being around, but he's managed to figure out how to follow the packet instructions on the back of a sausage casserole, so between that and the fast-food he's mostly been covered, although he could do with one of my Sunday roasts. I sigh before hitting reply and suggesting that if he keeps eating Big Macs, he will start to resemble one. I add that I am glad he isn't starving or living off cereal or poisoning himself with rotten milk.

Poor timing, as usual, I am startled as my phone buzzing in my pocket.

I thought Mal had been quiet today. He usually picks up the text frequency when he's at home alone, but he's only sent a few so far today.

He fire's text after text faster than I can open and read them.

16:00: 'Ring your sister see if that fucking dog is at her cunt boyfriend's house.'

16:03: 'Madeline?'

16:06: 'What the fuck! FUCKING CUNT! Get them to bring the cunt back and put it on its fucking lead before I GO AND GET IT MY WAY! CUNT FUCKING SLUT DOG!'

16:07: 'This is my fault, I shouldn't try!"

I grab the office phone and call Rosie, "Hey, is Tom home? Bess has gone missing, and Mal is really worried." I cross my fingers and hope, although I have no idea what I am hoping for.

"Yeah sorry sis, she's here. We didn't think anyone was home, we were going to bring her back once you got home from work?" Her voice is genuinely sounding remorseful that she hadn't messaged me to let me know they had her.

Opening my phone, I send a quick message to Mal telling him that Bessie is with Rosie and Tom.

"Thanks so much for taking Bess in, can you guys keep her there until I get home?"

"Of course, she's a sweetheart and Sheba just loves her," Rosie tells me.

"Sheba?" I repeat, confused.

"Yeah, that's Tommy's Mum's dog," she says as if I should already know this. Since we live on the same street, perhaps I should.

"Oh, the white fluffy one," I say absently while my phone goes crazy in my hand as message after message comes through from Mal. "I better get back to work, I'll come get Bessie when I get home." After a hasty goodbye, I hang up.

With dread, I reopen my cell phone and grimace at the sheer volume of texts I've just gotten. I don't know how to handle him, there's not enough time to reply before another comes through.

16:08: 'Just keeps pushing it doesn't it.'

16:08: 'Why didn't anyone fucking call or fucking txt to say it was there?'

16:11: 'I've been calling out for an HOUR! Your sister and that fuck head would have heard! Why the fuck didn't they tell me! CUNTS!

I try breaking in, saying not to worry and that I will go get her when I get home from work, but it's only a short reprieve before several angrier texts come through.

16:19: 'FUCK OFF I fucking txt OK keep it there. I don't want it here.'

16:20: 'I feel like a fucking fool trying for your dog. I give up Madeline I tried for you.'

There is nothing to say to this really, so I try to ignore him while he sends more texts.

16:30: 'Do you acknowledge that I've tried? Should I have left it tied up to shit on itself? Sorry for FUCKING TRYING! Do you SEE that? Selfish.'

I try to placate him again 'I'm sorry, she's ok. I'll get her when I'm home.' But it doesn't work.

16:31: 'Stop stressing me out,' he texts back.

16:43: 'You can't acknowledge that I have tried and put in the effort, can you? You don't see I tried for you? Thanks for appreciating my effort. I guess it was nothing.'

'I'm sorry,' I reply again and then follow it up saying that all the texts are stressing me out, that I am trying to work, but it's making that very difficult, but if I was hoping to elicit some empathy from him I am shit out of luck.

16:55: 'Why are you stressed out?' he replies. After that, he sends a few weird texts asking if I tried calling him, but I give up responding to him and try to focus on work. He's supposed to be picking me up at 5.30, but I am feeling sick about what sort of mood he will be in when he does. I have no idea what possessed him to even attempt to take Bessie of the rope, but I suspect it was nothing good.

CHAPTER NINETEEN

I step outside a little before 5.30 pm and send Mal text to say I'm ready and rock back on my heels. Trying to calm my breathing down, I let my mind wander. I wonder what Justin is doing right now. He's probably considering his take-out dinner options. Everyone is just getting on with their lives, and I am stuck in hell, and I am dragging my poor animals along for the ride.

I'll never forget meeting my beautiful dog for the first time, she was such a tiny sweet thing with paws the size of dinner plates. I was visiting the animal shelter with a friend who was adopting a cat, and as soon as I saw her, I knew she was meant to be mine.

I'm so impulsive, I see that now. I fling myself from one situation to the next, but I knew that dog was mine. I love her like she was my child, and now I'm not even allowed to feed her. I already told Mal he doesn't need to be the one to feed the animals, I am more than happy to do it, but it's like he is terrified of relinquishing any control to me at all.

My poor under the blanket in my bed dog doesn't even have a proper bed anymore. Not that she would want to come inside with him in the house. I wish Mal could see things the way I do, and understand how I feel, even if only for a second. I am trying so hard to make things work with him and for us to be happy. I want us, I want him. I don't want to be unhappy, and I don't want to be sad all the time.

I wonder if it's jealousy, but how can someone be jealous of an animal? I know I have had them for a long time, and that I brought them from my relationship with Justin, but I was so hoping for us to be a family. I wish he would understand that Bessie has feelings too, she can feel joy and feel frightened just like me. She tries so hard to please him and fails nearly as much as I do.

I wish there was a way to tell him all this and have him understand me, but what's the point. It doesn't matter how many times I try to write it down or talk to him because he won't listen.

Forty minutes later, he finally approaches the kerb. He shoots me an ominous black look with a deep scowl etched across his face. After the text barrage, he sent me this afternoon I have already tried to mentally prepare myself for his deluge of abuse.

I'm not sure if I want to get into the car with him, I open the passenger door cautiously and climb in, careful not to look him in the eye. He doesn't say anything to me, so I start to hope vainly that maybe he ran out of anger.

He doesn't talk to me, but he drives fuming all the way home, cornering too hard and crunching the gears. Then when he enters our driveway, he's going too fast and almost hits the garage door. He yanks on the hand break jerking me forward against the seat belt. I rub my shoulder, expecting another bruise. Of course, he doesn't bother asking if I'm ok and before I've got my seatbelt unplugged, he's got the house key in the door.

At first, I try to walk towards Tom's house to get Bess back as I told him earlier, but as I start to step away, Mal is suddenly by my side grabbing my shirt to hold me back.

"Where the fuck do you think you're going?" he growls, yanking me back towards him.

My eyes fly around the street searching for anyone who could be looking at us, fearful for my sister whose car I see parked in Tom's drive. The street is eerily quiet, but as he drags me towards the house, I think I see the net curtains across the street move.

"Get in the house, Madeline," he instructs me.

I'm not sure doing what I'm told is a good idea, but I have little choice with his hand wrapped around my throat. I do what I am told, terrified of the consequences of disobeying him. I walk as fast as I can up the stairs to the lounge, I place my work bag on the couch.

As I turn around, Mal hits me in the chest so hard, I struggle to draw a breath. He springs back grabbing the shoulder of my shirt along with a fist full of my hair and throws me to the ground.

"Have you got something to confess to me?" he over enunciates each syllable, making every word a weapon.

"I don't know what you mean?" I say in confusion, wondering what this has to do with Bessie.

"You FUCKING WHORE!" he shouts in my face. "I thought you were the one. I THOUGHT I could trust you! And it turns out you're just like the rest."

"I don't know what you mean?" I plead with him.

"Once a slut always a fucking slut, I should just cut this baby out of you right now, you don't deserve to have my child inside your whore body."

"What have I done?" I say, cowering on the floor as he towers over me.

His breathing is heavy with rage, and he seems very much like an enraged bull. I tighten my arms across my body where it still aches from his impact, and I struggle to get my breathing under control. I'm scared; I am very scared.

He takes the few steps away from me and reaches for a stack of printed emails and waves them in my face. "You fucking whore," he calls me again. "Did you think you were going to get away with this?" He is waving the papers around to quickly for me to see what's on them, but I'm now sure this has nothing to do with Bessie.

Just went I think he's not going to tell me what's caused him to be so angry with me he starts reading from them.

It's the email's I've sent to Justin over the last few days. My heart stops cold, and the feeling of ice slides across my entire body.

He knows. He's hit me again, and he knows. My mind races, I can't begin to understand how he got these emails.

"No one likes you, Madeline, why can't you get through your thick fucking skull. You are nothing but a filthy whore, and everyone knows it. Do you know what they call you?"

He leans down over me again until I can feel his breath on my face. He waits for an answer, but I have none, no words at all, I'm too stunned. He shunts me, and I slide at least a meter across the floor to the kitchen. I struggle to swallow the saliva building in my mouth and shake my head; it's all I can manage.

"Pancake tits," he spits at me. "That's what all they all call you, the slut with the Pancake tits."

For some unknown reason, this cuts me deep. My breasts have always been a part of my body I've felt the most insecure about. I've always thought they were too flat and now everyone else thinks that also.

I don't know why adolescent name-calling is upsetting me so much when I have a much bigger problem. Someone has forwarded the emails I exchanged with Justin to Mal. Did Justin do it, or did he get them some other way?

"No one likes you and don't think for a second that your so-called workmates are your friends. There is someone there who would be more than happy to ruin you any way they can. You better watch your back because I'm not fucking going too."

I'm heartbroken thinking someone at work might be out to get me, I thought that even despite how aloof I can be, I'd created myself a place there. I don't know how to respond to this information. Not that I have a chance to respond because he's not finished with me.

"Everything you told your so-called friend 'Megan' she told Justin, and now I know."

He punches the side of my fridge so hard that the indent of his knuckles is left in the metal and I'm left with no doubt in my mind that he wishes to punch me like that.

As he turns back towards me, he lashes out with his other hand and puts a similar dent in the side of the microwave that sits on top of the fridge. Two more of my things added to the list he's damaged or broken.

"How the fuck did you think you were going to get away with this Madeline? Don't ever forget who I am or what I can do. I know people, people who like me and are willing to help me. I can ruin you."

At some point in the evening, the doorbell rings. I'm still on the floor as Mal paces over me. I suspect it's Rosie and Tom as they still have Bess, but I don't want anyone seeing me like this and I don't want my poor dog anywhere near him while he's this volatile.

They ring the bell again, and just when I think they've gone, I hear a rapid knocking at the back door. The lights are on in the lounge, but they are off in the kitchen so they probably can't see us.

"Maddie? Mal?" Rosie calls, as she knocks again.

Mal places his hand over my mouth and stares into my eyes, warning me not to say a word. To think I once spent hours staring into his rich brown eyes thinking I could get lost in them, thinking that was a good thing. Now they are hard and accusing, and the only 'lost' I can get in them is a bad thing.   My phone starts buzzing as my sister tries to call me, but I am pinned under Mal and can't reach it. The second time it rings, he grabs it accepting the call and thrusts it at me.

"Hi," I answer with a crack in my voice.

"Weren't you coming to get your dog? Where are you?" she asks.

"I'm sorry. I had a migraine," I adlib, hoping she doesn't hear my desperation. "I went to bed and forgot. Can you keep her until tomorrow?"

The line is silent for a while, and I wonder what's going through her head. "Are you ok Madeline?" she asks finally.

"I just need some sleep," I tell her. I'm not sure she believes me.

"OK, I was staying over at Tommy's anyhow. But you better come get her tomorrow morning."

She hangs up, and Mal takes my phone away from me, ripping the last lifeline from my hands.

The phone call doesn't end his anger, it continues for hours, threat after threat. I cry so hard, and for so long, my throat is as tender and raw as my chest and shoulder. My eyes are so swollen from the tears I can barely open them. I pray for him to stop, but he's been saving the finale for bedtime.

"Have you even got your fucking money from this fucking prick? I bet he's just trying to get out of paying what he owes us. Why have you not called a lawyer yet? Is this part of some master plan? Are you just going to go back that fuck? I've got all the proof I need to take my baby from you, and you will never see her again. If you contact that slut friend of yours again, or even for one second think you can call that fucking retarded husband of yours, it's over. Don't you ever forget that baby is mine, not yours! You are a fucking bitch, you whore, and you're nothing but a slut."

I go to bed, hungry and exhausted. I lay on the edge of the bed and wonder what on earth has happened to my life.

CHAPTER TWENTY

There is no morning salvation for me today; I wish I could just stay home. I want to bury myself under the blankets and block the whole damn world out.

Mal flings himself out of bed like I have some incredibly infectious disease, so I pull the duvet over my head and rub my aching temples in circular motions. Well, at least the migraine I told my sister about was real.

"Get up," he says. "I'm going to get that cunt dog back. I've got to go to fucking work and so do you."

I don't reply, what's the point? He doesn't listen. Instead, I ease my aching body from bed to stand in front of the toothpaste stained bathroom mirror, staring at a person I don't recognise as me.

A sizeable angry bruise reaches across my chest and shoulder. Moving my arm is painful, and I hope he hasn't caused any lasting damage. At least it's below the collar of my work uniform. I ease my shirt over my head and try using cold water to shrink my eyes back to their normal size. I give up in the end and grab a pair of dark glasses, despite it being overcast, and 7 am.

I hear Mal outside, and I presume he is tying Bess back to the step. I have no idea if she's been fed or not, but he doesn't give me a chance to check as he rushes through the house and out the other side leaving me to chase after him.   I grab a couple of porridge sachets for my lunch and hope that today will get better.

Mal doesn't say a word all the way to work, but just as I get out of the car, he comments, "I'm coming back for lunch. Meet me out here at 12."

"Uh, ok," I reply. I sort of wonder if this means he will take me to the café? Maybe I won't have to eat porridge again.

In the office, I sit as close to the screen as I can and hope that Adele doesn't ask too many questions. If she does, I'll just say I had a migraine last night to cover my scratchy voice and puffy eyes. I delete the emails from Megan as soon as they ping into my inbox, and I don't reach out again to Justin. I'm not sure what I would say to either of them.

I think I know exactly who started calling me Pancake tits. I bet it was Brad, I'm sure. They are all blaming me, but it was Justin too. How could I have let this happen? But I only have myself to blame. Mal is only telling me these things to hurt me, I know that. But oh god, what am I going to do? I'm hurting, and I feel so betrayed by everyone.

I rub my chest and shoulder because it's still very sore where he hit me. I guess I can't trust anyone anymore, maybe not even Adele. He keeps blaming everything on me, but it's not just me, right? It's him too.

Dead on 12 pm, I am standing on the kerb waiting for Mal. I don't have to wait long for a change, and as he pulls up, I open the door and get it.

Apprehension and dread build within me as he pulls back out into the traffic and parks the car in the next side street.

Looking at me with a flatly, he asks, "Where's your lunch?"

How am I supposed to respond to this, he must know there is nothing in the house to take for lunch, and I'm sure he buys his?

"I just have porridge, "I tell him. "I've got to make it in the staff room."

"I'm not a fucking idiot you stupid slut, I know how to make porridge."

I give up and keep my mouth shut, I guess I'm going back to work hungry. I thought for a while that maybe he wanted to make some sort of amends for last night, but it becomes immediately apparent that all he is interested in doing is keeping an eye on me.

By the time lunch is over and he returns me to the front of the store I'm starving. I rush to the staffroom where I stand in front of the microwave, willing my porridge to cook faster.

I scald my throat gulping it down, but I'm not sure it matters much as it's still sore from last night. I get back to my desk only ten minutes late.

My phone starts buzzing in my pocket, alerting me to another text message. I pull it out without surprise that it's from him. 'Once I've stopped being angry, I will be hurt and cry.'

Maybe this is a good thing. I've been stupid, but at least there are no more lies between us. The hurt and anger he is showing me isn't just the hurt I caused. It's an accumulation of all the pain he's ever experienced in his life. No wonder he has trouble processing it all. I wonder if he'd go to counselling with me, I'm sure it would be beneficial for him. But I'll have to plan the approach very carefully.

I debate calling Megan and asking if she told Justin anything, I've told her, but decide not to risk it. I'm confused enough as it is right now, and I have no idea where to place my trust.

Instead, I tell Adele I am still experiencing morning sickness and try to focus on what is in front of me, rather than the battlefield of emotions that are warning in my head.

An hour and a half later, there is a knock at the office door. I swivel in my chair expecting to see Paul or Amy, but it's my Mother. My heart misses a beat, and I pull at my shirt, making sure that the bruise is covered. She stares at me with a face as dark as a thundercloud. She could give Mal a run for his money.

"Why didn't you go get your dog last night Madeline?"

"I'm sorry, Mum, I forgot she was there." I realise how lame this sounds. I glance over at Adele, but she stays diplomatically silent.

"How could you forget? Why on earth would you not let your sister in last night? What is going on with you? Bessie is your dog and your responsibility."

Her hands are propped on her hips, her face drawn in a line of disapproval. Years as her daughter mean I know she is not happy with me at all. This is the look I learned to be very wary of as a child.

Adele looks like she's ready to bolt, but my Mother is standing in the doorway blocking both of our escape. There really isn't much I can say to her, so I just stay seated and wait for her to blow off steam.

"Your father is not happy with you Madeline. We are a family and if Mal won't let us in your house then he worth nothing. Do you understand me?"

I stare her slightly dumbfounded. I don't know how to deal with this. "I'm sorry, Mum, I was in bed. Maybe Mal didn't hear them?"

"Madeline, that man is no good. You should just get rid of him."

Wow tell it like it is Mum, I feel like no one really wants to help me. Everyone has an opinion on what I should do, or how I should feel, and

I feel like my head is going to explode. No one is listening to me or what I really need.

I swallow my hurt, pain and anger and say, "Look, Mum, I've got so much work to do. Can we have this conversation later?"

"What? You can't even take a break for your own Mother?" She sounds incredulous like she can't believe her own ears.

I shake my head, trying to dismiss her as fast as possible. "I have to work Mum," I say harshly, turning back to my computer.

She stands there for a few more moments before huffing incredulously and walking away. I suspect she thinks that I have chosen Mal over my own family when all I really want to do is choose me.

CHAPTER TWENTY-ONE

When I was little, my Mother was very regimented, she ran a tight ship. She always made sure our clothes were ironed crisp and were never mismatched, god forbid our underwear didn't match our outfit. I just assumed that socks came in pairs and they never got separated. Beds magically got made while we were at school, and toys were always put away. She kept everything ordered and insured we fell into line as well.

If we didn't have everything out of the lounge before morning, Mum would bin it. If my room were too untidy for her standards, she would dump everything onto my bed. Occasionally she would dump it all out of the window.

When I was little, I would never have ignored her or answered back or walked away from her. Dismissing her so callously is chewing away at my insides like acid. I don't want to fight with my Mum, and certainly not about Malcolm.

Rock and hard place – that's me. I'm stuck between what Mal wants, and what my parents want. Only Mal wants to hurt me, Mum wants me just to do what she wants, and Dad just push, push, pushes me to agree that I'd be better off moving back home. All I want to do is scream and shout, "Hey Mum and Dad, I'm pregnant! Congratufuckinlations on becoming Grandparents!"

I just want out of this madness; I need to get away. I need some space to breathe. I can't be bothered with it anymore, any of it. I have had enough. I'm not laughing, but it feels like life keeps on playing jokes on me.

With Mum's visit cramming my head all motivation to get any work done evaporates. I glance around to see what Adele is doing before grabbing my Journal and chewing on the top of my pen.

I feel like I've spent my entire life trying to please everyone else, but I have no idea why I bother anymore. No matter what I do, it's never been good enough. Almost every important decision I have ever made has gone wrong.

God, what the hell am I doing?

How can I live the rest of my life like this? What happened to my fairy tale? Guess I don't deserve it.

I can't live the rest of my life like this. I can't live in fear of him. Is there a point where a person can't be saved?

I need to do something, anything just so I don't feel so stuck.

After staring a blank page in my journal for nearly ten minutes, I decide that to help my life move forward, maybe I should try listing some goals? Isn't that what they always tried telling us at school?

The first few on the list seem so basic I feel wretched that I even must write them.

Provide a safe environment for my child.
Be happy, feel safe.
Have a home where my family is welcome.
Have somewhere my animals are happy and feel safe.

Well they aren't too unattainable, are they? Next, I jot down all the things I need to find the courage to tell Mal.

I don't want this child to grow up without a father.
I don't want to live in fear of you.
I don't want to cry myself to sleep anymore.
You don't have a clue who I am.
You scare me.
You use power and control to me.
You threaten me, you say you are going to take away my baby and that you will hurt the people I love.
You always make it about everything else but never focus on the real issues.
You harbour so much anger, hurt and resentment.
I have lost my freedom. I can't even take a bath without you controlling it, it's either too late, or it's too early or whatever.
You even control my movements, i.e. Sit on the couch, I don't want you near me. You don't even let me do the washing up.

I pause to shake out my hand, I've written so hard and fast it's starting to cramp up. I glance up the list I've just written noting the similarity between what I've just listed, and the power and control wheel Adele gave me. I sneak it out from under some files in the top drawer and carefully reread all the sections before continuing.

WHAT I AM EXPERIENCING IS CALLED DOMESTIC VIOLENCE, JUST BECAUSE YOU, DON'T BEAT ME TO A BLOODY PULP DOESN'T MAKE IT ANY MORE ACCEPTABLE. I DON'T FEEL SAFE.

"Pushing me" When you push someone in the head it's a hit and even a push is OUT OF LINE.
I can't live like this, I can't be so sad all the time, I wake up depressed.

I hate how he twists my words, it's like he is some sort of lawyer. He gets my meaning so bent out of shape I no longer recognised them as my own thoughts, to the point where I don't even know what I am thinking. So, I tell him nothing. It's safer that way. His hate is killing me, it's like I am drowning in his jealousy towards everything in my life.
He has to let go of this hurt and pain, our relationship has gone past the point normal people part. He acts like he fears to lose this child, but then he torments me, and I can no longer believe he loves me. In fact, I think he deserves a big part of himself just to hate me.
When he hit me, when he had me terrified and pinned to the ground, I realised that I fell in love with something that doesn't exist. I thought I could tell him anything. After all the lies and deceit in my marriage, I was longing for someone I could just be me with, but I was wrong. I don't know if I love him anymore, my life has been replaced with hate and dread.
I've always pushed so hard for the things I wanted with little to no regard for the feelings of the people around me, and I honestly feel like this life I have now is a punishment for that. I am finding it so hard to love this child that is growing in my belly, and the guilt is consuming me.
Oh God, I'm so scared that I won't be able to love it, that every time I look at it, I will see Mal's face and all the mistakes I have made. I'm petrified I am going to resent this child, but I desperately don't want it to grow up without a father. I don't want to spend the rest of my life feeling like this, hell I don't even want to spend the rest of the week like

this. I have never been this scared in my life.

I can't even write those things; these feelings are so unthinkable I can't bear to commit them to paper. I can't erase this baby like it never happened, it doesn't matter what I decide I will be changed forever.

As scared as I feel I am also submerged in anger. Anger that Mal has let me down, angry that he treats me like crap and then makes out it's my fault. I can't believe how easily he has turned me into a victim and made me feel so hopeless and alone and scared and angry, so very angry.

He treats my dog like crap just to make me feel bad and taken away my ability to make decisions for myself. What sort of person dictates when another person can have a bath? I asked him every day for a week, and he said no.

I hate the fact that I even feel like I have to ask for his permission. God, I am angry with myself for letting him get away with it. We were so much in love; how has it all been taken away from us? I really think I am beginning to hate him.

I need some space so I can think straight, but I can't go anywhere. I have no car and no money; he still has my cash card and doesn't seem like he's in a hurry to give it back to me.

The list goes on, I can no longer read at home or write in my journal, and it's certainly not safe to keep that at home. He is violent and abusive, and I think he hates me. This is his cycle, right? That's what the power and control wheel taught me. How can I let our child experience this?

When I get home, I quietly sneak out the back door and sit on the step. My cats scoot closer and Bess puts her big head in my lap as I absently stroke their fur. I promise I will make things better for them, I just wish I knew how.

CHAPTER TWENTY-TWO

Mal has barely spoken a word to me all week, neither has he text me. I'm not sure if this is a cease-fire or an intimidation technique.

When he finally breaks his silence, I can't quite believe what I am hearing. "You need to tone down your emotions, I can't handle this."

I stare at him, processing what he's just said, it's not like I can handle it either. "I'm sorry," I say, leaning towards him in an attempt to hug him, but he pushes me away.

"I've got a migraine, no one can help me," he says as he walks away from me and into the bedroom.

I think I may have broken him, or maybe he's just stopped caring? I'm not sure of the damage I've done, and I am not sure how to handle this shell I've been left with. A cloud of depression has replaced his volatile anger.

I wait until Mal's been in bed for over an hour and I pull my cell phone out of my pocket. I saw my sister's car parked in Tom's driveway so while I'm sure he's sleeping I feel safe enough texting her.

"What are you up too? Want to go for a walk?' I send.

As I expected, she replies a few moments later. 'Meet me outside in 10 :)'

I grab the house key from Mal's bag as I don't have one of my own then pull out Bessie's lead by the back door. Shutting the door gently behind me, I click her lead to her collar as quietly as possible then make our way silently out to the road.

"Hey!" Rosie exclaims a tad too loud as she bends to rub Bessie's head. I glance up nervously to the darkened bedroom window, a gesture that is not lost on my sister.

"Come on," she says, taking my arm. "Let's walk."

It's twilight as we set off and there is a chill in the air, so we both walk a little faster than our usual pace. I think, can tell I have a lot on my mind, so she waits for me to talk.

"I'm really sorry about the other day. I crashed pretty much as soon as I got home." I wish I could be more honest with her, but I still haven't fully processed what happened.

"It's ok sis. Tommy's family think Bess is awesome."

After a long pause, I stiltedly begin again. "Mum wasn't happy; she came into work." Rosie shrugs and puts her arm around me.

I take several measured breaths before building the courage to tell her about the baby. "I'm pregnant." The words rush out a tad too fast, but as I say it, she stops in her tracks and grabs my arm.

Leaning in, she wraps both of her arms around me, "Oh my god Maddie! That's so freaking exciting! How far along are you?"

I pull up my sweatshirt and show her my bump. "Nearly 16 weeks."

"You didn't think to tell me this sooner?!" she accuses, but not in an angry way, more incredulous that I could have kept it from her for so long.

I don't mean to lean on her so heavily, she's so young, but I really feel like there is no one left on my side and the fact that she hasn't once tried to tell me what to do bolsters my bravery in telling her some of my fears.

"Things aren't very good with Mal right now. He's really depressed at the moment and angry all the time. I don't think he is going to stick around."

I can see her digesting this information before answering me, and when she does, I am struck with how much wiser than her years she is. "You will never be a single Mother Maddie. You have Mum and Dad and Me, and Jack."

Tears fill my eyes and spill down my cheeks as I hug her back much more fiercely and I think I'll cherish what she just told me forever.

"When are you going to tell Mum and Dad?" she asks.

"I'm not sure yet, maybe next weekend? I just need some processing time, you know."

"Well, just tell me when you are going to do it so I can be there too. They will flip out, Grandparents!"

"Yeah, they will flip out alright," I tell her. "Somehow I don't think they are going to be as excited as you are."

"It will be fine, Sis, you'll see," she says as she retakes my arm and we walk home.

I don't immediately go back inside. Instead, we stand on the street in the dark, quietly discussing what it will be like to have a baby in our lives. It feels so good to talk about this positively with someone who isn't trying to push their own ideas onto me.

I want to savour it, but movement catches my eye, and I see Mal standing at the bedroom window watching us. My stomach lurches with dread and the hopeful feeling that has blossomed with my sister withers and dies.

I take a deep breath, trying to still my fear. "I should go in; it's getting late, and I have work tomorrow."

Rosie hugs me once last time, "It's all going to be ok sis," she reminds me.

I watch her walk away from me, feeling suddenly bereft, but I turn and rush Bess back to her step and tie her as fast as possible. When I get in, I expect him to say something or at least be angry. I left the house without his permission, but his ambivalence is almost frustrating. He just gives me a flat-eyed stare and turns back to the bedroom.

On some level, I know I'm dreaming, but the feeling of suffocation is so real I can barely breathe. The alarm clock is ringing and ringing, but as hard I as I try, I can't get my arms to work well enough to turn it off. I jerk awake expecting to be late, but it's barely light outside.

Mal is still asleep next to me, his breathing steady and even. "What are we doing?" I ask him quietly. "How on earth are we supposed to raise a baby together? I love you so much, I've given so much up for you, and you just can't stop hurting me."

It feels somewhat better to say this to him, even if he is asleep. In a way, this is probably the only time I can speak to him. Everything I say while he's awake is wrong.

It's only 5 am so I have plenty of time to get ready for work since it doesn't look like I am getting any more sleep today I slip out of bed and head to the shower.

It feels good to have hot water pouring over my body. I can almost shut the world away and just enjoy this tiny moment of peace.

But peace flees the moment I hear Mal push the bathroom door. I've locked it, so when it doesn't immediately open, he shunts it hard enough to shake the whole house. I quickly shut the water off hastily wrapping a towel around me to unlock it before he breaks the door down.

"Why did you lock the door?" He asks as I exit the bathroom.

I shrug in response, "I don't know." But I do know. The bathroom is the only place I have left where I can shut him out. The feeling of sliding the flimsy lock shut means much more than its actual effectiveness.

Mal punches the door inches from my face leaving another imprint of his fist in the thin plywood. "Are you trying to hide something from me?" he demands.

"No, I'm just trying to get ready for work," I tell him evenly. Water is dripping from my hair and body; I feel exposed, standing here in only a towel. I pull it a little tighter and bite my bottom lip.

He stands there staring at me before moving aside, giving me only just enough room to move around him. I glance at yet another hole as I walk past the door, I have no idea how I will explain this to our landlord.

He stalks off, and I try to blink the tears out of my eyes, I should be used to this by now, all I can do is breathe through it. One foot in front of the other and get ready for work.

In the bedroom, I survey the chaos that he insists upon. The duvet minus cover is on the floor, and piles of both dirty and clean washing sprawled everywhere. Every single drawer is pulled open; I can only imagine what sort of fit my Mother would have if she saw this. I'm not the world's tidiest person, but I wasn't raised to live in this sort of disorderly mess. I don't like living like this. I don't much like living without choices either, but that's happened too, hasn't it?

I shrug my work shirt on, and then struggle to fasten the button on my skirt but give up after a few tries, it's become next to impossible.

Staring down at my belly, I realise that I have formed quite a noticeable bump. Instead, I search through my underwear draws and use a safety pin to keep it in place.

I turn to look for my hairdryer, but I can't find it. This house is a mess, but my hairdryer should be where I left it.

After wasting ten minutes moving everything around, with me even looking under the bed, I give up. I scrub my head vigorously with a towel and resign myself to going to work with wet hair. Not ideal, but not the end of the world. I go through to the kitchen trying to ignore Mal sitting at the computer desk doing up his work boots. I open the fridge to grab the milk, and I'm shocked to find my hairdryer in its place instead.

I glance over towards Mal, "Did you put this here?"

"Why would I touch your hairdryer?" he replies without looking in my direction.

I can't remember the last time I used it, but I am quite sure I didn't put it in the fridge. "Umm, ok," I say.

Mal finished with his boots moves toward me, "Is it my fault you're going fucking crazy Madeline. Take better care of your stuff. If you want a ride to work, get a move on."

I no longer have time to dry my hair anyway, I barely have enough time to grab some porridge, my work bag and follow him down the stairs and out the door.

I've also managed to forget my jacket, which is stupid because my hair is still wet and despite the fact, summer is around the corner it's cold out this early. Mal already has the engine started, so there is no chance he will let me go back in and get it. The wind whips around my head, making me shiver. I climb into the passenger side of the car and immediately fiddle with the heater. He slaps my hand away and turns it back to cold. I know he is doing this on purpose, either to punish me or just mess with my head, I don't know. I can't understand why he is so casually cruel to me.

I doubt he has to be at work so early, but he drops me at the front of the store almost 40 minutes before my shift starts, but I don't feel bad about this. I sit in the staff room with a hot bowl of porridge, a steaming mug of coffee and my journal in front of me.

I start with recording how I told my sister about the baby, how she's genuinely happy for me, and her pledge that if I left Mal, I'd never be a solo parent. I struggle to keep the tears from spilling over. I am not the only one in the staff room, and I'd rather not draw any more attention to myself.

One thing I can do when as deeply unhappy as I am right now is write poetry and, in the time, before I head to my desk to start my working day, I write a few lines.

This single tear that travels across my cheek is poetry for only me, my heart breaks, but no one hears a sound, my soul weeps, this pain is for me alone.

Very accurate, I think to myself. He doesn't understand that when I cry, it's not to try and manipulate him, but just a glimpse of my desperate sadness. All I have is tears, a locked bathroom door, and a journal left in my work locker. Everything else he has taken away from me. How did my life become so crazy?

CHAPTER TWENTY-THREE

Ten minutes before I am due to start Amy and Paul enter the staff room for their morning coffee.

"Good morning Madeline, it's lovely to see you so bright and early," Paul says.

Amy pats me on the head as she passes me, "Good, I am glad you are here!" She pulls out a stack of *Trivial Pursuit* cards and hands them to me. "Learn these by lunchtime, and I'll test you on them."

For a few moments, I don't understand what she is talking about, but then she hands an equal pile to Paul with the same instructions. "Oh, here's some for Rosie too, but you'll probably have to quiz her on the answers in your own time."

The Penny Drops, the team bonding quiz night. I've still not broached the subject with Mal, given the current atmosphere at home I'm not sure if I will be given permission ever to leave again.

Of course, I don't tell Amy this; she's so enthusiastic about her impending winning quiz team that I don't want to be the one to crush her right now. Instead, I take the stack of cards and promise to forgo all work for the morning in lieu of becoming part of the most knowledgeable team in the building.

"I'll learn them," I promise, not that I hold out much hope of the information staying in my brain. Part of me is wondering if I did put the hairdryer in the fridge. I have become so scatty recently, is that part of pregnancy?

Of course, I fail Amy's quiz test at lunch. I can't really afford to spend all morning memorising facts, but I've committed enough to memory to make her happy. A pinkie-swear later and she's satisfied with my promise to continue to study them at home.

The look on Mal's face as he pulls up in the car alerts me to this being another bad night. He shouts expletives at different drivers who he feels have cut him off or generally flaunted the road rules. I stop listening to him after a while because it's the same old words on a different day. Idly I imagine him reaching across the space between us in the car and hitting me in the face hard enough to bruise. When did I become so melodramatic?

He must have noticed my lack of attention because he barks at me, "Am I boring you?"

"I'm sorry. I was listening, I'm just tired."

"Why do you feel the need to lie to me all the time, what did I just say?"

I open my mouth to answer, to try to force out anything but I can't. My mind is blank.

"For fuck's sake, Maddie, I don't know why I bother." After that, he stays quiet, but it's not long before we are home, and he is marching me inside and upstairs.

Louder than necessary, he announces, "I've found somewhere else to live. I think I should move out."

I freeze where I am while I absorb what he is telling me. I wasn't expecting this turn of events, so I'm having trouble processing this massive bombshell.

"I'm sick and tired of you lying and going off and cheating on me with your fucking cunt husband. I don't know why you waste your time with that slut either. They don't like you anymore, once a cheater always a cheater."

Salty tears trail down my cheek as he reminds me of the loss of my connection with Megan, not to mention having no idea who I can trust anymore. I swipe at the tears and turn my head away, doing my best to hide my face from him.

He carries on ignoring my tears, "Well, that's not going to be my problem anymore is it, because I'm going. Don't you dare expect me to sign your kid's birth certificate because it's probably not mine any way."

I can't believe he is telling me this. I sit down heavily and try to get my breathing under control. Is he really going to go? How can he tell me he won't have anything to do with this child? He brought it into the world with me, how can he abandon us?

"I am not going to be paying for another kid that's not mine, I've had one slut try and trap me this way, and it's not happening again."

He hasn't said much since he admitted to me that his Ex has been pregnant. The most he's ever said was he thought the baby was his and it turned out she was sleeping with some guy.

He leaves me sitting on the couch as he starts opening and then slamming the cupboards in the kitchen. He ignores me completely as he starts making himself dinner.

Despite all his promises to pack his bags and go he doesn't leave, and I am finding it hard to be in the same room as him, he hasn't shut up all evening. All he's done is lecture me for being a cheating slut and put two more holes in the living room wall. I don't feel like I can sleep in the same house as him let alone the same bed.

I finally ease myself off the couch, I'm hungry enough to risk moving without permission, but when I get up shouts, "Get back here, get back here, do you want me to slap you in the face?"

I freeze, pulling my arms across my belly. "I'm hungry," I say. "The baby, it's growing."

"I don't care. Sit back down," he commands.

I start to move back to the couch, but I can't stop crying, I try so hard never to let him see how he is hurting me, but I just can't hold in the hurt.

I cry my heart out, but all he can say to me is, "Stop grizzling, don't carry on like that."

Finally, I break and shout, "Then stop tormenting me!"

He pushes me to the floor; in a panic, I clamber up, flying to the bathroom to lock the door behind me. I don't know where my brazen courage has come from. Turning I try to examine my back, it doesn't look bruised, but it still hurts.

I'm only in the bathroom a few moments before Mal shunts right through the lock and barges in on me. He stands there, with his hands on hips and just glares at me, like had I invited him in.

"Get into bed," he says.

My bravado dismantled with the lock, so I do what I'm told. I feel a lurch in the pit of my stomach when I see it hanging by one screw. So much damage to both me and this house in such a short space of time and I'm not sure how well either of us can be fixed.

I lay awake long after he has fallen into a fitful slumber. When I'm sure he is sleeping soundly, I utter, "You break my heart over and over and over again. Why do I keep letting you do it?"

He wakes in the morning, acting like last night's drama never happened. He makes no attempt to pack his bags, and I'm not brave enough to ask if he still plans on leaving. I just feel numb now, which is a weird feeling. Me, who was once so resilient against all the bad things in life can no longer see my life improving. I've done so much I'm not proud of and have no way of explaining away. I think I've accepted what I did wrong, the hurt I dealt to Justin and the damage I caused. I certainly feel like I am paying for those mistakes.

I have a new responsibility now and no matter what it's going to have to come first. I'm left with such mixed feelings about this child growing so rapidly inside me. I can't fathom how much my life is going to change, I mean how I could? I'm such a different person to who I was a year ago. I will always remember that I brought this child into the world on purpose, and we both wanted it so much. I wish I could understand what went wrong between us. I don't think I will ever understand him, he's beyond my reach, I don't know how to help him heal himself, or if he ever will.

However, if we do part, I just hope he doesn't walk out of our child's life too. All I want, what I truly want is him back. To once again feel what we did such a short time ago. I want to feel that consuming passion that told my body and my soul that I couldn't live without him. I miss him so much, and it hurts to see him so changed, and so in pain – he has isolated himself so much. Is it too late? Have we already lost him? I feel so lost.

He barely speaks a word to me as we move around each other; the only time he has spoken to me in the last twenty-four hours is to tell me what to do. "Go turn the bedroom light on." Or "Leave the door open."

Just before dinner he rips open a draw because I hadn't shut it properly and yells, "You are such a fucking lazy slut! Why can't you just keep this shithole house tidy?"

I don't know why he feels the need to call me these names, bitch/slut/cunt. Can't he see the hurt he's doing to me? Can he not see the damage he is doing? Damage I'm afraid can't be undone.

I have no idea why the draw wasn't shut; I can't even remember the last time I opened it. I don't understand why he gets so mad about a draw being open when it's his crap all over the place. I don't know how to communicate with him anymore.

And then later that night he does 180°, he comes up behind me and rubs my lower back, leaving me feeling unbalanced. "You must be getting sore now," he says in a quiet voice.

I shrug, "It's ok, I can feel the baby move now, though."

"You can?" he asks, surprised and slides his hands to my belly.

I freeze. It's been a long time since he's touched me in anything but anger. The Baby is starting to feel heavy in my womb, and I'm feeling it wriggle more often inside me. "If you keep your hand still you may be able to feel it move a bit."

We stay like this for quite some time, I almost relax, almost. He seems so calm with the baby moving beneath his touch, so I decide just to go ahead and ask him about seeking some relationship help.

"Mal, with the baby coming, I thought it could be good for us to see someone, like a counsellor?"

He jerks at my request but doesn't remove his hand, "and how much would that cost?" he asks cautiously.

I'm prepared for this question. "It's free from the family court."

He doesn't say anything for a while, and I am sure he's going to say no, but he surprises me instead. "Okay, I'll give it a go. You have to set it up though."

I nod and smile a little, hopeful for the first time in ages. I have a lot riding on this working. While I am feeling brave, I also ask "I can't keep this hidden for much longer, I have to tell my parents. I have to tell them soon, or they will guess before we've had the chance to say anything."

"I'm not ready yet," he states. "Maybe next week."

I decide not to push him further; I'm surprised I've managed to get this much communication out of him. It's a small thing, but it feels like a win.

CHAPTER TWENTY-FOUR

As soon as I get to work the next day, I waste no time in locating a counsellor. I pull out a copy of the white pages and wipe the dust from the top. The first call I make puts me on the correct path, and it's not long before I'm speaking to a lady at a local facility.

The receptionist listens attentively to why we need to see a counsellor and arranges for me to meet with a lady named Ruth the following week. Crossing my fingers, I text Mal and let him know when our appointment is. I get the reply 'OK', and the breath I didn't realise I was holding escapes sharply from my body.

I am shoving away the phone book when Adele walks in with her morning coffee.

I smile at her triumphantly.

"Hello dear, you look happy?" she asks me questioningly.

"Mal and I are going to counselling." I'm bursting to tell her about the progress I feel we are making.

She looks at me for a while studying my face then replies, "That's good to hear. It will be good for the two of you to talk about your problems. Especially before the baby gets here."

"That's the idea," I reply. "I can't just walk away; I need to make sure we both tried our hardest to make it work."

"I know love, I really do."

The morning of our first scheduled counselling session tension runs high. I can tell Mal is searching for a reason to back out, but I'm not having a bar of it, so I try extra hard to give him no reason to change his mind. I keep my behaviour impeccable during the morning and make sure my phone is in my hand so I can reply to his texts immediately. We will be going directly to our session once we finish work which is a good thing if we had to go home before our appointment, he may not want to leave again.

I spend the day fussing and worrying and trying to avoid Amy, who is on the warpath with her quiz night preparation. I park the concerns about Mal letting me go; maybe we can discuss it in therapy. During my lunch break, I jot down some things I'd like to talk about during our sessions, letting a sliver of hope in with every line.

At the end of the day, I am waiting kerbside glancing at my watch every few minutes. He screeches to a halt in front me only ten minutes late, but he's cutting it fine if we're to get to the counsellor's office in time for our meeting.

We arrive without being too late thankfully; I waste no time in unbuckling and propelling myself towards the building.

Mal grabs my hand as I make a beeline for the door and says, "I'm doing this for you, you know."

His grip on me doesn't feel affectionate, it feels like he is trying to hold me back, but I don't pull away from him.

Mal pushes open the frosted glass door which opens into what looks like some one's living room. A desk is pushed up against the wall near the entrance with pamphlets labelled 'Parenting through separation' and 'Living through grief'. There are a few couches scattered around a coffee table which is stacked with well-thumbed magazines. I wonder how many people spend time in the waiting room.

"Hello," says a lady who seemingly materialised out of nowhere. She has short dark hair and round glasses. She's maybe in her forties and a little taller than me. "I'm Ruth," she introduces herself. "You must be Madeline and Malcolm?"

"Hi, yes, that's us," I reply and hold out my hand to shake hers. She takes my hand easily, then offers it to Mal, who takes a little longer to respond.

"I'm going to be your counsellor, let's step into my office."

We follow her down a passageway to what appears to me like a second lounge. The evening sun subtly lights the space through net curtains that obscure the view of the back garden. There is a three seated couch under the window and a single chair facing it, between them, is a similar coffee table to the first lounge, only instead of magazines sits a full box of tissues. I glare at the tissues like they are a bad omen.

We sit on the couch with a good meter of distance between us, and

Ruth sits opposite.

"So, let's start with some ground rules. This is a safe space for both of you. Both of your opinions are to be respected and heard. I don't like to take too many notes but will jot down a few things so I can remember where we are up too for our next session. You have 6 sessions approved, but we can apply for more if we need them."

So, with a little prompting from Ruth, I begin to give her a small synopsis of what's been happening in our relationship. Even though I don't mention the physical abuse as I speak, I see Mal's jaw tense up. Ruth glances in his direction.

"Would you like to add to this at all, Malcolm?" she asks him.

"I had to quit my job to move to this shithole town for her. I left my well-paid job to work a shitty one, we live in a shitty house, and I get treated like shit by her family, does that about cover it?"

It doesn't take long for Ruth to see the crux of our problem; she responds to us by telling us that she was the abuser in her relationship with her ex-husband. "I was out of control," she tells us.

I really like the way Ruth expresses 'Anger Management' she calls it 'Violence Management.'

"It's ok to feel angry, anger is a normal emotion. But violence is never ok, and that's what we have to deal with. People resort to violence when they feel like all other paths of communication are exhausted, so let's work on opening up nonviolent forms of communication," she says to us both.

"I just get so mad at her; I can't think straight, and it's like blackness is taking over my brain and body, and I can't control what I say or do. I just want to shut her up."

I'm surprised by Mal candidness. I thought even though I got him to come, he wouldn't talk to her. But I can see he really is opening up to her. I can see how hard it is for him, but he seems to respond to Ruth, and I'm proud of him. It's weird, though, hearing him talk about his feelings, and what happens to him when he loses his temper. I only feel the end results as he yells or pushes and hits me.

"What would you like to get out of these sessions Maddie?" she asks me.

I don't have to pause for long before answering, "To be happy again and to feel like I have some control over my life. I just want to feel happy again."

Ruth wraps the session up and sees us out. By the time we get home, Mal is notably quiet.

"How was that?" I ask him timidly.

"I think she understands what I'm dealing with on a daily basis. All the things I have given up for you and you just take for granted. But do I think she will be able to help you with all your problems?" he shrugs, and I am a bit taken aback. It was apparent to me that Ruth homed in on his behaviour over mine. I was really hoping to make some progress in our relationship, not solidify his belief that I am at fault.

"Um," I reply. "I guess we will continue to talk about it next week?"

"Yeah," he says.

After several more sessions with Ruth's help, I finally get him to agree it's time to tell my family about the baby. Mum's surprise is evident when I call her and ask if it's ok for both of us to come over for dinner at the weekend. Mal rarely visits anymore, and I'm hoping she will see this as some sort of peace offering.

"Of course, darling, we'd love to have both, why don't you come a bit early and help peel the spuds?"

"Okay, Mum, we'll see you on Sunday." I feel nervous, but I lost the ability to hide this baby a month ago.

The result of this small win over Mal's controlling behaviour is paid for by lunchtime. He doesn't like the way I'm cutting up an apple, he grabs the knife, and in doing so shunts my favourite fruit bowl onto the floor.

As it shatters into thousands of pieces, I am reminded of how he has worked his way through my entire life-shattering and running everything. I don't know why I expect anything different.

CHAPTER TWENTY-FIVE

Despite Mal's foul mood, I don't cave and tell him we don't have to go to my parents. I know he still isn't happy about telling them about the baby, but unlike everything else in my life, I hold my ground. I carry on as planned, and we arrive at their house just before 6 pm, later than my Mother had planned but better than not at all.

My brother Jack answers the door which surprises me as it's unusual to see him at home in the evening; he's usually hiding out at his girlfriend's house.

"Hi Jack," I say as I lean in to hug him careful not to bump him with my expanding tummy. I'm wearing a baggy jumper over an old tee-shirt that is also rapidly becoming too tight. I'm a bit hot given how close we are to summer, but I'm not quite ready to expose the baby yet.

"Hey big Sis," he replies, kissing me on the cheek. The only acknowledgement he gives Mal is a slight nod of the head, then he turns back to the living room.

My whole family is here, including Bella, Jack's girlfriend and Tom. I start to feel awkward and wonder if we should have done this with less of an audience. As if the baby knows I'm about to chicken out it does a small summersault, reminding me that there is, in fact, a tiny human inside my tummy that will not remain hidden for much longer.

Mum is in the kitchen, putting the finishing touches on the roast pork. She's gone all out with so many of us being here and has even produced crackling. Just smelling all the delicious foods makes my mouth water. I'm not sure how well a baby grows on porridge alone, my body is crying out for some variety in my diet, some meat and vegetables. I'll probably get scurvy if I don't start having a more varied diet.

"Hello, darling," she calls.

"Hi Mum," I say as I hover between the kitchen and dining room. I glance over to where Mal is standing awkwardly with my Dad. I strain my ears to hear Dad ask if Mal wanted a beer, he says no. I've never seen him drink. Dad pours him a diet coke instead, and I inhale softly, so far, so good. He hasn't bitten anyone's head off yet or gutted them.

Mum is busy talking to me, but I'm so focused on what Mal and Dad are doing. I don't hear a word of what she's saying. I try to tune back in and catch the end of what appears to be a conversation about her scrapbooking   group.

When it seems to be the right moment to comment I say, "Oh, I'd love to see what you're working on," and hope that it doesn't sound too desperate or random.

"Oh, you will love the gorgeous new die cut I've got," she tells me with enthusiasm. "Your Dad was so proud of me. I got it on sale! I saved over $50."

"That's great, Mum." It's rather hard to maintain interest with so much playing on my mind, but I conjure up a smile.

"Girls, please lay the table, dinner will be ready in 10 minutes," she tells us.

Rosie peels herself off Tom and comes to help me. It's always been left to us 'girls' so we move in comfortable unison as we grab plates and cutlery.

"How are you feeling?" Rosie whispers.

"I'm a nervous wreck, we're telling them tonight."

She glances at my tummy and giggles, "Well, it's not like you're going to be able to hide it for much longer."

She's right, I can barely lean across the dining room table to arrange the knives and forks.

I look around my childhood home, evidence of this spread out everywhere. Mum still has crude stick figure drawings we did at kindergarten pinned up on the inside of the pantry door, and old school photos of the three of us in varying stages of embarrassing clothing and bad hair framed around the lounge.

If things don't improve with Mal, then this is not the sort of home our baby can look forward too. Right now, our walls are adorned with holes from his fists, and he hasn't allowed me to put up any artwork or photos to cover them. A wave of sadness flows over me, but I do my best to brush it off.

I have no idea how to tell them I'm about to provide them with their first grandchild, but I do know it has to be tonight. From the look on Mal's face, we won't be coming back anytime soon, so I best make the most of it.

Rosie and I help carry the food to the table, it's a good thing it seats 8 people as we need every chair tonight. I take the seat I always did as a kid, and Mal sits down next to me displacing my sister. She doesn't make an issue of it though and moves to the other side to sit with Tom.

I glance to my left, "Hi Bella, how are you?" I ask my brother's girlfriend.

Bella offers me a tight smile, "I'm good."

She's not an easy woman to get to know, but then I wonder what my brother has been telling her about Malcolm and me. Mum told me that she used to live with her reclusive parents several hours north of Auckland and was home-schooled, so perhaps she's feeling a little overwhelmed by our family, I would be.

Sitting at this table throws me right back to when I first introduced Mal to my parents. It's such a stark contrast to what my life is like now. My Dad really liked him, in the beginning, both my parents did. I have to hold back tears when I think of Mal sitting not so far away from where I am now, his arms wrapped securely around me, whispering that he wanted to make a life with me, that he loved my family and couldn't wait to be part of it.

This was less than a year ago but feels like a lifetime, like it never even happened.

Once everyone is seated, my Dad urges us all to dig in. I pile my plate high with meat and potatoes and eat like I don't know when my next meal might be, I don't worry about there not being enough for everyone else, Dad has a rule about roast potatoes, they must always be plentiful.

People make small talk, Mum natters on about what is happening to a distant cousin, and Dad talks about a new car he is thinking about buying. Tom and Jack make conversation about some computer game they both like and Rosie does her best to bridge the conversation between myself and our Mother. The only two at the table who don't say much is Mal and Bella.

After the food is finished, but before there is a chance to clear away the dishes I look over to Mal and ask him, "Shall we do it?" He shrugs, but it's got my parent's attention.

"Do what?" asks Mum as her eyes narrow with suspicion.

"Uh," the words stick in my throat. "I'm pregnant." Not the most eloquent announcement of their impending grandparenthood but I'm at the point where I just want to get it over and done with.

For a few seconds, everyone at the table stares at me. Then Mum half shrieks accusation, "You're not!"

I stand and pull up the jumper I am using to hide the baby. Yes, I am showing sufficiently to shock nearly everyone at the table, bar Rosie. I am very proud of her acting skills.

"How far along are you?" asks Mum incredulously.

"Uh, six months," I admit reluctantly.

Mum and Dad look at each other knowingly. "We didn't announce until we were almost seven months pregnant with you." they confide.

Then I am sucked into a circle of hugs and congratulations. I keep tabs on Mal noting that he suffers the handshakes and pats on the back with reasonably good humour.

I'm so relieved that the announcement has gone well, and now over. I was so worried they'd hit the roof I almost feel like I can do this.

As we move back to the table to clear it, Dad takes the plates out of my hands and tells me to go sit down and rest. That will take some getting used to, but it's nice for them to make allowances for my pregnancy since Mal spends most the time pretending it's not happening.

"Who's your midwife?" asks Mum, dragging me back to reality.

"Oh, I don't have one yet."

Mum looks at me with wide-eyed incredulity. "You need prenatal care, Madeline," she scolds gently.

"It's on my list for this week. I have a few numbers to call, but I've just been so busy at work," I reassure her, lying smoothly. I've not thought about midwives or prenatal care at all. Life has been full just dealing with Mal.

Not long after finishing dinner, I can see that Mal has had enough. He's inching towards the door and refusing to sit down like everyone else.

I yawn with theatrics before saying, "I'm so tired, I think we should probably go home Mal."

He's standing back rigid and arms crossed, he looks ready to bolt at any moment.

As I get up, Dad asks, "Would you like some tea before you go? Rose, go put the jug on."

I stall him before she can get up. "It's OK, Dad, I'm really quite tired."

I let my family hug me one last time with more congratulations and exclamations of excitement from Rosie about all the things she will get to do now she's going to be an Aunt. Then Dad walks us to the car.

He holds open the passenger door and silently hugs me one last time before we get in and drive away. I wonder what he's thinking. I expect quite a few mixed emotions and perhaps more than a touch of anger at Mal. I must commend him though because he hides it well.

As we pull out of my parent's street, Mal lets out a sharp exhale and exclaims, "That was fucking torture! I thought they were never going to let you leave."

"Well, at least we've told them about the baby,' I say to fill the silence.

"Yeah well, knowing your family they will probably make it all about them."

Not a positive response from him, but better than what I was expecting.

The days following dinner at my parent's house pass in relative calm, and the relief on Adele's face that I've told my parents about the baby is evident. After that, the news of my pregnancy spreads like wildfire through the shop floor. Less than forty minutes later, Paul and Amy arrive at our office door clutching a tray of coffee cups and a paper bag from the bakery.

"CONGRATULATIONS!" they shout in unison, causing me to jump and overturn a stack of papers.

"We got you a present." Amy passes a coffee to Adele and another cup to me. "We got you a hot chocolate Mama to be," she says.

"You are a dark horse Mademoiselle, how are you hiding a baby in there without us noticing!" Paul reaches to pat my tummy, making me feel awkward.

Since I no longer have to hide my bump, I am not wearing my trademarked bump hiding jersey, so sidestep him and stand up to show them how much I am showing.

"Really?" asks Amy. "You've got to be at least six months? How!" she hands me the brown paper bag with a flourish. "Babies need doughnuts," she explains.

"Well I don't know about babies, but I certainly do," I reply taking the bag from her and peeking inside.

Leon appears next in the doorway. "I hear congratulations are in order," he says to me.

"Yes, Um, thanks," the awkwardness returning.

"I'm sorry for giving you such a hard time for being late Maddie. I remember how sick my wife got in her first trimester."

I'm overwhelmed with their kindness and generosity and thank them all profusely before retreating to the staff room to savour the sugar and cinnamon doughnut. I love doughnuts. They are a reminder of a simpler time, one where I thought all lives had a happy ending, and I was safely cocooned in my bubble-wrapped childhood.

My Granddad would buy us each a doughnut then sit us at his kitchen table and tell us if we could eat the whole thing without licking our lips, he'd give us a dollar. These are some of my best childhood memories, spending time with my grandparents, covered in sugar, in fierce competition with my siblings to be the best at not licking our lips. Remembering makes me smile, and I wonder what sort of childhood memories my child will make.

When I get back to my desk, there are five more *Trivial Pursuit* cards with a note from Amy *'Baby brain doesn't buy you a free pass. Learn these!'* I stare at the cards and grown inwardly; I need to ask Mal if I can go, though I need to find a midwife before my Mother throws herself to the task.

I pull out the yellow pages and flip to the M section. There are five midwives listed in our area, so I set about calling them. It doesn't take long for me to realise that none of them has space for a woman who is already 25 weeks along. Panic starts to grip me, and I imagine myself with no midwife, giving birth to my baby in the bathroom.

By the time I make the call to the last name on the list, I am miserable and fighting to hold back tears. My voice cracks when I tell her how far along, I am, and she takes pity on me. She gives me a number for the local maternity hospital and lets me know that there is a new midwife there who has just arrived from Britain and will likely be able to take me on.

I tap my fingers on the desk in nervous repetition and wait to speak with Carla Wright. I am slightly taken aback by her thick accent, I'm not one hundred per cent sure but I'd pick somewhere in Northern England.

"How long have you been in New Zealand?" I ask her

"Just under 4 weeks Love, but don't worry I'm over the jet lag," she reassures me.

"And you can really take me on?"

"Since I've not been here for long, I have plenty of space for your gestation. Can you make it to the Maternity Hospital for 9 am tomorrow morning? We have a Clinic behind the main building."

Relief floods me, "I've not seen a Dr since my six-week scan. I'll be there.

"OK, Maddie, I'm looking forward to it," she tells me, giving me the address.

Come hell or high water I'll make it to my appointment tomorrow.

After hanging up the office phone I pull my mobile out, I already have four texts from Mal. I skim past them without reading what they say and instead tell him about the midwives' appointment. Leaning back heavily, I bite my nails and wait for a response.

'I suppose I have to drop everything then,' he fires back within minutes.

I sigh, fighting the urge to respond I slide the phone back into my bag and try to focus on work for a change. At least I am going to be meeting with a midwife now, and my parents know about the baby. In the bigger scheme of things, it might not seem like a lot, but in my world, we call this progress.

CHAPTER TWENTY-SIX

I wake long before Mal does, lying as still as possible I stare blankly at the wall as the sunlight creeps further into our bedroom. I pull the duvet closer around my neck; it's still without a cover. The clean sheets I intended putting on our bed weeks ago are still in a basket in the corner.

As Mal rolls towards me, I instinctively shuffle away, but he grabs me and pulls me closer. I don't know why he's so much more affectionate in the morning, but it's one of the best times of my day, of my whole life. As he holds me with his arms wrapped around my waist, my eyes slide to the clock on the sideboard, I really don't want to be late to meet with the midwife.

"Mal, we have to get up, we have an appointment with the midwife in half an hour."

He groans and rolls away from me. Weighing my options, I decide I can't wait for him any longer and make a move toward the bathroom.

I rotate my body to a sitting position and place my feet on the ground, but as I attempt to heave myself up, he startles me by barking, "Where are you going?"

"I really need to pee," I lie, hoping the baby will remind him to be gentle with me. "Baby is doing summersaults on my bladder."

It must work because he frowns at me but doesn't say anything else as I get up. By the time I wash my hands and put some clothes on he's up and standing at the fridge drinking milk from the bottle.

He shoves it back in the fridge and closes the door with more force than necessary, then grabs the car keys and makes towards the front door. With no time for breakfast, I hasten to follow him out. My tummy grumbles in protest, but I ignore the empty feeling, it's slightly easier to ignore that now the baby is taking up more space.

It doesn't take long to drive to the maternity hospital, only a ten-minute car trip. Mal navigates down the long drive beside the shabby fading building and parks in the indicated parking space.

He looks around sniffing in disdain. "This place is shit."

I give him a small shrug in response as he snags my hand, holding it tight like you would a toddler and heads towards the entrance.

I allow myself to be towed along behind him, he's happier when he feels like he is in charge. We march up the ramp and into the central part of the building, where a soft-looking elderly lady directs us to the rear of the hospital.

These buildings seem even older, I know this place has been here as long as I can remember, but it doesn't look like it seen much upkeep in the past few years. The gardens are pleasant enough, but I can tell Mal isn't happy about it as his mouth is turned down in displeasure. I think we both must look slightly dishevelled when we arrive at what I assume is the reception to the community midwives.

"Hello, you must be Maddie?" asks a lady about 4 inches shorter than me with a platinum blonde pixy cut. She has a strong British accent, so I assume this must be Carla.

"Hi, yes," I replied shyly and thrust out my hand not entirely sure on the protocol of meeting your midwife for the first times. "Uh, this is Mal," I add as an afterthought. He steps forward and awkwardly shakes her hand also.

"So, you're the Midwife?" he challenges her, eyes searching behind her. Perhaps he's hopeful a 'Kiwi' midwife is lurking in the shadows.

"Well as Maddie knows from our phone conversation, I'm Carla Wright. I've only lived in New Zealand for four weeks, but I've been a certified midwife for 15 years, and I have delivered thousands of babies. You're in good hands." She smiles up at us, I feel instantly reassured by her calm, confident manner, and I can only hope Mal feels the same way.

She ushers us into a small office and motions for us to both take a seat. "So, you mentioned you'd had a scan at six weeks? Did you bring the results with you?"

"Oh, I'm sorry I had no idea you'd want to see them?" I say as I glance cautiously at Mal.

"That's ok, plenty of time for us to get them. Have you been taking any prenatal vitamins?"

"Vitamins?" I repeat stupidly.

"Like folic acid?"

I purse my lips, "I was, but only what the doctor gave me, they ran out."

I note Carla's glance in Mal's direction and wince.

"Well, I'll write another script." I think she must feel the tension we are both under, so she smoothly changes the subject. "Roll your sleeve up love, and we will see what your blood pressure is doing."

I sit motionless as she places the cuff around my upper arm and slips a stethoscope under it. It starts to hurt as she inflates it and my fingers begin to tingle. She frowns as she watches the little air bubble flutter down. As it hits the bottom, she repeats the procedure and then jots the numbers down on the new chart she has gotten out for me.

"Your BP is a bit higher than I'd like so I am going to suggest you start to take it easy, are you working?"

"Umm yes, but it's just desk work."

"You'll probably need to start thinking about maternity leave around the 37-week mark, ok?"

Without skipping a beat, she weighs me and then asks me to hop up on the bed. "Pull up your jumper love. We are going to use this thing called a Doppler to listen to baby's heartbeat." I do what I am told and pull up my sweatshirt.

"I've just got to put this gel on your tummy first. It might be a tad cold."

My mind starts to drift as Carla fiddles with the nobs on the box attached to the Doppler so I am taken by surprise when suddenly I can hear my baby's heart beating for the first time. I have no idea what it's supposed to sound like, but it seems fast.

"Is it ok?" I whisper.

"Don't worry," she reassures us. "Baby has a nice strong, steady heartbeat."

"It's so fast?" I worry.

"That's totally normal for a foetus love."

A tear slides from the corner of my eye and starts a slow descent down my cheek. Before it hits the pillow, Mal crosses the few steps from the door and holds my hand.

"That's our baby," I say in quiet wonder, and he squeezes my hand gently.

After wiping off the gel, Carla pulls out a tape measure and measures from my navel down to my pubic bone and writes some more information in my chart. It's all quite overwhelming, and we still aren't done with what feels like a somewhat invasive procedure. She asks us questions about both our family histories. I can answer nearly all the ones related to my side of the family, but Mal struggles to answer even the simplest about his. I think it's because he is so reluctant to reveal any personal information to anyone, but maybe he really doesn't know.

"Okay, just a few more things before you get on your way," Carla chirps. "I need to dip this stick here in a little bit of your wee to check for protein in your urine, fun eh!" she laughs as she holds out a little plastic container and shows me to the toilet.

It almost feels like I am about to take another pregnancy test as I deliver my little tub of dark yellow urine to Carla and make a silent promise to myself to be more hydrated the next time, I visit her.

After she examines the colour, my urine has stained the stick she advises us that she will arrange for me to do a follow-up diabetes test I can do in my own time after fasting and writes out a form so we can have the 20-week anatomy scan.

As we leave the maternity hospital, I can't help but feel like I've missed out on so many of those early pregnancy experiences that so many other new Mum's gets. I haven't been able to join an online forum or meet up with other pregnant Mums for a coffee group, I'm not taking any vitamins at all, and I have no one I can really share this with. Mal pretty much immediately dismissed the idea of an antenatal class as a frivolous, unnecessary expense, so I am pinning my hopes on Carla being able to coach me through this. For a moment I let the panic of the baby's impending birth sweep over me and wonder how on earth I'm supposed to manage this with Mal at my side?

"Are you sure there isn't anyone else who can do this?" he asks me, rousing me from my silent hysteria.

"Do what?" I reply stupidly.

"Deliver this fucking baby!" he says with a raised voice.

"I've called every one, there's no one else."

"She sounds weird. How do we even know she's qualified?"

Taking a breath, I try not to let him get to me. Replying as carefully as I can I tell him, "I don't think we have much of a choice."

Even if I hadn't liked her myself, his disdain would have been enough to sway me towards wanting to keep her.

"Well I don't know if I trust her Madeline, so you may have to start looking elsewhere."

I try not to listen to the rest of his rant about how dilapidated the hospital grounds were. Instead, I stare out of the window and try to fill my mind with other things, cramming out his words.

CHAPTER TWENTY-SEVEN

He drops me off right outside the front entrance to work, so I make a beeline towards the stairwell. I'm relieved Amy hasn't spotted me as I've still not spoken to Mal about the Quiz Night, but really, I can only handle one crisis at a time. I see her restocking racks of underwear so stealthily dart in the opposite direction. Tonight, I'll talk to Mal, I promise myself half-heartedly.

I can't wait to tell Adele about hearing the baby's heartbeat; it's the first thing that burst from me as I sit down in our office.

"I'm so glad you're finally getting some prenatal care, Maddie, you must start looking after yourself. It's not just about you and Mal now, soon enough you will have a baby," she reminds me.

"I know, but there is just so much to take in."

"How's the counselling going?" she asks after I get settled at my desk.

"We've had a couple of sessions now," I tell her. "I feel like I hardly get to speak, though."

"How do you mean?" Adele probes

"Just that we are doing a lot of talking about his stuff." I shrug it off like it's of no consequence, but I know deep down the reason why Ruth is so keen to nut out Mal's issues. She sees right through him. She may not have raised the subject of physical abuse, but I can tell she knows that there is more to our story than what I'm willing to say to her.

"Well, I expect it will take a lot of work on both your parts. But if he isn't going to make an effort dear you need to put yourself and your baby first."

I know she cares, but all I can feel is pressure. This is not what I want or need right now, not from Adele, who is generally supportive of me. I get enough of that living inside a pressure cooker with Mal.

I'm so sick of him calling all the shots, deciding where we go, what we do, even what and when I eat. I doubt he even knows he is doing it. I don't know why I am holding on so tight, I already feel like a single Mother.

Later that night, long after I should have been in bed, Mal looks in my direction and tells me, "I'm going out." I glance at the clock surprised he is heading out so late.

"OK?" I say. "Do you know when you'll be home?"

"Does it matter?" he barks back.

"I just wanted to know if I should wait up for you."

"Don't bother," he says as he grabs his jacket and keys and heads out the door.

I move as quietly as I can to the front window to watch him get in the car. The headlights cast a long shadow across the lounge as he pulls away. I breathe out a sigh of relief, this feels like a free pass. I pull out my phone and text Rosie hoping she might want to come over, but I get a text back a few minutes later to tell me she's gone out with a few friends from work. I sit on the couch for a while longer trying to get interested in what's on the telly, but I rarely get moments like this to myself, I don't want to waste it.

Knowing he won't be home until much later gives me the perfect opportunity to find my phone. Even if I can't use it around him, just having it back might give me some sense of control over something. Then if I still have time after that, I'll have a bath before bed.

I tiptoe downstairs with a torch, just in case he comes home earlier than expected. I don't want him to catch me down here with the light on. I enter the room he uses for storage and look around. There have been more boxes of crap dumped here since my last effort to look for my phone. I poke through the top of a few of them, but it's just a jumble of more army surplice store stuff. Why on earth does he need five pairs of army issue boots and six jackets? God knows what he intends on doing with them all.

Doing my best to memorise where all the boxes are positioned, I make my way towards the back. I intended to attack some of the boxes I helped pack when he left Christchurch, but my eyes are drawn to the ones with DOM written in bold black ink.

Curiosity getting the better of me as I gently ease open the top box and flash the light inside. I see the top of a faded photo album and carefully pull it out. Sitting cross-legged on the cold floor, I open it. I'm greeted with the faces of two little girls, two little girls who look exactly like Mal. I turn the pages wondering if they're the younger sisters he told me about. But it becomes undeniable the further into the album I get that these children are his.

The shock I feel is immense, and I drop it like it holds some sort of nasty disease. I shuffle away from it, half wishing I hadn't seen it, but I am drawn back into the box it came from and where I find a stack of letters addressed to a person named Dominic Neill. Why does Malcolm have so many letters addressed to someone else?

Once I start digging further into the box I can't stop, I'm having trouble processing what I'm seeing. It's like someone else has connected all the dots, but they've done it the wrong way, and the picture is scrambled.

Cold dread seizes my heart, he's not who I thought he was at all. I stare for a solid 5 minutes at an old ID card with Mal's photo and Dominic's name on it before things start to fall into place. His name is not Malcolm McPherson, it's Dominic Neill.

This is too much for me right now, rushing without care of how it came out I replace it all except for one photo of the two little girls sitting on the bonnet of a blue car. The older one looks to be about five, and the other just a toddler. I don't see any photos of their Mother, and I wonder where they are now. He already told me he could walk away from us and never look back. Now I know he means it.

A wave of anger washes over me as I ascend the stairs back to the lounge. Any thoughts I had of finding my phone or having a bath have fled.

How am I going to talk to Mal about this? Do I even want too? Maybe I should just pack all my stuff and run now before he gets home.

I let this thought develop for a while, but I don't. Instead, I boil the kettle and make myself a cup of crappy tea. I drink it weak, with a large splash of milk and try to steady my breathing. The photo of the girls is on the breakfast bar in front of me. I don't know what possesses me to leave it there after I go to bed, but I do. Rocking myself to sleep tears slide down my face, maybe tomorrow will give me answers.

CHAPTER TWENTY-EIGHT

The weak morning light illuminates the bedroom as my eyes flutter open. Slowly I focus on Mal sitting next to me on the edge of the bed. He is facing the curtains and still dressed in what he was wearing yesterday. I have no idea what time he came in, but it must have been a long time after I wept myself to sleep.

As I stir, he turns to face me, he is holding the photo in his hand.

"Where did you get this?" he asks quietly.

Gauging his mood, I sincerely regret leaving that photo out for him to find. It's the most rebellious thing I've ever done to him.

"I was looking for one of my books," I lie cautiously. "And I found this wedged between the boxes."

I don't feel guilty about bending the truth. He isn't who he told me he was, and it's obvious we must confront this, I need him to focus on what part of this important and not obsess over me digging through his stuff.

"Do you want to tell me who they are? Who Dom is?"

He sighs heavily and shifts his weight. As he moves his body, I instinctively cringe. The anticipation of being hit is forefront in my mind, but he keeps his hands to himself. "I wanted to tell you, so many times Maddie."

After a few minutes, it's obvious he needs a prompt to continue. "Tell me what?"

"I've not always been Malcolm, and these are my children."

Although I had already deduced this myself, I still feel dismayed shock hearing it from him.

"How? This doesn't make any sense," I stutter.

"I can't tell you, and trust me, you don't want to know."

"What do you even mean? You aren't who you say you are; you've got kids I didn't even know about." I'm being brave, but I have to know.

"God Maddie, if you looked hard enough online, you'd find out. I got into some bad stuff, and I can't have that following me around, so I changed my name, end of story. I already told you what I am capable of, so leave it alone."

Too shocked to dig any further I change tack and ask about the girls instead. "You have daughters?"

"I made some mistakes, and I paid for them, and now I'm not allowed to see them. I don't want to talk about this anymore, so just drop it. I'm sorry I didn't tell you sooner, but how the fuck do you tell someone that? Believe it or not, I'm sorry."

I can't believe I just heard those two words come out of his mouth, not once but twice. The man who never apologises for anything and who I've witnessed chase a man across town and block him in his driveway just because he didn't like the way he looked at him, never EVER says sorry.

"It's ok," I hear myself say even though it's about as far from ok as it can possibly get.

He leans over, wrapping his arms around me and hugs me tightly. I reciprocate the hug and wonder if this is the barrier that has been standing between us all along.

"You must really miss them," I whisper.

"I do. But we have a new little baby on the way."

We stay like that for some time before Mal says quietly, "I hope it's a girl."

"A girl," I ponder. "That would be nice. We could find out at our next scan?"

He shakes his head vehemently. "No. Let it be a surprise."

"OK," I agree, but a large part of me starts to hope that I'm carrying a boy, I can't help it.

Just when I think he's fallen asleep, he suddenly says, "Everyone has always let me down. I try and try, and every time people just end up using me. Are you going to be another one in a long line of girls to fuck me over? I really hope I can trust you, Madeline, because right now I have a lot of bad thoughts about you in my head."

I'm confounded, how can anyone keep up with his mood changes? He gets up and walks away from me, leaving me sitting on the bed alone as the warmth of his embrace leaves me. I can't get my mouth to work, to reply to him, to call him back or just to say anything at all. I have missed him so much, and I'm so desperately in need of comfort that even this tiny scrap he just threw me then snatched away breaks my heart. How hard is it to see that I have fallen apart, that I am broken?

His deception about his true self-tears me deep inside, taking root. It pours more pain into my already fragile state and poisons my soul. Every day he causes me more hurt, but he doesn't see what he is doing to me. It leaves me angry and hurt, devastated and completely unable to do anything about it.

It's so hard to have glimpsed at everything I thought I'd have with him; we were so happy, and it felt so right. I felt like I had no choice, we were meant to be together.

I rub my temples, trying to remember when thing started going so horribly wrong. Has it only been a year? It wasn't supposed to be like this, we were supposed to be happy. I couldn't and didn't want to imagine a life without him. I couldn't understand how those other girls could let him go. I thought if he were mine, I wouldn't ever let that happen.

He was so beautiful to me, he treated me with such love and respect and care. I don't understand why he felt like he couldn't trust me enough to tell me the truth about himself, especially right now when I need him so much.

I feel like my life is over. Is this my punishment for being such a bad person? My life has dissolved into a kaleidoscope of anger, hurt, violence and fear. That is mostly all there are these days, and I just don't know if I will ever feel happy again

Despite my whole world being rocked with Mal's revelations, the weekend brings a sense of normality and with it a small amount of peace. I spend a lot of the time trying to process a sudden shift in my perception of Malcolm or Dominic. It's given me a lot to think about, but I have no idea how to broach the change of name with him, and he hasn't mentioned it again or given me any sign the subject is still up for discussion.

I have no idea if he's changed it legally, how do you even do that? I don't know what I'm supposed to put on this baby's birth certificate, or even what name it will take once it's born. I wish I had access to the internet so I could find out what it was he did that was so bad, bad enough to warrant a change of name. But he put a password on my computer months ago, and after repeated baulked attempts at cracking it I gave up trying.

CHAPTER TWENTY-NINE

After successfully avoiding Amy for almost three days, she finally corners me outside work, while I stand kerbside waiting for Mal. She's in high spirits telling me how well prepared she thinks we are for the Quiz Night. I may have embellished the truth somewhat, like having looked at any of the trivia cards she's been flooding us all with or being able to go as I haven't said a word to Mal yet. The longer she natters on, the more anxious I feel, and nausea starts building in the pit of my stomach. He will be here any minute, and I'm worried she will say something to him before I've had a chance too.

I instinctively appraise his appearance as I see him approach us. My concern is well warranted; I can tell already. I pull open the car door and Amy smile brightly at Mal. She's totally oblivious to the frown painted on his face as she excitedly confides in him her master plan for winning the quiz night.

"I do hope you can come too!" she exclaims. "My fiancée is coming as he knows all about sports, well Rugby and Cricket mostly. How much do you know about New Zealand Colonial History and Maori relations?"

"What?" he exclaims incredulously. "Just because I'm Maori you just assume, I know shit about it, that's a bit racist, isn't it?"

His outburst stops Amy in her tracks. "I'm sorry. I didn't mean to offend you."

I stand uncomfortably on the kerb, completely frozen by the scene unfolding in front of me.

"Get in the car Madeline," Mal tells me, ending the further

conversation.

I hurry to do what I'm told, and Amy reaches towards me as I climb down into the passenger seat. "I'll see you tomorrow," I say to her as I yank the car door closed.

As soon as he pulls into the flow of traffic, he speaks, "What the fucking hell was that cunt talking about Madeline?" He enunciates each syllable of my name with a hard edge, using it as a weapon

I can't answer him, and after a few moments of my continued silence, he flies into a rage. "HOW am I supposed to trust you if you never tell me the god damn truth? Were you planning on sneaking off with that slut?"

"She's just talking about the work team-building exercise. It's a quiz night." I pray that believes that it's nothing sinister.

"You ARE cheating on me, aren't you? Otherwise, why didn't you invite ME! Are you ashamed of me? Is that it?" His accusations come hard and fast, how does he so successfully change it around and make it my fault? Any attempt to defend me dies before they reach my tongue. I remain silent and try to hold back the flood of tears that are threatening to overflow.

"Can you just help me not hurt someone else, just do what I ask and be fucking honest with me."

"It's just a quiz night, it's not important," I finally say quietly, willing him to calm down. His driving has become erratic, and I am beginning to feel very scared. "Please slow down," I beg him.

"Shut the fuck up Madeline, or I'll drive this car into a lamp post and kill us all. Is that what you want?"

How can he say these things and still blame me? I'm so scared of him; he must realise this? He wants me to do EVERYTHING he says, and if I don't do it immediately, he gets wound up and goes mental at me, making it all my fault.

I clutch the car door and glance in his direction, I should have just told him about the quiz night.

"You are making me do this Madeline, this is not my fault. You should know I can't control myself when I get angry."

"You can come, of course, you can. You're more than welcome, too," I plead.

"If you think I am going anywhere with your slapper work friends you are very much mistaken. Take your slut sister with you, she thinks she knows it all anyway."

Just like that, I have permission to go, and with Rosie too. It doesn't feel like a victory, though. His behaviour in the car has left me shaken, there is a massive part of me that believes he would kill this baby and me if he felt I had wronged him enough and that thought is utterly devastating. I thought having a child would bridge us together, but I couldn't have been further from the truth.

"I feel sick, and my head hurts," Mal tells me. I'm not sure if he wants me to do something about it or say something. I choose silence. This isn't the first time I've heard this following an 'argument'. I use argument in the loosest sense. When you argue with someone, it usually implies it's a conversation where two people are disagreeing. Generally, I do disagree with him, but I am far too scared and conditioned to tell him how I really feel.

In this case, I think his headache has more to do with the work quiz night I'm trying to get ready for because Rosie is picking me up soon. He's been sullen and difficult for the entire week leading up to today, and in the last hour, he's ramped up the complaints in frequency and volume.

After seeing him rub his temples and grown a few more times, I relent. "Do you want me to get you some Panadol?"

"What's the fucking use? It won't do anything. I'm probably dying because of that stupid job I'm forced to do. I hate it. I should never have left Christchurch."

I dismiss the last bit and go to get some painkillers for him. I rustle around in the medicine box, and my hand brushes an old bottle of Lorazepam. It's supposed to have relaxed me during a dental procedure, but I never took them in the end. Briefly, I wonder what they'd do to Mal if I gave them to him, but I quickly brush the thought aside and fill a glass with water. I leave it along with the Panadol next to him on his desk.

"My sister will be here soon."

"Whatever," he replies sulkily.

I turn back to the bathroom to clean my teeth and wash my face. After some searching, I locate my makeup case shoved at the back of the wardrobe. It's dusty with disuse, I can't remember the last time I even put makeup on but seeing as I know my sister will be wearing some, I want to make an effort.

Staring at my reflection in the bathroom mirror, I wonder where the Madeline of the last 25 years has gone. My eyes look puffy, my hair, even though I washed it this morning looks limp, with way more split ends than I would have permitted 2 years ago. I decide not to worry about the foundation and settle on a tiny bit of light brown eyeshadow and one quick pass of mascara. It will have to do.

Once upon a time, I would have thrown several outfits around my room looking for the perfect combination of spunky and cool, but a growing belly dictates that the majority of my wardrobe no longer fits. Out of desperation, I settle for my stretchy work skirt with a plain black tee-shirt that I used to only wear in bed.

I grab my jacket from the back of the door and go back to sit on the couch. Mal is still at the computer, he doesn't seem to be paying any attention to me at all, but my tummy is still tied up in knots. I can't help but think I will pay dearly for this night out.

But I rally and think of the list I have written in my journal, all the things I want back in my life. Thankfully it's safely tucked in my work locker. I desperately want to claim my independence back, and I know that if I don't start trying now, he will lock me down for the rest of my life.

I glance at the clock and check my cell phone, but the last text from Rosie was over an hour ago.

"Hah!" Mal shouts. "Is your sister even coming?" He gets up and walks towards me. "What the hell are you wearing on your face?"

I hold my breath without meaning too as he leans down closer towards me.

"Why are you wearing makeup? Fuck Madeline? Are you trying to attract a new man?"

"No, of course not," I try to defend myself.

"I really hope you aren't turning back into your old self Madeline. Are you trying to make me worry about you going off with your slutty sister?"

'Fuck you' I think to myself while trying to hold it together. Fuck you, you don't know the first god damned thing about me.

My silent bravado doesn't do much to calm my nerves, but luckily, I am spared the rest of his views on 'sluts who wear makeup'. I've heard it all before anyhow. I see the lights of Rosie's car pull into the driveway. I heave myself up and move out of the house before he can stop me.

"What time are you coming home?" he calls as I almost make it to the bottom of the stairs.

"Umm, I'm not sure. Not too late, I'll text you," I say.

"You better."

I race out the door before my sister has a chance to get out of her car. I've left it unlatched in the hope I'll be able to get back in if he's gone to bed. He won't let me carry a house key with me, so I really need to make sure I am back before he goes to bed.

"Hey!" Rosie says as I climb in the car. "How are you? Sorry, I'm late. Mum was on the phone to Aunty Jo, some drama with Nana June taking a fall."

"Oh, is she ok?" I start to worry; our Nana is well into her nineties but still fiercely independent.

"Just bruised, I think. 'Nothing a good drop of whisky, won't fix', that's a direct quote from Nana."

We both roll our eyes. Nana June believes that a drop of whisky could cure pretty much anything. And what whisky can't fix, ice cream and chocolate cake would. I wonder how much alcohol and sugar it would take to fix my current predicament.

CHAPTER THIRTY

"So, this is at the Sports Club?" Rosie asks after fiddling with the radio. Dance music starts to fill the car, as she turns it up, I reach in discreetly and turn it down.

"It's just past Pizza Hut," I clarify.

The further away from Mal, I am, the more I start to relax, but he's never far from my thoughts. As we pull into the car park the first text message from him arrives. Well for better or worse, I've made it out the house to a place that does not work without Mal chaperoning me. I try to brush aside my feeling of unease and focus on enjoying a rare night out.

Before I've even found my seat my phone buzzes again, I glance at the screen discreetly, hiding my phone from Rosie. 'Do we not have any more Panadol? Head is KILLING me.'

It can't have been 30 minutes since he last had some, but I tell him where I put the rest, almost immediately he replies with, 'Don't worry I found codeine.'

Where on earth could he have found codeine? I think for a moment of the Lorazepam tucked away in the medicine box, but Amy has spotted me and is towing me to a table half-filled with people from her department, and a man who I assume is her Fiancée.

"Hello, Mamma," Paul waves. "Nice of you to finally join us, now let's win this thing!"

"Oh god, I really hope you weren't pinning all your hope on us?" I ask.

"Well speak for yourself Mads, but I'm ALWAYS on the winning team," says Rosie as she brushes past me and plonks herself into a vacant chair.

"I'll get the first round, order up!" Volunteers a guy I recognise from the shop floor. He looks in my direction first, but my tongue sticks to the roof of my mouth. I can't return the favour because I can't even pay for my own drinks.

When I asked Mal if I could take some money with me earlier in the week, he had hit the roof. "What the fuck do you want to buy that I can't get you?" he retorted. When I tried to reason with him, he insisted that since it was a work function, they should pay for everything. "Besides," he said. "You can't drink while you're pregnant and water is free from the tap." I have no idea if the water is free in a bar, but since he was still letting me go, I gave up.

"Um I'm pregnant," I remind everyone and hoping that would be the end of it.

"Coke then?" he tries again.

"Diet, she drinks diet thanks," supplies Rosie. "And I'll have the same because I'm driving, and I have to get my sister home in one piece."

Satisfied, he takes orders from the rest of the table, and the banter resumes. Worry gnaws at me, fraying my nerves. I hope I can avoid having any more drinks bought for me by nursing my coke.

It's beyond a joke that I can't spend my own money, and soon enough I won't be earning any at all. I have no idea what's going to happen once the baby gets here, I don't know if I am going to quit my job and stay home or be forced back to work. I am sick of him threatening to leave, I'm sick of him always making it my fault, why does he NEVER take any of the blame?

With everyone else engrossed in conversation with each other, my mind wanders. How many times does he have to hurt me and break my heart before he is satisfied? Are our problems really all in my head? I am so sick of his dark moods, his stomach pains and headaches. I'm sick of him calling me names and slagging off everyone left in my life. I'm tired of feeling sad all the time, and I am sick of him calling me a slut and a whore for no reason, and then accusing me of cheating on him just because I am wearing makeup.

Then he gets on his high horse about how he hates girls who get dressed up and put makeup on like this wasn't how I dressed when he first met me. He says they look like sluts that are up for anything, is this how he thought of me to start with? I like to wear makeup and dress nice, but I do those things for me, I don't do it to attract anyone else to me. How does he make me feel so confused about things I used to take for granted?

My pity party is broken by Mr Jamison, the big boss of our store talking on a PA system. I can barely see his thinning grey topped head over the crowd, but I can hear him as he taps the microphone a few times until he is sure he has everyone attention. "Welcome, Staff! We have set up, and the Quiz Master is ready to go!" Muffled talk continues as he explains the rules to us, but he smoothly ignores the continuing chatter. "We are shouting you all a lovely glass of champagne, so after the first round the staff here will bring out some finger food to soak it all up. We aren't going to tolerate any cheating so leave your mobile phones in your pockets. Yes, Brian, I am looking at you. But most importantly have fun!" he concludes to a round of applause.

I try to relax as the 'champagne' gets distributed. I discreetly pass mine to Amy who lines it up with her other glasses.

"Don't worry," she says dismissing looks of amusement from our team members, flashing her fiancée her most winning smile. "I'm not driving tonight!"

Someone else at the table laughs mockingly. "Make sure you sit her on a plastic bag on the way home with a doggy bag if she keeps drinking like that."

"Amy, you won't be much use to this team if you're drunk!" says someone else.

"HEY!" Amy shouts with a smile, not offended at all. "I got this!"

The conversation around the table is easy, with everyone enjoying themselves. I force myself to at least appear relaxed. It turns out that I am hopeless at answering any of the questions, but thankfully my sister really is the promised 'know it all'.

"Oh, damn it!" Amy swears. "Bloody hell, Neil Finns christened first name is? It's right on the tip of my tongue."

"A Gin and Tonic?" Paul supplies helpfully.

My sister rolls her eyes at us. "Seriously guys did none of you study for this! Cor-ne-li-us Mullane Fin. How can you not know this?"

We scribble the answer down and move on to answer the next question. But I'm stuck thinking of Cornelius Fin who changed his name. I guess I can understand why he'd not want to be burdened with a name like that in the music industry, but Mal changed his entire name. I wonder if he told his parents he's changed his name. I don't have the first clue what his parents are like, I've never met them, and as far as I know, he's not told them about the baby or me either.

Not before long round one is over, and the nibbles are being delivered to our table. My tummy grumbles with anticipation of a food group that doesn't consist of microwaved past its best before date porridge. I ignore the humoured looks people cast in my direction and pile my plate high with mini potato topped pies, tiny quiches and cocktail sausages.

"Wowser!" Rosie's exclaims. "Pregnancy sure makes you hungry."

"I haven't had dinner," I defend myself.

With the quiz in the intermission, I pull my phone out. I'd hate for our team to be disqualified because I was firing off a text to Mal every few minutes. His last texts claim he misses me. I'm in two minds, whether I should return the message. It's like a double-edged sword when dealing with his unpredictable temperament. Deciding that any response is better than none, I reply, 'Missing you too.'

Thirty seconds later he sends back, 'What time will you be home?'

Ugh, I have no idea when I'll ever get another night off ever again, I don't want to spend it playing text tag with Mal. 'Not sure, just finished first-round, can't text while the quiz is on,'

'You BETTER not be drinking!' is his response.

What planet is he on? 'Of course not, got to go, quiz back on,' I fire back and slide my phone back into my bag, trying to focus on the conversations around me. By that time, I manage to tune back in I've lost track of what they were talking about. So, I ignore the buzz after buzz of my phone and try to enjoy the friendly banter going back a forth around me.

I know I can't ignore Mal's text messages forever, but instead of giving in to my urge to respond I leave it in my bag and smile while Amy regales us with stories about the last time she and her Fiancée went to town.

Once Mr Jamison and the Quiz Master tally the results, he taps on the microphone to get our attention. "We have the results in so hold onto your hats and let's find out what you might just be taking home with you tonight."

He pulls a bed sheet off the table behind him to reveal 'the prizes. I stand up to get a better view of an odd assortment of bits and pieces that have obviously come from the store we work at.

"Oh!" exclaims Rosie, "I want the toaster oven."

"Why?" I laugh. "Mum does all the cooking!"

"Well, I'm not going to live there forever." She winks at me.

After lots of shouts and cheering it's announced we've come third. Rosie doesn't get her toaster oven but picks out an alarm clock that throws itself around the bedroom floor if you don't turn it off. I stare at the collection of knickknacks and after some thought chooses a Galileo thermometer. There is something about the colourful floating balloons inside the glass cylinder that makes me feel happy, I shake it slightly and watch them bob around.

My phone buzzes again inside my bag, so I slide it out. My sister is still happily chatting with our team members and distracted enough not to notice my attention has wandered. I have another ten texts from him all along the lines of, 'How much longer do I have to wait up for you?' Which is laughable, as it's only 10 pm and he usually makes me wait much longer than this before I can go to bed. It doesn't matter how many times I promise myself I'm going to make a stand against him that familiar feeling of anxiety tightens its hold on my nervous system and ensures I obey him. I text him back promising I will be heading home soon and for the benefit of my sister pretend to stifle non-existent yawns.

It doesn't take long for my play-acting to take effect. 'Let's get this tired Mummy to be home. See you all soon!" she promises her new friends. They have arranged to go out the following weekend. She's in high spirits and talks animatedly about how much she's enjoyed the evening out with me.

"We should so do this again before the baby gets here," she gushes. "We haven't really hung out in ages."

"I know I should make more of an effort. Just between work and being pregnant, I don't have a lot of energy."

Rosie reaches across the short space of the car and rubs my shoulder. "It will be OK, you know; you'll figure it out."

"Thanks," I reply. I'm not so sure she's right, but I appreciate the sentiment.

I clutch my new thermometer to my breast as we travel. I've not had anything new that was mine in over 18 months. It's more precious to me than I can allow myself to accept. A symbol of me defying Malcolm and doing something just for myself.

I see him standing in the front window as Rosie pulls into our driveway. I'm relieved he is still up, but I'm still scared about what sort of mood he will be in.

"Are you heading home tonight?" I ask.

"Yeah, I could do with a night of good night sleep," she winks at me and then glances up at the window Mal is occupying. "Looks like someone is happy I managed to get you home in one piece."

I bark out a laugh, "Something a bit like that, I suppose." I lean over the hand brake to kiss her on the cheek. "Thanks for coming with me tonight, I had fun.”

“Anytime Sis, I mean it. You call, and I’ll come to get you.”

I stare at her, with so many words unsaid and smile sadly. After climbing out of the car, I stand and wave as she reverses out of the driveway.

I must have stood there longer than necessary because Mal slides the window and yells at me. “I’m not going to stand here waiting for you all bloody night!”

Frantically I look around at the neighbour’s houses hoping that no one heard him. Thankfully I don’t see any movement, sighing inwardly I go inside, it feels a lot like walking into a lion’s mouth.

My chest tightens as I ascend the staircase to the lounge and enter. I gently close the door behind me, and he is standing inches away with his arms tightly folded across his chest. I freeze where I am, unsure of what I should do next.

“What’s that?” he asks as he nods his head in the direction of my thermometer.

“I won it tonight, we came third,” I reply, my grip tightening like he might try to rip it from my hands and smash it against a wall.

We stand there for what feels like an eternity before he steps aside to let me into the room.

“You can put it down there,” he commands, pointing to the floor next to the TV.

“Eh ok.” I don’t think that this is the best place for my prize, but I do as I’m told and put it down next to the TV. It’s quite pretty with its floating glass balls, and I hope that maybe the sun will catch it and reflect the colour on the wall.

“I’m going to bed,” he says, walking away from me.

I make a move towards the kitchen for a glass of water and to go outside to feed Bessie, but as I open up the back door he slides around the corner and shouts at me, “Where do you think you’re going?”

“I’m just feeding the dog?” It comes out like a question like I am asking permission.

“I’ve already fed the mongrel; do you want her to get fat?” I look at him dubiously. The dog roll doesn’t look that much shorter than it did that morning. “I told you I fed your stupid animals, didn’t I? Go get into bed!”

He snatches the dog roll from my hands and I back away in a flurry. Tears slide unrestrained down my face as I brush my teeth. My heart bleeds for my poor animals. He is not feeding them anywhere near enough. I know the cats will catch mice and birds, but my poor dog will starve tied to the steps.

I promise myself I'll wait until he's sleeping and sneak her some food. I can't let this continue, he's going to end up killing one of us, all of us maybe. I just wish I could think of a way to fix this; I'm starting to think I should have left Bess with Justin. Perhaps he'd take her back?

Mal would flip if he thinks I'm contacting him again, but maybe Dad might call him, or know someone willing to take her in. I can't let this go on. I'm selfishly keeping her with me, but she means far too much to me to let him destroy her.

Before leaving the bathroom, I wipe the tears away and splash cold water on my face doing my best to reduce the red puffiness that always plagues my face after crying because he thinks my tears are another manipulation tactic.

I'm pulling my nightie over my head as he enters the bedroom. I glance in his direction, just by looking at him, I can see he is going to make me pay for my night out.

"Why on earth are you putting that on?" he says, gesturing towards my nightdress. It's halfway pulled over my bump as he reaches towards me and tugs at the hem. "You don't need this, take it off."

He reverses my motion and pulls it back over my head. I stand with my arms wrapped around my breasts as his eyes rake over my naked body. My skin crawls with apprehension, feeling degraded by this treatment.

The minutes drag by as I remain motionless as he stares at me in silence. A cool breeze chills my body as I stand next to the bed, my flesh raised in goosebumps.

"I'm cold; can I get into bed, please?" I finally ask him.

"Well, what are you waiting for you, stupid cow?" he says as he walks out of the bedroom shaking his head.

I climb between the chill sheets taking care to tuck the duvet around my body, pulling my knees up until they touch my bump. I hug myself tightly, willing my body to sleep before he returns.

CHAPTER THIRTY-ONE

Almost an entire week passes before I build the courage to call my Dad about finding Bess a new home. I know it's the right thing to do, but my heart aches when I think of losing her. She needs a safe home I reassure myself, it's just a matter of time before he permanently hurts her, or worse. She's already missing her bottom teeth thanks to him, and I'm sure he's whacked her more than once on the spine.

Dad picks up on the sixth ring, and I let out my held breath in one big rush. "You got Sam," he answers, in his usual informal way of picking up a work call.

"Hey Dad, it's me,"

"Hey, Babe, what's up?"

The words stick in my throat, I can't answer him.

"Are you OK, Maddie?" I can hear the deep concern in his voice.

"Oh, yeah, I'm fine. It's just I was wondering if you could speak to Justin for me."

"Justin? Why?" he asks, I can tell I just earned his full attention.

"I'd do it myself, but it's kind of awkward. I was wondering if you'd ask him if he'd take Bess for a while. With the baby coming and everything," I can't finish the sentence. My voice breaks and I struggle to hold in a sob.

"Are you sure you're OK?" Dad asks again.

It would be so easy to ask him to save me, ask him to make it all OK again. Make this bad man go away and erase all the bad horrible things that have happened to me.

But I can't, because I believe Mal when he says he will hurt him, so instead I hedge my bets on his first grandchild being the most important thing. "Please, Dad. I just don't want Bess to get neglected because I'm busy with the baby."

"I hope you're not doing this because of Mal?" he says, immediately doubtful of my motives.

"No Dad, this is what I want."

"She's your dog Maddie that makes her your responsibly."

"She's Justin's dog too," I retort instantly regretting it, but the pain I feel at doing this is almost too hard to hide from him.

"Well, OK, I'll call him soon, but this better be what you want and not what you are being pressured to do."

I hope this is the most painful part, although I don't want to think about actually saying goodbye. I've secured a happy future of my beloved puppy, at the expense of my own comfort. My feelings are so mixed, half of me hopes Justin will immediately drive up and get her, but the other half hopes he says no and I get to keep her. The rational part of my mind knows I have to do what's best for Bessie, though, not me.

The only thought in my head that comforts me is of holding my dog, my Bessie because she asks so little of me and gives me everything in return. Why is this so god damn hard? Why can't I have what I want for a change? It's not like I am asking for an enormous amount. I want Bessie, but I may as well be asking for the moon. I want to be happy again. I don't want to feel like this anymore. I want to feel safe, and I want some fucking god damn control over my life.

I bite my nails until they bleed while I wait anxiously for a reply from Dad. I can't focus on work when my brain is so full up. Adele picks up on my distracted mood and sends me a few querying glances, but I avoid eye contact and bend my head closer to the computer monitor. I don't want to talk about it, I'm too mentally drained to rehash this with anyone else.

Finally, I feel my cell phone start to buzz against my thigh. I take a deep, breath and answer, "Hi, Dad."

"Hi Babe, I've spoken to Justin, and he's agreed to come and get Bessie, but he can't do it until after Christmas. He's going to visit his parents so there won't be anyone home to look after her."

"OK," I say slowly. "Thanks, Dad."

"Madeline, that man still loves you. He'd take you back, you know."

"What, pregnant with another man's baby? I highly doubt that" I scoff.

Dad sighs, exasperated with me, "Yes, Maddie. I believe so."

"Thanks for calling him Dad. I better get back to work."

"Justin will call me when he knows the exact date."

And just like that, it's done. Bessie will be going back to her home, with a man who loves her. I try to feel happy for both, but it's hopeless. I wish I could go with her.

"You need to call Ruth," Mal tells me a short time after getting into bed that night.

"OK, why?" I ask.

"I don't think we need to see her weekly anymore. I think fortnightly will be enough."

WHAT? I think to myself. We have a session tomorrow evening, and I've already confirmed we will be there. "What about our session tomorrow?" I remind him.

"I don't feel like we need to go tomorrow, we'll go in a fortnight."

"OK," I say, biting back the disappointment that is starting envelope me. It's pointless to argue when he's made his mind up. But I really wanted to go, I need to tell him that Justin is coming to get Bess, but I don't want him to get the wrong idea and think that I've been talking to him again. How on earth are we supposed to work toward making things better if he has no interest in trying to make it work at all?

I try to relax against the pillow, but it's starting to become hard to get comfortable. I shift my belly into an easier position. My heart hurts. I've missed him so much; he's laying here next to me, but he may as well be a billion miles away. I desperately need comfort, why is it so hard for him to see that I have fallen apart? There's this deep hurt inside me, it's burying itself deeper, and pain pours out of me and poisons me. I just don't know anymore, every day I'm hurting, and he can't see what he's doing to me. I feel like he is killing me.

It hits harder at night when I have nothing to occupy and distract myself from how broken I feel. I don't believe I have ever been this unhappy in my entire life.

I really hoped that counselling would help us because I don't know what else to do. I was once so resilient against all the bad things in life, so convinced that everything would work out well, in the end, I thought my family had already been dealt all the bad stuff it was allocated.

Sleep doesn't come easy, not with billion worries and fears cramming my head, but finally, I do fall into an exhausted sleep and wake again with a damp pillow.

CHAPTER THIRTY-TWO

I find myself biting my nails again and whip them from my mouth. I know I must call Ruth soon and it's causing my stomach to knot. The office clock seems to have turned into one of those crazy carnival clocks that spin too fast for reality. Every time I glance at it another hour is gone, and I am that much closer to Mal coming to pick me up.

Eventually, I reach for the phone and punch in the number. After a period of ringing, it's finally answered.

"Central City Counselling Services, Ruth Speaking." Damn it, I was hoping to leave a message.

"Uh, Hi Ruth, it's Madeline," I talk faster to get this over. "We can't make it tonight. Uh, Mal has a work commitment, and we can only come fortnightly."

"Okay," Ruth draws the word out, taking her time to digest what I've just told her. "I'll have to charge you a late cancellation fee, though."

Oh crap, Mal's going to love that. "Um ok, how much is that?"

"It's $45. Shall I keep you scheduled for next week?"

With a sinking heart, I tell her yes and hang up. I glance at the clock; I've only got half an hour before it's time to go home.

Adele startles me from my melancholy by asking, "Have you made plans for Christmas?"

"Yeah, I guess we will spend the day with my parents." I hadn't really thought about it, even though it's already December.

"My Daughter and her family are coming up this year." She smiles brightly. "The last time we spent Christmas together was at least five years ago, so I'm sparing no expense. I'm going to roast an enormous

Turkey and do a Baked Ham."

"That sounds great," I tell her, rallying some enthusiasm to disguise how flat I feel about the 'festive' season. In truth, I just don't want to think about it. I don't want to think about approaching Mal to talk about doing the usual family things. Or how to buy gifts for my family when I am sure there is no way in hell Mal will want to fund presents for my parents and siblings.

I look down and realise I have twisted a piece of paper into thousands of tiny pieces, creating a snow scene on my desk. I use the back of my arm to sweep it all into the wastepaper basket and grab my things, it's time to go home.

As I walk out, Amy bounces over with a broad smile on her dimpled face. "Guess what!" she asks.

"You're running away to join the circus?" I guess.

She looks at me puzzled before blurting, "We've set a date!"

"Oh, really, when?" Jealously unexpectedly grips me.

"The first of June next year so only 6 months away! Please, you've got to help me! Can you come over after work and help me go through some wedding magazines?"

"Um, I'd have to make sure Mal doesn't have any plans."

She grabs my arm and pouts, "Please, I really need some help."

I rub her arm, trying to placate her into letting go of me. "I'll do my best OK."

She flashes me a smile as she runs off towards the staff room.

I'm glad I didn't make her a promise I know I can't keep. I can already imagine what Mal would have to say about me hanging out with her, and none of it would be good.

I am standing kerbside as Mal arrives to pick me up; his face the dark thunderstorm I have always begun to expect. He slams the car to a halt and flings the door open. I jump back to avoid being whacked by it.

"I hope you cancelled that damn appointment."

"Yes, but," I reply, leaving the cancellation fee hanging.
        "But what?" he barks.

I reply in a small voice, hoping that he won't hit the roof when I tell him. "We will have to pay a late cancellation fee."

"What the fuck is that? I thought these sessions were free?"

"They are, but we she told me we have to pay a cancellation fee if we cancel late."

"Jesus fucking Christ Madeline, do you think I am made of money?"

His knuckles whiten as he grips the steering wheel tighter. I keep my mouth shut; instinctively, I know we have crossed into entirely irrational.

"I supposed you haven't contacted anyone about getting what you are owed from that fucking ex-husband of yours either?"

Oh shit, I hadn't even thought about that.

"Have, you, contacted, a lawyer? It's that easy Madeline."

"I'm sorry I've been so busy at work, I'll do it next week, I promise."

"Like fuck, you will. Can you just help me not hurt someone else? Just do what I ask! Do you want me to drive this fucking car into a lamp post and kill us all? Don't make me do it, Madeline."

To prove his point, he speeds up and jerks towards the kerb. Narrowly avoiding a lamppost, he mounts the pavement and swerves the car back onto the road. My heart is in my throat and my blood pressure skyrockets, for a few seconds as he aimed the car towards the lamp post, I really believe he would kill us.

"You know I can't control myself when I feel like this," he tells me later when we are home. He wraps his arms around me, rubbing my back. "We need that money Madeline; you have to get it. You have to call a lawyer first thing in the morning, do you understand?"

I understand. He wants more from me, and there doesn't seem to be anything I can do about it. I know he will make it my fault because I didn't get the money from Justin. I know I am dragging my feet on the divorce settlement, but I still feel so guilty for leaving Justin, how can I take more from him?

It's set to be a long weekend, or at least it feels that way. It's not long until Christmas, but I can't even focus on what's happening right now let alone something that is still a few weeks away.

I get up Saturday morning to find my Galileo thermometer in pieces on the floor. Assuming that Mal has kicked it over, I carefully pick up the glass. The liquid is all over the carpet; it smells like turpentine and burns my nose. I am heartbroken by the loss of one of the last items left in this house that was truly mine, a symbol of defying him, even if only for one night. I swipe at a tear and shove my anger with him down further.

I'm dumping the damp smelly towels I've used to clean up the mess into the washing machine when he surprises me by shouting, "You need to figure out what to do with that dog of yours. I've had enough of her shit, the whole fucking yard stinks like dog shit."

Biting my lip, I try to think if I should tell him that I've already solved that problem, or ask him what happened to my thermometer, but something holds me back.

Instead, I try to clear my mind and focus on my breathing as he carries on listing all the transgressions my dog has supposedly committed against him. I am unsure how he can think that my loving her takes away from him, but apparently, it does. He hates and breaks everything if I can't love anything other than him, I wonder what this means for our baby.

"Are you even listening to me, Madeline?"

"Yes, yes, of course, I am," I lie.

"I'll probably catch fucking rabies," he continues.

I refrain from remarking that it's highly unlikely considering we live in New Zealand.

Suddenly I am stuck with insight that this isn't about my dog at all. Before I've had a chance to stop myself, it slips from my mouth, "It's not about the dog is it?"

Mal stares at me for a few seconds, his gaze intense with disapproval.

"What the fuck is that supposed to mean?" he asks.

Carefully I try to compose my thoughts. "I just mean, I feel like this is about something else, maybe something from your past?" In my head, I can almost imagine Mal as a baby, or a toddler being bitten maybe.

Eyes flashing, he slaps me across the face, shouting, "How dare you tell me how I feel?"

I shuffle back as far as I am able, but he lunges towards me and grabs my throat. He pins me down and breathes into my face. "It's not about the dog. Fuck the dog and fuck you. You are such a fucking bitch."

I can't breathe, my arms flail to push him off me, but it just makes him squeeze tighter. Lights flicker in my vision, and I feel the fight leaving my body. I feel him changing me, pushing me into something else, someone who lets a man treat her this way.

I stop struggling. I give up. This is how he ends my life.

Just before I pass out, he pushes me away, and I gasp desperately for air. I look towards him, seeing both hurt and fear in his eyes. I see now that he is holding onto his pain so tightly that he may never be able to heal. I'm not sure I can ever forgive him, but I have part of him I can't give back.

CHAPTER THIRTY-THREE

"Don't be a gloomy bum." He tells me a few days later.

The bruises start to emerge in earnest, and I can still feel the burn of his hand around my neck. He changed me that day; I believed he was going to kill me that I was going to die.

How could this have happened to my life? I don't understand this at all. How can he use such horrible words and treat me with so much anger and disrespect, then in the next instant extend a sliver of tenderness? He is hurting me so bad that I don't know what to expect from one moment to the next.

I am stressed, but I also recognise that I'm depressed. I desperately need someone to be here for me, and that someone was supposed to be him. He isn't here for me, and he isn't here for our child.

He is crushing my spirit, crushing and suffocating me as surely as if he had succeeded in strangling me on Saturday morning.

At some point, I will have to face the fact that I may have lost him for good. Can I blame myself for that? I don't believe I have changed, I am still essentially the same person, and the only changes made to me are the ones he has wrought. I wonder if it helps him to hurt me.

I reach down and rub my belly, and the baby moves under my touch. It's hard to imagine this baby will be here soon. Harder still to acknowledge we may lose Mal for good. I don't know how I feel about that either. If he were truly gone then so would the hope that we may regain him if he were gone, he would never come back, and our child would never know him.

I miss the beautiful amazing, loving, caring man he was when we first met. I miss him so much it burns in my heart, but I'm more scared that my life won't get any better.

As if answering my silent question, he reaches towards me and lays his hand on my tummy, on our child. I wonder what thoughts pass through his troubled mind. But I know what I want, what I need. I need to feel safe; I need to feel happy, and I need to be able to share the joy of our child with him. I just want him back.

Before I know it, it's Christmas. I can barely stand the happy chatter from the people at work. People planning their perfect Christmas breaks and all I want is to get through the day without someone yelling at me, or expecting me just to do what they say, or do what they want because they think they know what's best for me, or think they have the right to treat me that way.

I've finally summoned the courage needed to tell him Mal that Bessie is going to a new home after Boxing Day. He asked who was taking her, but I just say that it's someone Dad knows. I can't bear to bring up Justin again and give him something else to hate me over.

After he strangled me, things have been almost normal between us, and I am beyond surprised by Mal's involvement in the lead up to Christmas. I allow myself a little hope that he may come and give me one day of normalcy.

He even purchased gifts for my whole family, including my Aunty Jo and Uncle Geoff, so I let myself feel like things might be getting better.

"Mum said to come over at ten for breakfast," I remind him casually on Christmas Eve.

"I don't know Madeline," he tells me. "You know that Christmas is hard for me."

I don't know that, because he hardly ever talks to me about his past. Deflated, I ask, "Are you going to come over later?"

"Actually, I thought I'd stay here and tidy up the spare room."

"Oh, OK," I reply. I don't know why I feel so crestfallen; the day is sure to be more enjoyable without his malevolence.

I hoped that the interest in buying presents meant that he might want to be included in all my family traditions. Why am I always hope, he will 'change back' into the man he was when we first met?

I try to hide my disappointment from him and instead invest some hope that he will create a space for the baby once it arrives.

"Mum is coming over soon to pick me up. I'm going to the supermarket with her to pick up the last few pieces for tomorrow." I've already told him this, but I don't want any margin for error.

"Well OK," he says dubiously. "We need more milk, and some bread and I want some more muesli bars."

He hands me $20. It's the most money I've had in my possession since I surrendered my EFTPOS card to him. I stare at it for a few seconds before I shove it into my bag. I have $20 whole dollars to take with me to the supermarket. Should this feel so wonderful? A year ago, I'd have taken this for granted.

I feel almost buoyant as Mum toots from the drive, and I make a mad dash for freedom.

"Hi Mum," I greet her as I pull the seatbelt across my belly.

"Hello darling," she replies as she backs out of the drive and heads towards the local Supermarket. "Thanks for keeping me company. Rosemary claimed she had to work to do, so it's just us. I think she's working on Tom having Christmas Dinner with us."

I stay silent on the subject; I don't want to bring up the fact that Mal won't be coming. Instead, I reach for her list and double-check she has everything on there.

I can't express how it feels to be wandering up and down the Supermarket's isles, to just feel like a normal person. I casually push the trolley behind Mum and call out items from her list and make sure she hasn't forgotten anything. And then I see it, its something small and stupid, but this time last year I brought Bess a rope toy with four plastic sausages on it. I have no idea what happened to it, but she loved it. Before I give myself a chance to process what I am doing, I lift it from the shelf and place it in my small pile of groceries in front of me.

It's fitting that I should send Bess off with a special gift from me, I know that she won't understand, but it feels like sending a child off with a security blanket. Mum just pats my arm and thankfully doesn't say anything at all.

A big part of me was hoping that Mum and Dad would offer to have Bess for me, but I know that was just wishful thinking. As far as Dad is concerned, I shouldn't have to give her away at all.

I have mixed feelings after Mum drops me back later that day. I've managed to ignore most of his texts, but I can't avoid him forever.

I place the grocery bags on the counter before opening the fridge door and putting the milk inside. I'm just about to put the bread away when Mal pulls open the bag and pulls out the dog toy.

"What's this?" he says dangling the plastic sausages in front of my face. "Where the fuck is the receipt Madeline and where is my lotto ticket?"

"Lotto ticket?" I stutter stupidly.

"I fucking text you, stupid slut!"

"I'm sorry," I beg with a whimper.

He reaches towards me, snatching my purse from my shoulder. I swallow bile as he pulls out the few dollars I have left and the receipt. He glances at it and sweeps his coffee off the kitchen counter. The boiling drink splashes against my bare legs stinging me, but I don't have enough time to give that any consideration because of Mal in my face.

"Why do I have to miss out for your dog again?"

My whole body starts to shake as I cower in fear of him. In my head, I feel his hand wrapping around my neck again, but instead, he spits in my face as he yells, "I knew I couldn't trust you!"

He stalks off to the bathroom. When I'm sure he's not coming right back, I run a tea towel under the cold tap and press it to my scalded legs.

I knew he would be mad at me, that I spent five dollars on a toy for my dog, five whole dollars of money that I earned I should add. Angry thoughts start to whirl around so fast in my head that I can no longer think straight so I go grab a scrap of paper and a pen and sit outside on the back deck, close enough to get some comfort from my dog, but not so close that it would set Mal off.

When I'm sure he's not watching me, I start to write before my heart ruptures.

Another broken cup to match my broken heart, why do I let him do this to me? I don't know what to do anymore. When will he be satisfied, I have been hurt enough? My heart is bleeding, I'm hurting, and I know I will never have him back, and if I stay all I will have is hurt and pain and misery and fear and nothing.

After a few minutes, I feel a little calmer and reach to turn the handle on the back door, but I find it locked. I knock quietly at first, but he doesn't answer. I rattle it again and knock, but instead of him letting me back into the house I hear my car's tyres screeching out of the driveway. He has locked the back door, and now I can only get back in if he returns.

Part of me is shocked that he had driven off when he knew I was out here. He doesn't care about the baby or me at all. I think I should just let him go, but how can I?

An hour later he still isn't back, but at least I have some quiet time to write some more. I think I'm pretty good at looking on the bright side.

Did he really think we were going to win lotto? Why am I holding on so tight?

There is nothing left, and no one else knows how much I'm hurting.

No one except Bess and I are losing her tomorrow too. My cats have come to sit with me; they know how unhappy I am.

I wonder when he's going to come back, I wonder if he's going to come back. It's well past 8 pm, and there is still no sign of him. I don't even have my phone on me so I can't text my sister to come and get me. I briefly entertain going over to Tom's house, but I can't let them see how crazy my life is. It's bad enough they can probably hear him yelling at the animals and me.

I really hope he comes home; it will be dark soon, and I'm getting cold. Why does he hate me so much? Does he care about this baby and me at all? I tuck my paper under my shirt and hide my pen in my bra before leaning up against the back door.

That's where Mal finds me when he gets home way past midnight. Cold, alone and sleeping on the back doorstep.

Merry Christmas baby, Merry Christmas Maddie. I think silently to myself as I make my way to bed.

CHAPTER THIRTY-FOUR

When I wake on Christmas morning, Mal is already up and dressed. I wander through to the kitchen to find he has made me a coffee and left it on the breakfast bar. Next to my cup lays a green envelope.

I starc at both in confusion. It's been so long since he gave me anything other than bruises I don't know how to react.

"Is this for me?" I ask cautiously.

He rolls his eyes and pushes it closer to me. "Yes, for Bubba and us."

"Oh." Stunned, I carefully run my finger on the inside of the sealed flap and extract a gift voucher. "This is amazing," I tell him as I look at a family Zoo pass, he has got for us. "I love the Zoo."

"Yeah, I know."

We had our first clandestine date at the Zoo and in particular a shared kiss amid the artificial rain forest. Briefly, I recall the light misting of rain collecting around us. Ignoring how stiff I feel from a night outside, I start to wonder if our baby can have a slice of that happiness too.

"That's a great present Mal, thank you so much." I reach towards him and pull him into a hug, and ever so slightly, he squeezes me back. "I better get ready to go; I need to leave soon. Are you sure you don't want to come?"

"No, you know I'm not feeling well, my head hurts," he claims.

I don't try and argue with him; instead, I gulp down the coffee and head off for a shower.

I stand under the steady stream of water and try to fortify myself against the worse part of the day, Bessie going back to Justin.

After towel drying my hair and telling Mal, I had to leave, I walk outside to where she is tied up on a rope that is far too short. I unclip her tether, and she follows me silently and hops up into the back of the car. Her tail starts to thump in a slow rhythmic pattern and her tongue lulls of the side of her mouth. She looks happy and trusting, and even though this will be painful, I am grateful that she will be well looked after.

I put the remaining dog roll and biscuits into the boot, next to the presents and hand her my hard-earned string of sausages over the back seat. She takes them gently and wags her tail a little faster.

She will be staying with Mum and Dad until Justin arrives the day after Boxing Day. I wipe away a stray tear with the back of my hand and pat her on the head. It's for the best I remind myself.

As I back out the drive, I see Mal standing in the living room window watching me. I shiver and try to shake off the intense feeling of dread.

Fifteen minutes later, I pull into my parent's driveway and Bess bounds towards their house, dancing in small circles, barking her excitement and joy. I must smile despite my misery at losing her. She's going back to her Dad, back to a man who loves her. I am trying to focus on the fact that this is the best I can do for her under the circumstances and that I am not just one giant failure.

Dad opens the door as I raise my hand to knock. "I heard the 'dog-bell'."

I laugh a little manically at his 'dad joke', and he takes the multiple bags from me. Bess follows Dad happily into their house, rushing around to greet everyone with the sausages still in her mouth.

Rosie is sitting on the kitchen counter with a coffee in her hands wearing oversized sunglasses. "Shhhhhhhhhhh," she says, exaggeratedly to my dog. "I had a late-night Dog with too much beer, but I wouldn't expect you to understand."

I poke her in a rib, "I have no sympathy. I thought you were 'working'."

Mum laughs, "Make yourself useful and unstack the dishwasher."

"Augh," she groans. "Why can't Maddie do it?"

"Because she's carrying my first grandbaby AND helped me yesterday. Off you go I need you to carry this out to your Father first." She pats her on the back and slaps a tray in her hands. "I love you, my Rosie-Posy, I really do."

I laugh out loud at the use of her childhood nickname, and she sighs in an emphatic exacerbated fashion, but she still does our Mothers bidding.

"How are you, darling?" Mum asks while looking behind me, "Isn't Malcolm with you?"

"It's not really his thing, Mum."

"Christmas isn't his thing? What kind of family is he from?"

I shrug, I wish I knew.

She remains silent, but her body language speaks volumes. She's not happy with this arrangement. I guess it's only a matter of time before they start asking why I don't leave him.

Not long after I arrive, Jack turns up with Bella in tow. "Hi, aren't you spending Christmas with your family?" I ask her.

She looks at me, doe-eyed, "They don't mind. I'll see them tomorrow."

"Is Mal with his family?" Jack asks.

"Uh, he's got a migraine." I really hope we move off the subject of Mal's absence. But I do wonder how he's doing.

The kitchen conversation moves to recipes, and I relax, but I feel my cell phone buzzing in my pocket.

'Hope you're having a nice day,' his text says.

'Good so far, Dad is cooking breakfast,' I text him back.

'Missing you …' he replies.

This is all so weird. I don't know where all this affectionate behaviour is coming from. Only days ago, he had threatened to kill us all in a car crash, then he almost strangles me to death, and last night he locked me out for hours, and now he's acting all-loving. It's confusing and painful, and I don't know how to take it.

'I miss you too,' I text back.

'I've been thinking about you.'

'What have you been thinking of?' I reply, wondering if he'll send me a poem like he did when we were first getting to know each other.

'Kind of … I'm not really happy, all I see is you pushing and hurting and frustrating me more and not compromising and only doing what you want for you.'

Well, that didn't last long. I'm so tired of this, why can't he see I am the same? It's him who has changed, why does he always make it my fault? Why can't' he see the effect this is having on me? Am I as selfish as he thinks I am?

The family activity blurs into the background as Mal texts me over and over telling me how I have taken away his chances of winning Lotto this year, how I stole from him for my 'fucking dog' and that the only thing I had managed to get right in the last year was getting rid of her.

I stifle a sob and text back that I am sorry, but I'm not sorry. God, I am so confused; how can he not see what he is doing to me? I am so angry and tired. I have had about enough of this as I can manage. I know he is sick, but this is wearing me down.

I see my brother and his girlfriend sitting on the couch with their arms draped around each other, my sister is blissfully happy sharing a private joke via Skype with Tom and even my parents chuckling with each other in the kitchen and I feel a surge of anger at how my life is playing out.

I can't believe he keeps thinking I don't compromise! I heave my heavy body off the couch and head towards the bathroom. On the way there I grab the notepad and pen my parents keep beside the telephone. Angrily I start to list all the things I want but don't get. That I don't even ask for because I know it just starts another argument.

I title it: My Christmas wish list.

1.   I want my EFTPOS card.

2.   I want to be able to spend my money – not a huge amount, but I should be able to make that decision for myself.

3.   I want to be able to drive my own car whenever I want too.

4.   I want to be able to fold and put away towels since Mal won't do it and insists I don't do it correctly.

5.   I want to be able to visit a friend without Mal acting like I am going off to cheat on him.

6.   I want not to have to jump every time I get a text, I shouldn't always have to tell him who it is, he doesn't tell me who texts him.

7.   I want to be able to plug the landline in and have people know the number.

8.   I want my family/friends to be able to come into our home.

9.   I want to be able to have friends.

10.   I want to live in a clean house.

11.   I want a key to the front door!

12.   I want to be able to buy my dog a toy or food or whatever and not feel like I am depriving him of something.

13.   I don't want to have to give my dog away.

14.   I want to be able to wear makeup without Mal telling me I look like a slut or that I am wearing it for anyone else except myself.

15.   I want to be able to wear clothes I like without wondering if Mal thinks I look like a skank.

16.   I want to be able to be in a bad mood.

17.   I don't want to constantly have to watch what I say so I don't end up saying something that upsets him.

Is that list so unreasonable? I just don't know anymore. I stare at it for a few minutes before another surge of anger prompts me to rip it to shreds. I fling tiny bits off into the toilet bowl than watch as what I really want for Christmas gets sucked away, leaning my back against the bathroom door I carefully lower myself to the floor. I shove the back of my hand into my mouth to quieten my sobs and think back to last Christmas, my last Christmas with Justin.

My feelings for him were so mixed; he'd already been away for months when he came back fleetingly to spend a few short days with us. I was dragging my guilt with me over having slept with Mal a few weeks before and how I felt like I was falling in love with him. Justin was so loving and attentive to me, investing in our marriage in a way he hadn't done in the last few years. Maybe on some level, he must have known I wasn't in a good place mentally. I'd begged him not to leave before he went and now, he was back I was trying to distance myself from him emotionally.

Maybe if Megan hadn't moved away, then things might have been different, but I was falling apart, and even today, I have no idea how I was managing to keep everything together. He must have known, maybe not about me being a lying cheating double-crossing bitch, but certainly, that something was wrong.

I accused him of trying to ruin Christmas when he shoved a wrapped box at me at five minutes past midnight. "What will I have to unwrap after lunch if you let me do it now?" I asked him.

"I'm not going to ruin Christmas Maddie, just open it!"

Trying my best to raise one eyebrow, I finally relent and open it. I wondered what got him so excited. I peeled back the wrapping and was rendered speechless. "A new cell phone?" I finally managed to get out in disbelief. I was staring at the top of the range smartphone. "How can we afford this, Justin?"

"It's my present to you, don't worry about it."

So, I pushed my worry aside until he surprised me again that afternoon with a diamond eternity ring to match my wedding set.

I held him so tight that night, hoping to mend some of the rifts I had torn between us. I cried for two days solid before he had to go away again. I begged him not to go, I begged him to find some way to stay and not leave me. He probably thought I was hysterical, and that I'd be fine once he left. But I knew better. I knew that once he left, that would be it.

I felt physical pain when I dropped him off at the international terminal. The moment after I kissed him goodbye at the departure gate, I ran as fast as my legs could carry me to watch him walk through into the duty-free shopping area below me. I watched in silence as he walked under me, unaware of my presence. I watched until he was long gone and out of sight. I stood crying silently, waiting until I felt more composed because it was time to go back to my parents' house and start planning some sort of future from this wreck I had created.

CHAPTER THIRTY-FIVE

It takes days for the melancholy of losing Bess to start to fade. I try to find some comfort in knowing that she will be much better off with Justin, but I feel like I am trapped in a vacuum.

"My ex has been texting me," Mal announces smugly, quite out of the blue. I had been watching telly, trying to focus on the mind-numbing but familiar weeknight soap opera.

Mal knows he's got my attention though as my eyes are drawn in his direction.

"What does she want?" I ask perplexed.

"I don't know, but she wanted to know how I was." He holds my gaze for a few seconds before adding, "She says she misses me."

"Oh, OK." What am I supposed to do with this information? I'm at a loss wondering why he's telling me this.

"I might get to see my girls Maddie."

This new statement freezes me. He hardly ever talks about his daughters, but it broke my heart to see how much he loves those two girls, and how much he suffers because he's not allowed to see them. I steady my breathing and bite my tongue, wondering what revelation may come next.

"Did you know if that slut hadn't cheated on me, we would still be together? But I didn't know if the youngest was even mine. How was I supposed to live with that? That's what happens when people betray me. I walk away, just like that. Bet she regrets it now."

My hand drops to my baby bump, wondering if he could walk away from our child too. I'm not sure which path bothers me more, that I allow myself to think I could leave him or that my baby could grow up without him. I'm scared of him, and I don't know how much more abuse I can take. How much more is he going to make me suffer?

It is way past midnight before he lets me go to bed, and I am thankful to be sucked quickly into a deep sleep. It doesn't last long before I am woken by his whimpering cries.

I lay rigidly while deciding how to respond as his whimpers change to a chant of, "Hold me, please, hold me."

So, I hold him. Pulling him closer, I stroke his hair and talk soothingly, hoping the things I say are comforting. "It's ok baby," I say. "I'm here, I'm here for you,"

I say the same thing over and over again until he starts to settle. He wakes up two more before sunrise and both times I hold him until he falls back to sleep.

At 5 am, I am woken by him again, but he is rubbing my back, not crying. I stay where I am hoping that he might think me still asleep, but I can't deceive him, and I doubt it would have made much difference even if I was sleeping.

"Come here," he says as he pulls my hips closer to him. He wedges my legs apart and enters me from behind, not caring that I am as dry as sandpaper.

As his movements become faster and more erratic, I wonder if I should be feeling like things are starting to improve. He let me hold and comfort him last night, and now he is attempting to make 'love' to me, even if it is awkward with baby extending my belly so much.

I wonder if he is trying to push me away from him. Well if that is his plan, then he has succeeded. He has pushed me to the very edge of my sanity, and I have had enough. He talks about a compromise like some foreign word I don't understand and makes it seem like something I am incapable of doing it.

I don't think he even knows what it means, he only cares that things are run his way.

I am so angry and sad and mad at myself for all the stupid decisions I've made. I just wanted to be with someone who would accept me for who I was and create a space where I could just be me. Was that too much to ask for? I can't even speak my mind anymore without him becoming furious with me. I am so unhappy, and he is so selfish, he can only see his own misery. I don't believe he cares about our child or me at all.

As all my anger and resentment collide, he spends himself inside me and pulls me closer to him, snuggling his head on my shoulder, he sighs with what sounds like contentment and goes back to sleep.

Just like every damn thing else in my life, I am trapped under him.

I fall asleep on the couch long before midnight on New Year's Eve. My Aunt and Uncle had invited us over to their place to celebrate, but Mal said he wasn't feeling well, so we didn't end up going.

I made a resolution, though, and as soon as I get to work the next day, I write it in thick black capitals 'STOP BEING SO JUDGEMENTAL'. To try and act a little more positive about my future, I time my lunch break to coincide with Amy's.

"Any plans for your day off?" she asks.

Smiling as wide as I can muster, I have an actual answer for a change, "Yes actually. Mal got us a Friend of the Zoo pass, so we're going to go tomorrow."

"I love the zoo!" She exclaims.

"Yeah, me too," I smile with her enthusiasm.

"You know I've thought we should plan something special before you go on your maternity leave, Maddie. Did you have anything planned?"

"Um, no," I hadn't given it any thought at all. In fact, I hadn't even thought about when I should start my maternity leave.

"Leave it to me, sweetie, I'll plan everything," she promises me. "You know Jenny had that great idea last month, with the cakes."

Yeah, I remembered, it really was a great idea. She made two cakes, one pink and one blue then told everyone to make their guess by taking a slice in the corresponding colour. I feel a pang of jealousy thinking about how she could just whip up a cake for work. Give to other people and not feel guilty, like she was taking food out of her husband's mouth.

"Yeah that was a great idea," I echo, but inwardly I start to question the wisdom of taking my break with her.

She natters away absent-minded for the rest of our half-hour, and I relax a little and before I know it the break is over, and I am back sitting in my office staring at the wall clock.

I think I spend more time looking at the clock than my computer when I am startled by the sound of my cell phone ringing silently. I reach for it cringing; instinct preparing for Mal, but it's Megan's number flashing on the display.

I answer tentatively, "Hi." I haven't spoken to her in so long.

"Hey hon," Megan says. "Good news! I'm coming up to Aucks for a few days, wanna catch up? Please say you will."

"When?" I ask.

"On the fifth of Jan, so that's only four days away."

"Sure, I'd love to," I say against my better judgement. "Um, did you want to come to see me while I'm at work?"

"If that's what you want, hon. I miss you."

Tears slide silently down my cheek as we arrange the date. I push my apprehension aside, hoping that Mal won't find out.

Fear that Mal will somehow figure out that Megan has called me works its way into my gut. I check and recheck that my call log is deleted. I'm so preoccupied that I am totally taken by surprise when he announced during dinner that he plans on purchasing a new vehicle.

"I've seen a truck for sale, and I think it would be a great investment for us. It's one from where I used to work," he tells me while he chews. "It's a great price too, but we don't quite have enough to buy it outright."

I wouldn't know as I have no idea how much money he has or doesn't have. He cuts the chicken and scraps his knife across the plate, the sound grating my eardrums. I close my eyes; I hate that noise.

"Look, Madeline, I'd get the loan myself, but there's no way they'd give me one after my Ex screwed me over. So, I'm going to need you to ring the finance company tomorrow, I've already started the paperwork."

"Do we need another car?" I ask.

"What the fuck do you think? That we're going to carry our baby around in your death trap?"

I guess not, although calling my hatchback a death trap is a stretch, I'd always maintained meticulously.

"Look, it's not like it's going to be forever. If you'd just call a lawyer, we'd already have the money."

He's so blasé about planning what's going to happen with the money from my divorce settlement that my breath gets caught in my throat. I will need that money. We need to buy things for the baby, I want to be able to plan for my child's future, but I can barely get through the day.

"Jesus Madeline! Do you think I'm stuck here? My Ex text me again, and she's more than happy to take me back, so don't you dare think I am stuck here with your fat arse."

My heart constricts in pain. Realistically I know this must be nonsense, he told me over and over again how much she hurt him. Tears blur my vision as I struggle to hold them back. "Don't you think we could use that money for the baby," I try reasoning with him.

"Fuck it!" he spits at me. "All I want is money, and I don't care where

I get it. I'm getting that truck, Madeline! Stop trying to turn yourself into a victim."

I stare at him stricken as he goes to the computer desk, the rest of his dinner forgotten on the bench. Is that all I am for him, a paycheck?

"I've already signed the sale of the purchase agreement," he tells me, as he grabs a stack of paperwork and thrusts it towards me. "You just have to sign here and here and call the finance company in the morning. I can't spell this out any clearer for you."

He shoves a pen directly into my hand and stands there with his arms wound tightly across his chest as I woodenly I take it and sign where he has indicated.

I feel sick. When did I become so powerless that I can't prevent this from happening? How can I be forced into a loan I don't want, for a car that's not even for mine?

"Where's your driver's licence, I need to copy it," he says once I'm done.

He smiles at me arrogantly as he waits for me to get my licence from my bag. He has no concept of what he is doing to me, and it's obvious he doesn't care how I feel about it. I am hurting so bad, and I really am alone in this. Well kind of alone, there is the baby after all. But I am too scared to make a decision; the last time I made a choice for myself, I ended up here, being abused. But one thing is sure, I can't live like this forever. It's destroying me.

I wait until the printer has finished copying my driver's licence and try to retrieve it, but he slaps my hand away from the scanner bed and reaches it first.

"I still need it," he claims as he shoves into his wallet, next to my EFTPOS card.

The sinking feeling in my stomach descends lower, and I swallow bile.

I go through the motions of eating dinner, of watching TV, of following him to bed. I lie awake for the better part of the night as I silently cry out my pain.

Friday is the worse day of the week for me. Most people look forward to it, but weekends signal no escape from him at all. At least I don't need to worry about getting up for work, not that I can even remember the last time I was on time. Leon has given up scolding me for being late. As long as I get my work done, he pretty much avoids me. He's probably worried I'll cry on him again, which is highly likely given my current predicament.

With only a month until the baby is due to be born, I figure this weekend I really need to start thinking about planning a hospital bag. At my last midwife appointment, Carla gave me a list of items that I'll need, but I've been too scared to approach Mal about it yet.

I make a mental catalogue of what we have so far. A nappy bag that Mal brought, only it's not a nappy bag at all, it's a chilly bin. It's quite a good picnic bag, but will it work as a nappy bag? I guess I'll just have to make do, although, at this point, we don't have nappies to put in it anyway.

We have some baby clothes and a car capsule that my Aunt Jo gave me not too long after Justin and I got married. Wishful thinking on her part because they have sat dormant until now.

And that's it, nothing else. This baby is due to arrive in approximately four weeks, and we have pretty much nothing.

I'm beginning to think that it will come home from the hospital to makeshift tea towel nappies and sleep in a cardboard box. Well, at least breastfeeding is free.

That night after I finally fall asleep, I have the most comforting dream I've had in a long time. I'm holding a tiny baby in my arms, he as bright blue eyes, a halo of dark hair and he's perfect. In my dream, I'm happy, safe, and secure. I gaze lovingly into the eyes of my son, who I call Liam, it all felt so right. I haven't felt anything that right in a long time.

CHAPTER THIRTY-SIX

I wake up clouded in a haze of semi-happiness, and as I start to try and haul myself out of bed to relieve myself, Mal snakes an arm out and nuzzles into my neck. Instead of making a break for freedom I try to ignore the nag of my bladder and enjoy this tiny slice of day where things haven't turned completely shit yet.

It's a good thing I snatch these moments when I can because they are fleeting. Does he not realise he is pushing me away? He is blind to the fact that I am no longer coping, that at this point, it would be easier for me to walk away. I wish he would just do what he keeps promising to do and leave because he's made it abundantly clear he doesn't want to be here anymore.

It takes an effort to get out of bed now, and I really can't ignore my increasingly urgent need to pee. I make a move to get out of bed, but he holds me tighter.

"I need to go to the bathroom," I tell him.

"Go then," he replies hurt like I'm abandoning him.

"I really have to go Mal; I'll be right back." I'm just going to the toilet for crying out loud, but he is acting like I am packing my bags and moving out.

The rest of Saturday morning is just going through the motions, putting one foot in front of the other. Go to the bathroom, then get some breakfast. Try to get the dishes done before Mal tells me to leave them and they stay on the bench for another day. I try hard to anticipate Mal's needs, which means asking him if he wants a coffee or backrub, but nothing works.

"Why would I want a back rub?" he asks. "Are you trying to spy on me?"

He turns his back, so I can't see the computer monitor, and I am lost for words. I hadn't been thinking about the computer at all, but now I am starting to wonder if he does have something to hide.

I take a shallow breath before replying carefully, "No. I was just trying for us to have a good weekend." I wasn't sure if using his own words against him would pay off, but he seems to relax visibly.

"No, I don't need a back rub."

"Oh, ok." I close my eyes, wondering how to approach my real goal. "I thought we could talk about what needs to get before the baby arrives."

"What sort of stuff?" he asks me warily.

"Um well, I need to pack a hospital bag and …"

He cuts me off immediately. "You already have a bag; why do you need a new one?"

"No, not that. I know I have a bag, but I need some things to go in it," I explain.

When he continues just to stare at me and say nothing, I try again, "I need maternity pads and some stuff for the baby. And Mum says I need to think about getting a decent nursing bra."

"Well if your Mother thinks bras are so important, she can buy you one can't she."

"But," I manage to get out before he interrupts again.

"You don't need that shit, and I'm not giving you money to waste on bras. PLUS, the hospital will give you pads, don't you know anything? For fuck's sake Madeline, I thought we were going to have a good weekend?"

I forgot he's already had kids, but I'm pretty sure that the Midwife said I needed to supply my own Pads. The simple fact that he's already done this should mean he knows what a baby needs. Why is he acting so obtuse?

I bite the inside of my lip; does he not realise how humiliating and degrading it is to beg for money from him? I work 43 hours a week for nothing. The way he makes me feel for having 50 cents in my pocket like I have stolen it from him is sickening like he has a right to everything I earn and own, and my body too.

He has conveniently forgotten how he hits me, left bruises on my skin and on my heart, how he accuses me of not compromising daily but cannot do so himself.

I feel like I am suffocating, I don't know how much more of this I can take. I can't have a baby and have him be like this. How could I have been such a fool? I loved him so much, and it felt so right. How could things have gone so terribly wrong? What else is going to fuck up? I'm hurting so badly.

Since the counselling started, he seems to think that telling me that he is getting angry is enough. But I will not say thank you to him just because he has identified that I have made him mad. That is not dealing with his issues as he seems to think.

Then he goes on and on about how he has had to make all the compromises in our relationship. Moving to Auckland, leaving a job he now says he loved, leaving his family behind although I've never met them and he never talks about them, I don't even know if they know I exist.

He acts like I got pregnant to trick him into staying with me, and then tells me he is going to leave me for his ex. I didn't fool him! He wanted this too, and it makes me feel so alone. I have tried to involve him, but I am fighting a losing battle. I feel so angry, but at the same time, I can't fight this depression.

It hurts to hear him tell me about how happy he was about his daughters, but he can't feel the same way about my child. The fact that he doesn't feel the same way makes me furious.

I can't believe what he said about only wanting money and that he doesn't care where it comes from. But I shouldn't be shocked, right? He takes everything I earn and does god knows what with it. Not that God cares, I've repeated the Lord's Prayer so many times over the last year and has he helped me?

I feel sick about this so-called 'Truck'. I can't believe I signed the paperwork, what was I thinking? Spending all this money on a vehicle we don't need is entirely unnecessary, how selfish can one man be? We have a baby on the way, and it doesn't even have anywhere to sleep.

He knows exactly how what to say to hurt me for the maximum impact. The truth is, I believe I would be better off without him. I am tired, tired of it all. He is becoming more and more irrational, and I am sick of him believing it's my fault.

He says 'Don't ruin our weekend' but I have more right to say that exact same thing to him. If our weekend gets ruined, it will not be by me. He needs some serious medical help. I believe he must be sick; no rational person acts like this. He needs to do something to change because I can see no future for us otherwise.

I can't live like this for the rest of my life. I can't do it for me, and I certainly can't do it to our child. I have lived a dog's life for almost a year, and I will not do this forever.

CHAPTER THIRTY-SEVEN

'Good' days are few and far between, but Sunday seems to be shaping into one. Sleeping half the day limits the potential for things to go wrong, though.

Out of the blue, Mal suggests we go for a walk at the Botanic Gardens. Wandering hand in hand, I can almost trick myself into believing it's just like it used to be.

"Are you hungry?" he asks me.

"A bit," I reply. It's a bit of an understatement, seeing as I always feel like I'm starving these days.

He drives to a nearby bakery, and then we take our filled rolls and apple turnovers to a play park. Swaying gently on the swings, I wonder if I should attempt to talk to him about all the things that are causing me to feel scared and angry in equal measures. But it's easy enough to set him off on a typical day; I don't want to risk flicking his switch, so instead, I decided just to enjoy the calm.

The day stretches out, and I briefly try to make a few notes to write in my journal, so that I never forget how we can still have good days. No matter how sparse they are.

It takes a long time for me to drift to sleep because I don't want to forget today, we have so few days where he is truly here.

I'm woken abruptly by excruciating pain in my lower back. Instinctively I pull up my legs to protect my pregnant belly. Mal is having another nightmare I reassure myself, he's probably not aware that he's just kicked me in the spine. I shudder to wonder what might have happened if I was laying the other way around.

Reaching across the expanse of bed, I try my usual technique of comforting him. "Shh, it's ok, it's just a dream," I whisper. Instead of calming him though he swats madly at my hands, so I back off and leave him to his terrors.

Now fully awake with an aching back, I am overly aware of the pressure building on my bladder.

As I slip silently from the blankets, I hear Mal's voice lilt, "I was stabbing that cunt dog of yours. It felt good killing her. I guess you're lucky someone was dumb enough to take that stupid mutt."

His words are like ice water, and I'm not so sure he was sleeping when he kicked me. I shut myself in the bathroom and spend the remainder of the night with my back resting against the door.

The days start to slide together with the monotony of my daily survival, but I worry daily about my impending rendezvous with Megan. We've arranged to meet at the café around the corner, and I pray like crazy that this doesn't get back to Mal.

She's already sitting in a booth when I arrive. I hang by the door and watch her for a while before she notices I'm there. Seeing her again drags all my shattered hopes and dreams to the surface and tears start to pour down my face before I've even reached her table.

"Oh Maddie, look at your bump!" she says, ignoring the tears for the time being. She pulls me into a tight embrace, and I sink thankfully into her arms, and for a while, we are content to just stand like that.

She's the first to pull back but holds me at arm's length staring intently into my eyes. "Are you ok hon? You look so tired."

"I'm fine." I've not spoken to her for weeks, my heart tells me I can trust her, but I already feel nauseous that Mal will find out she's here. My head has been so warped it's hard to ignore the warning bells screaming in my head.

"You have options, Maddie," she reassures me. "You can come live with me! He won't find you, I promise."

"Yeah, but I can't hide my whole family." Bile builds in the back of my throat; I wish I could tell her the full extent of how much of a horror story my life has become.

She's worried, very worried. But she understands that she can't push me, which is a relief because everyone else in my life thinks they can.

I don't want to leave her and go back to work, but I also don't want to risk Mal turning up and discovering us together. So, we say our goodbyes, and she promises to look in on Bessie for me when she is next in our old neighbourhood.

I return to work with a heavy heart. I check in with Adele and tell her that I have some tummy cramps and escape to the staff bathroom.

With the door locked firmly behind me, I let my grief and frustration drain out of me.

Without telling me, he was arriving early Mal appears abruptly in our office and bangs unnecessarily on the door jamb causing Adele to squeak in surprise.

He must have seen the irritation in my own surprised look because with an air of superiority, he demands, "Are you not happy to see me, Maddie?"

"I wasn't expecting you so soon," I placate him, trying to correct my earlier folly. I glance at the wall clock. I still have 45 minutes until the end of the workday. Glancing dubiously at Adele I try to decide the best course of action. Thankfully Adele steps in and saves me.

She eyeballs Mal as she says in my direction, "Why don't you knock off early Maddie darling. You look so worn down. You should be resting this close to the baby's arrival, not working."

Mal's gaze slides to me as he appraises my appearance. I know I look terrible, but I am still stung by the look of disgust on his face. I grab my things, being careful to shove my journal further under a stack of ignored paperwork, praying it would be safe and that Mal didn't spot it.

Close on my heels, he follows me out of the building, and as we approach the car, he growls, "Get in the car bitch."

What little food I have managed to eat today starts to curdle in the pit of my stomach, and I pray hard that he hasn't learned from the time I spent with Megan during my lunch break. I hasten to do what I'm told and slide myself awkwardly into the passenger seat, anxiety flooding my body.

"Do you have anything you want to get off your chest? Anything you might have been hiding from me?"

I bite my tongue, unintentionally holding my breath too. He turns the wrong way, heading away from our home and panic truly starts to set it.

"Where are we going?" I ask hesitantly.

"I'm going to take you somewhere where no one will hear you scream."

I force myself to breathe as my chest constricts. I wonder how much damage I'd do to myself and my baby if I try to jump out of a moving vehicle.

"Please let me out," I beg him, "Please, think of the baby."

"Don't you think you should have thought about your bastard baby BEFORE you went behind my back?"

"Oh, god, please let me out." I grip the seat belt praying that he realises what he's doing is mental.

"Shut the fuck up, or I'll knock you out."

I sit immobile in the passenger seat, knuckles turning white with my tight grip. I am beyond petrified he's really going to do it; he really wants to kill me.

He swerves the car across the road, shouting, "Do you think I care if you die? I don't love you. I don't give a fuck what happens to you."

His driving is becoming more erratic, surely someone will call the police? I certainly hope so.

I have no idea where we are but the sporadic residential area, we were driving through soon gives way to dense bush. I spot a Military signpost, warning trespassers to keep out, and I can't breathe. Literally, I can't breathe. The shallow breaths I manage to suck into my body aren't enough, and I start to feel faint.

He glances in my direction, disdain dripping from him. "Don't be so gullible Madeline. If I was going to kill you, do you think I'd warn you? I'd just do it." He yanks on the hand brake, spinning the car until it's facing in the opposite direction. "Why did you do it Madeline?" he exclaims.

"Do what?" I ask him in a small voice.

"Why ARE you cheating on me with your fucking husband? Did you think I wouldn't find out? I FIND EVERYTHING OUT!"

I'm confused, I don't understand what he's talking about. I haven't spoken to Justin since he found out I'd been in contact with him.

"I know he's got that slut dog of yours. I try and try Madeline; I try so hard for you and you just fuck up and fuck up. So, guess what, I'm not going to bother trying anymore."

He punches me in the face, my head snapping back from the impact. I stare at him stunned, my hand slides up to cover the sting of my cheek, and for a moment I can't decide if it hurts or not. It hurts.

"From now on I am going to make this really easy for you to understand. If you lie to me, I'm going to hit you. Nothing else seems to work with you, so you better pull your fucking head in before I knock it off completely."

He glares at me before releasing the hand brake and stomping on the gas. I hold my cold hand to my face and stare off into the distance. I have to get away from him; I just wish I knew how.

It feels like a lifetime until we are home, plenty of time to think about how I can escape him. Before I manage to heave myself from the seat, he races around to the passenger side and helps me out of the car.

He holds my face, gazing into my eyes and begs me, "Please Maddie, please just help me out and stop lying to me."

"OK, I'm sorry. I won't lie again," I promise as tears threaten to overwhelm me.

He crushes me in a hug, "I don't want to hurt you, but you won't learn."

He doesn't pay me any attention after we get inside. He just sits at the computer with his back to me. I go to the bathroom and hold a cool flannel over my bruised cheek and rub my neck. I feel like I have whiplash.

I stare at myself in the mirror and try to keep my sobs as quiet as possible, so he won't come and discipline me again. When did I become this person?

Trying to recall the sequence of events this evening has left my brain feeling scrambled. I've never been this scared in my entire life. I don't believe I will ever be happy again.

The next day he drags me to help him with the final stages of purchasing the truck. Standing in the car yard next to him, he clutches my hand tightly as if he's afraid I'll bolt.

"Just remember Maddie, this is your truck, so you need to act like it. Sign the paperwork, and we can drive it right off the yard."

Not long after that, I am trying to wedge myself into the driver's seat of my Mazda and carefully follow him home.

I study the truck as we navigate the suburbs. It's faded forest green with gold trim, fitted with something he tells me are 'running boards' along each side. I don't understand why on earth you'd need such a thing, which makes me wonder again where Mal used to work. I am not much impressed with this new burden. It looks big and intimidating, and I hate the thought of Mal charging around town in it. I worry for the safety of every other person on the road.

Seeing as I already have so much to worry about, I try to clear my mind. I can't control what he does, but I can control how I respond. After we get home and both vehicles are parked in the driveway, I leave him outside washing his new pride and joy to seek some solitude while he's distracted.

I look around at the mess that has become my home. Dishes piled in the sink, washing lying piled on the bedroom floor, bed unmade, the duvet void of cover strewn aside. Perching on the end of the bed, I try to fathom how this baby will fit in here.

CHAPTER THIRTY-EIGHT

Carla has ordered me to finish work, my blood pressure has been erratic at best, and it's obvious she's worried about me. So, I'm starting my maternity leave, and I am so depressed I can't even be bothered to write in my journal. He missed his doctor's appointment last week, but I still hold on to some hope he will make another. If he doesn't get medication or try to work on his issues, then we will never work. How can I spend the rest of my life in fear of him?

The baby will be scared too, my dog was insanely petrified of him, he just had to look at her, and she peed herself, and he just didn't care.

Lying in bed, I consider our last meeting with Ruth, our counsellor. I don't know if we accomplish anything at all going to counselling. He never listens to Ruth or me, he's full of double standards, and he will never see my side. I am exhausted both physically and emotionally, so tired I just want to give up.

I don't think he realises that Ruth focuses on him every session. I know I'm not without my faults, but they are of his making, he has made me this way. Then he spends the rest of the day ignoring me, even when I asked him if he still loved me, even a little bit. How can he not see how much he is hurting me?

I am beginning to hate him and hate myself even more. Why do I love him? Why do I find it so hard to say, 'No more', why am I not ready to say it's over? Why can't I give up on him?

Yesterday he came to work, he held my hand and led me up, and down the department store aisles and in one secluded spot he stopped me, leant down and placed a soft kiss on my forehead. For a fraction of a second, I felt loved by him again. I just want the beautiful man I fell in love with back.

Today he told me his stomach was hurting again, I'm beginning to wonder if he is getting ulcers or something. He is angry all the time, all that stress can't be good for him.

I look up as he enters the room. "Have you seen that blue bowl of mine?" he asks.

I have no idea what he's talking about, as far as I can remember we haven't ever had any blue bowls.

"Oh my god Madeleine, how are you going to take care of a baby if you can't even take care of this house?" he yells and starts pulling stuff from cupboards.

As he builds momentum, he starts to get more haphazard with where he puts the things he removes. Plates start to smash at his feet and as they begin to take flight I back away.

"Where do you think you're going?" he asks.

"Nowhere," nowhere at all. I wrap my arms around my bump, and more useless tears slide down my cheek. I am too weary of trying and hiding the deep-seated sadness that has enveloped my life.

Mal pauses in his destruction and glances in my direction. "I bet your kid is going to be as useless as your fat ass. Am I going to have to teach it to behave too?"

His words sink in, and a prickle of anger simmers to the surface. "You are not going to hit our child," I say carefully.

"Well, you should have had your kids with Justin then."

Losing it totally for the first time in months, I spit, "Shut the fuck up! Just shut up!"

I don't have time to process my mistake before Mal is up in my face, leaning over me so close I feel his breath on me.

"Do you want to repeat that?" he says in a low dangerous voice.

"Why is it different for me? You speak to me like that all the time." I have no idea where my bravery is coming from, but I don't expect him to answer me. In fact, I'm expecting him to hit me.

My courage flees me as he shakes his head. "I'm getting out of here. I've got some people I need to go see."

I am stunned that he just walks away. He grabs the truck keys and his wallet as he passes the computer table and leaves.

I can't believe he just dropped it; I can't believe I stood up to him. I can't say I feel buoyant about this small victory, but it floats a little hope. My life seems so surreal like I am trapped in some crazy movie. How did this happen to me?

Staring at the mess, he has left behind in the kitchen, I sigh as deeply as my pregnancy allows. I can feel my baby moving, I push him a little as his body moves so does the surface of my tummy. "Not long now Liam and I get to meet you." I hope all this sadness isn't damaging our precious child.

Struggling to reach the floor, I salvage what I can, placing it all in the sink, then I grab the broom and sweep it all into the corner. The floor hasn't been cleaned in months, so I also manage to capture a lot of other debris. I wonder what it might be like to be a normal expectant Mum, I am feeling such urges to create a special home for Liam, but I am trapped by Mal. I hate my life, and I hate me. What have I become? In response my baby wriggles again, pushing and making reaching the floor with the dustpan and brush next to impossible.

Focusing on the positive I make a simple meal out of bread and jam and get to enjoy it in peace. I also have my 'baby shower' tomorrow at work, which I promise myself is something better to focus on that it is my last day. I'm not sure how I am going to cope being trapped at home 24/7, but I push that thought aside. He's not here right now.

I'm 37 weeks pregnant, and this baby is going to be coming very soon. I feel like he has taken my voice, I don't know who I am anymore. He has stripped so much from me I don't know what I have left.

My heart is breaking in a thousand different ways, but he can't see my pain. Everything that has made me is pouring out. I am astounded at how selfish he can be. Little snippets stand out in my mind like, "Stop nagging me, I'll tidy up in my own time." "Just leave it the fuck alone, I told you I want to do it." "Just be grateful for what I have done and stop going on about what I haven't."

He blames me for everything, and I have no way of defending myself against him. So, all I can do is cry myself to sleep at night and pray he doesn't hear me sob. I cry myself to sleep and then try to make things better for myself by writing a different story in my head. These tears are my pain, and they are not to show him how much I am hurting. They're for me.

I was so sure that once we were together, everything would be fine, so I wasn't prepared for the man he has turned in too. I am afraid I fell in love with a man who doesn't exist, but I can't help but hope the man I fell in love with is the man he wanted to be, that maybe still wants to be.

I promised I would never give up on him, but how much longer can I live like this?

With him gone I feel brave enough to write, I haven't written in so long, I guess because he has so effectively muted me. I am just so very sad.

My pencil pauses on a scrap of printer paper, and I push my sadness into a poem.

Broken heart dragging down
cheated of a broken crown.
Bruised, abused, un-whole.
Burning pain, dismembered soul.
Something missing, lifeline gone.
No warning, no heralding song.
Devalued, demoralised, can life start anew?
A secret kept, shared by few.
Pain everlasting that none can see
Is this how life should be?

CHAPTER THIRTY-NINE

I arrive to work on my last day with a heavy heart. It feels a lot like I'm giving up the final part of my life that I have managed to keep for myself. I wish I could stay longer, but this baby is making it impossible to get any work done and going on maternity leave is kind of expected.

Mal wanted me to work right up until the baby arrived so we'd get as much paid maternity leave as possible. I told Leon that I would be returning to work, but to be honest, I don't see the point. Why leave my baby with strangers all day just for Mal to spend my money on god knows what?

I am 25 years old, and I feel like I've already written the story of my life. I don't have too long to feel sorry for myself, though, as I hit the stairs, Amy bounds towards me. She embraces me in a tight hug exclaiming, "Happy last day!"

"Thanks, I think," I tell her.

Paul saunters in our direction putting his arm around me too. "Oh, it's your very last day. We're going to miss you, are you going to come back?"

"Of course," I lie. "What else would I do?"

"Live a life of leisure?" Paul asks innocently, and both Amy and I laugh at the absurdity of it.

"You do realise I am leaving to have a baby, right?" I reply. "I'm not sure I'll get lots of leisure time."

"Dreams are free," He promises.

"We will miss you, though," Amy tells me as she gives me another hug. "See you at lunchtime!"

As they both head back to their own departments, I haul my heavy body up the staircase reminding myself this is the last morning I'll be doing this. When I first got my job after just moving home, I was just looking for any job so I could get myself back on my feet. I fell into it, and even though I could do more, I love the people I work with and the atmosphere. I feel sad to be leaving this place behind.

Sitting at my office desk, I start to assemble my personal effects so that my replacement can fill it up with their things. I don't have much here, just a photo of Megan and me both significantly younger, and slightly drunk. I stare at the picture, remembering a time when I at least had the resemblance of contentment. I doubt Mal would be happy to see this on the wall at home, so I tuck it into the back of my diary. I'll need to find a new hiding place for that too.

"Oh, hello love," Adele says as she bends down to kiss me on the top of the head and passes me a takeaway cup. "A little treat for your last day. But don't worry, there's more to come at lunch!"

"Oh, I'm looking forward to it," I assure her.

There may not be pink, and blue guess the gender cake, but my work colleagues have really pulled together for my last day. Amy has blown up several balloons and artily arranged them around the selection of mini pies, quiches and cakes resting on the table. Everyone congratulates me and wishes me well, but despite eating cake for lunch, I can't shift this heavy feeling of dread.

Before leaving for the last time, Adele gives me a tiny pair of lemon-yellow hand-knitted baby booties. "I don't knit, but when I told my neighbour a friend was expecting she produced these. You are braver and stronger than you give yourself credit for Maddie. This baby will have to be the most important thing in your life now. Please stay in touch."

She hugs me one final time before I slip out the back avoiding more messy goodbyes. Silently, with a little trouble, I manage to get myself up into the passenger seat of the Truck.

"How was your last day?" Mal asks as I try to get the seat belt to reach around my belly.

"Oh, well, my boss got cake," I tell him.

He looks in my direction, running his eye over my small box of personal belongings. "Didn't you bring me any?"

I shake my head mutely. "Sorry, it was in the staff room, everyone kind of ate it."

He sighs and shakes his head like I've done him a disservice. Biting my lip, I refuse the tears that threaten to spill over; instead, I stare out the window and silently read the street names as he drives us closer to my prison.

While on maternity leave several things are generally accepted as usual from an expectant Mother.

Firstly, people assume that the Mother will want to nest. As I look around my house, I think to myself I'd settle for a vacuum.

The second is that the Mother to be will want to wash every scrap of baby clothes in her possession. I can't do much about the first thing, but I can make a start on the second. I drag the bin liner of clothing my Aunt Jo gave me and emptied them out onto the couch. There aren't too many newborn items here, but there is enough to make me feel more secure. So, I wash them and hang them in the sun to dry and then recheck that my diary is safely wedged under the couch.

I can't risk him finding it, I've written to many things that would get me killed, but I must have some release from the emotional anguish he is putting me through.

He accused me of stealing his wire strippers, but it turned out he had flung them down on the couch. When he shoved me out of the way, he told me, "Of course they'd be under your fat arse." And when I said I wasn't fat; I was pregnant, he threatened to stab me in the eye with the soldering iron.

He's up and down so much it's hard to keep up, I mean he did glue the babies draws back together and did a minimal amount of reorganising around the computer, but it is so frustrating not being able to move anything and it's driving me crazy that I can't touch anything.

I lay awake at night for hours being so mad at him, for all the things he puts me through. I'm becoming bitter and twisted, but I'm helpless to stop it. He will yell at me for all hours and then bring me home *MacDonald's* for breakfast. I don't understand him, and I don't want to anymore. I wish he would just leave. How can I continue to live like this, I can't do this, not forever?

While he was out yesterday, I found a power of attorney form, and when I asked him about it, he acted outraged and kept yelling that if something happened to me then what would happen to him, that my parents would get all my money. I can't believe he thinks I am going to sign it, I told him I wouldn't trust anyone with that. What on earth was he thinking? That I'd just sign the rest of my rights over to him? I don't want to give him anything at all.

Thinking of all the things I still must do is stressing me out. I need to see my midwife again as there isn't long to go and I need to call Ruth to make another appointment, not that it's doing any good. He only cares about himself. I'm so unhappy and so scared, what sort of parents are we going to be?

CHAPTER FORTY

A sharp pain that extends from my cervix to the very top of my belly wakes me from another restless slumber. I think I have been experiencing Braxton Hicks all week, sharp pains where I would usually get menstrual cramps that feel a lot like the baby is trying to headbutt its way out.

My midwife assured me that everything is progressing correctly, but this doesn't mean that my mind is at ease. Baby has been super active over the last week, with lots of uncomfortable pushing, so I guess that means he, and I'm convinced he is a boy, is running out of space.

The tightening across my abdomen feels very different from the stabbing pains though so perhaps I am starting to labour. I don't see the point mentioning anything to Mal yet. Everyone has already told me that labour takes a long time and I don't want him to stay home with me all day, which I know he will if I tell him.

Instead, after I watch him drive away in the Truck, I call my Mum.

"Good morning, darling is everything OK?" she asks me.

"I think I might be in labour."

"Oh! Have your contractions started? Would you like me to come over?"

Oh crap, I think as I look around our messy lounge. "That's OK Mum. I'm going to call Carla soon. And Mal," I add as an afterthought.

"Well, let me know how it goes, I can always come if you need me." She tells me as I hang up.

Standing back, I survey the home where my child is supposed to live. Panic starts to set in, and I struggle to catch my breath. I need to get things in order, but this house is far too messy even to begin to think how I'm going to get everything done. We don't even have a cot or anything, but at least I can try. I'm beginning to wonder if a banana box is adequate sleeping quarters for a newborn baby.

I do my best to gather all the clothes from the bedroom floor and sweep them into the washing machine. With the laundry on, I turn my attention to the dishes. The only bright side with Mal breaking most of our plates is there aren't so many for me to wash.

I find myself trying to time my contractions so I can reach the basket at my feet and hang the clothes out. 'This is stupid' I tell myself but push on determined to finish what I have started. By the time I flop down on the couch and turn on the TV I'm exhausted.

I sigh inwardly and pick up the phone to call Carla and let her know how my labour is progressing. It's a good thing I found where he had stashed the landline; otherwise, I'd be screwed. I don't have any credit on my cell phone.

I must have dropped off for a while because I'm woken with a sudden jerk as Mal slams the front door. I rub my eyes sleepily while trying to order my thoughts. "Um," I say as he enters the lounge.

"What?"

"I've been having contractions."

"What?" he repeats.

"I'm in labour," I say slowly. "The baby is coming."

"No," he says slightly too loud, shaking his head at me. "I'm not ready for this yet, you are not having this baby today."

I stare at his back as he walks away from me and towards the computer. I am completely dumbfounded as I hear the computer start to spring to life. What does he mean I can't have the baby today? Is he out of his mind? Babies come on their schedule.

Shaking my own head, I try to ignore him and stay on the couch, staring blankly at the TV, I have enough to focus on just trying to breathe through contraction after contraction.

"Mal," I cry out after an unusually powerful one.

He looks at me flatly, assessing the situation. "This is your problem, deal with it. Stop acting like someone's is stabbing you."

But it does feel like someone is stabbing me, it feels like he is stabbing me in the heart. The father of my baby is supposed to be loving and attentive. He's supposed to be supporting me, rubbing my back and telling me how proud he is of me, not yelling that I am exaggerating the pain.

Time progresses slowly and finally by 10 pm, my contractions move to under 20 minutes apart. "Mal, I think it's time we call Carla again."

He ignores me, so I grab the phone and call her myself, as she answers another contraction starts.

"Oh, sweet pea," she reassures me with her strong British accent. "You still have ages to go if you're talking to me through a contraction. Why don't you have Mal run you a nice relaxing bath?"

"OK, I guess I could try a bath, it might take some of the pressure off."

"Call me if things start to speed up and we'll have you come in."

A bath does sound good, so with Mal still ignoring me I stand over the bathtub and try to figure out how I am supposed to reach the taps, let alone get in it if I managed to fill it up. Something about this situation makes me feel hysterical, and a bubble of laughter escapes me. Finally, I can run a bath without fearing Mal's reprisal, and I bloody well can't fill it up.

Anyhow, the contractions seem to be getting so much closer together, I think it's a much better idea to go sit back down. I make my way back towards the lounge, but I don't get even halfway before I'm standing in a puddle of water.

The pressure that had been building up in my belly rapidly dissipates, but the sharp tightening of my cervix reminds me that someone is very soon going to be making their entrance in my crazy life. I stare down at my feet and gaze at the pile of now drenched towels on the floor and think, *how fortunate that I didn't wash those.*

"Mal?" I call. "Mal, my waters just broke!"

"Well, you better call the midwife then?" He stares at me but doesn't make the phone call himself. *'What planet are you from?'* I think incredulously to myself as I hobble back to the phone. It's not even been five minutes since our last conversation.

"Wow, you're progressing fast! How about I meet you at the maternity hospital?"

"Yeah, um is 20 minutes, OK?"

"Perfect, don't panic Madeline, you still have lots of time," Carla tells me before hanging up.

Okay, don't panic, just Pack. I haven't packed my hospital bag. I could have kicked myself for not having done this earlier. I shove a few things into my backpack, but as I reach for my hairbrush the contractions get so close together, I can't breathe, and suddenly I'm overwhelmed with the urge to go to the bathroom.

I just about make it in time to sit down, waiting for what I expect to be my bowels evacuating before birth, but the pushing sensation is not in the right place. "Mal!" I call for him as my hand automatically goes to my vagina. Oh, my god. I can feel a foot. "MAL!" I scream in fear.

Finally, something captures his attention and he bolts down the hall and flings the bathroom door open.

"I think I can feel a foot, oh god the baby has pushed its foot out." Glancing down between my legs, his face pales. "Don't panic Maddie baby, I'm calling Carla. It's going to be OK."

CHAPTER FORTY-ONE

And like a light switch, he transforms, and for the first time in months, he is here for me.

"Carla says she's on her way." He traps the phone between his ear and his shoulder and puts his arms around my back to walk me to the bedroom. I try to keep as still as possible; I can't focus on what he is saying to Carla, I can only think of my baby. He hangs up and his next call to the emergency services.

An ambulance, oh fuck. Oh god, oh god, what is happening? I'm going to lose my baby. Panic clutched at my chest as hear Mal putting the phone on speaker.

"Get her to get on all fours, OK? It's really important that she doesn't push yet, do you understand?" He eases me into the suggested position and slides the large glass door open in the bedroom.

"What are you doing?" I shriek at him.

"I need to hear when the ambulance gets here," he says gently.

I can't speak much more, I need to focus, but that cold air wafting is surely going to make my baby breath, and he won't be able to do so, and he will die.

That's it I decide; this baby isn't going to come out until I am in a hospital. Having Mal change from a manic crazy person into the gentle, loving man I first thought he was is helping to keep me calm enough to do what I need too.

He slides his hand across my back, rubbing it in a way I'd have loved him to do an hour ago, but I can barely manage a grunt to shift him away. The slightest touch to my skin is too much for me to bear. It takes all my concentration to focus on keeping this child alive, I don't have anything left over for Mal, or the Ambulance or anything.

A dark thought unfurls in my mind, about what life would be like if this baby dies. In fact, I am pretty sure we are both going to die. Apparently, it's not unusual to have such thoughts during childbirth, but in my case, every single horror story I have ever heard about labour and breech births are firing through my already stressed and broken mind.

I am convinced that this is happening as a direct result of my life with Mal, that all the pain and misery that I am living through has caused this to happen. I think that the tears I have shed and all the bruises he has given me has already affected this child, that he's going to enter this world already scarred by life.

It feels like an eternity, but eventually, we hear the Ambulance arrive, with Carla's car not far behind. The lights from the Ambulance bounce around our bedroom and Mal flies out to the balcony to wave them up.

"Hi Maddie," says Carla. "You're doing so well. I just need to check to see how things are going, OK?"

I don't answer, I can't. She does an internal check and clucks her tongue before telling the ambulance staff and Mal that I am fully dilated. I don't hear what they say, I can't focus on what they decide, but since I am so determined to get to the hospital Carla pushes my baby's foot back up into my cervix and between them, they help me to my feet.

The pain is immense as I walk half-naked down the internal house stairs. It's a battle of epic proportion, as I wage war between the urge to push and the panic to keep my baby inside me. I can't believe that no one realised my baby was the wrong way around; he was supposed to be head down and engaged.

We arrive at the hospital at 11.45 pm, my vision shifting from one mundane item to the next. I am pushed into a room not far from the ambulance bay, and my eyes fixate on the tapestry behind the head of the Doctor.

I don't see his dark hair or tanned skin or notice he is talking to me. I am sure what he is saying is important, but it's hard to listen when all your focus is centred inwards. I catch only part of what he's saying, "Usually if a baby is footling breech we would deliver by caesarean section, but in your case, that would distress the baby further."

I have no idea why he is telling me this, this baby is coming now, and there is no time for talk.

But as I am laid back on the bed, and my feet placed in stirrups, the doctor subjects me to the most intense pain I have ever felt. Apparently, baby's hands are above its head, and they need to be pulled down before

I can attempt to deliver.

The doctor takes both my hands in his, and it is the most comforting feeling that I have felt in a long time, I stare into his warm brown eyes, and somehow, I feel reassured. "You're doing great," he tells me. "But you're the only one who can do this. You have to get this baby out."

I glance at the clock; I can do it. So, without even a contraction to aid me, I push harder than I ever thought possible and my beautiful baby is born less than five minutes later.

The overwhelming relief that I managed to birth my baby cancels out the significance of the absence of an infant screaming. I don't even look over to where a group of doctors are frantically trying to save my baby's life. I don't understand how drastic things are for him, that my baby is sick.

But Mal does, he stands there next to the bed staring at the table where the doctors are crowded.

"Is it a girl or a boy?" I ask him.

When he doesn't reply, I asked again a little louder, it takes five more attempts until I gain his attention.

"Girl or boy?" I ask one last time.

"Boy," he finally replies.

A boy, I was right. "His name is Liam, ok?" Mal is in such shock that he just nods his head as the doctors place our tiny son in my arms.

It's true what they say, that you don't ever forget the first time you lay eyes on your child. They give him back to me, wrapped in a soft blue blanket. He is so unbelievably perfect, but his lips are tinged blue, and that fills me with a different kind of panic. "Is he ok?" I ask. "What's wrong with him?"

"You can have a few more minutes with him, and then we'll take him up to the NICU. He's going to be fine," Carla reassures me.

I stare at his tiny face until they take him from me. "Go with him, you are not to leave him," I demand of Mal, and entirely out of character he does what he's told.

I hate this feeling of being without my baby, it's like a limb has been severed from me. Carla helps me climb out of bed and shower, so by the time Mal returns, I am feeling slightly more human.

"Is he ok?" I ask immediately, but Mal just stares at me. "Is he ok?" I ask again, starting to fear the worst, now my son is here I can't imagine the world without him in it.

He starts to cry. Not the silent tears I hide from him but big body racking sobs.

Oh god, I think to myself. Something has happened to Liam. I start to pull myself out from under the sheets and head towards the door. I must find my baby, but he grabs me and pulls me back. I cringe, expecting him to be rough with me but he pulls me to him and holds me.

Between sobs, he manages to tell me our son is fine and instead of the harsh, angry man I've been living with for the past year he drops to his knees. He wraps his arms around my back and lays his head against my now deflated stomach.

"I love you, Maddie, will you marry me?" he asks in a quiet voice. "Let's be a real family, you, me and bubba."

I am stunned to silence. How can I trust this? He's offered me no apology for his for the way he treats me, but he is crying and clinging to me like I'm his life preserver. Maybe this birth was what he needed to shake him into treating me better.

He's changed back, I promise myself. Somehow our child has brought back the man I loved.

"Maddie," he begs me, looking deeply into my eyes.

His cheeks are stained with unaccustomed tears I'm not used to. I'm not sure I understand this role reversal, and I can't stand him kneeling in front of me a moment longer. "Yes, of course, I will. We are a family," I reassure him. "Can you take me to Liam now, please? I need to see him."

It's a short walk to the Neo-natal unit, but the nurse in the delivery suite insists I use a wheelchair. I am grateful she did as fatigue starts to saturate my body.

We are admitted onto the ward and Mal pushes me past rows of tiny babies encased in incubators. I glance around nervously, feeling overwhelmed. We are led to an area with open cribs, and Mal walks up to the one in the middle. I stare at the tiny infant within it, but I can't understand how this child could be mine. Why is he connected to so many wires and tubes, how could this be our baby? How could he be so sick?

"Are you sure this is our baby?" I ask Mal, feeling like the world's worse Mother for not immediately recognising my son.

"This is him, Madeline."

Mal slides his hand under my arm and helps me out of the wheelchair, and I stand transfixed, staring at him afraid to even touch him until a nurse comes over and asks if we'd like to change his nappy.

"We can do that?" I ask in amazement. It feels a bit like the wires make him untouchable.

"Of course, let me help you." She smiles and pats my arm.

He's so beautiful and tiny, and I am scared I am going to hurt him somehow. Changing his nappy is terrifying, and I am glad I have Mal there for support because he seems a lot less fazed by this new experience.

"You know, I really should call Mum and let her know they are Grandparents."

"Do you think it might be a bit early to call?" Mal asks.

It's unlike him to be so considerate of their feelings, so this must be a good thing. "I can call them; they will want to know."

Not long after that, the Nurse suggests I go back to the ward to rest. I call my parents as Mal pushes me in the direction we have been given.

My mother answers the phone, her voice full of sleep, "is that you Maddie? Has my grandbaby been born?"

"Yes, Mum, it's a boy. We've named him Liam."

"Liam, I like that Maddie. What does he look like?"

"Hmm kind of like Mal, only more squished," I tell her.

Mum laughs, "Yes, they do tend to come out that way."

"What's going on?" I hear Dad say in the background. He sounds grumpy.

"You're a Grandpa at long last! That's news to wake up for!" Mum tells him. "We'll all come and visit tomorrow, OK, Darling?"

"Sure, I'd love to see you. But umm, I'm at the main hospital, not the maternity one."

"Why? What happened?"

"What's wrong?" Dad says in the background.

"Shh, will you be quiet, I can't hear her," she snaps at him.

"It's all OK Mum, just a change of plans. I'll tell you all about it tomorrow."

I lean back against the wheelchair after hanging up and close my eyes. I'm exhausted, but with my heart left at the NICU, I am not sure I'm going to be getting much sleep tonight.

CHAPTER FORTY-TWO

Reluctantly I let Mal lead me away from my baby and towards the wards where I will be staying. We stand awkwardly at the entrance, unsure what to say to each other.

"Are you going to be ok?" he asks in the short space before the nurse answers the buzzer to let us in.

"I'll be fine," I lie because I'm wrecked. I don't want to be standing here; I want to be with my baby.

"I can ask to stay a while longer if you want?"

I am touched by his consideration and lean into him, he wraps his arms around my back to pulls me closer, placing a kiss on the top of my head. "He's going to be OK. He's a strong little fighter, just like his Mummy Bear. I'll see you tomorrow."

He turns to leave, and I follow the Nurse. She offers to carry my bag for me, so I let her; I'm too tired to protest. She walks me past rows of open doors where the sound of newborns makes my heart ache.

She gestures to the room I will be sharing with three other women whose curtains are all closed. The sleepy noises of the babies are much more acute now I'm inside, and the absence of my own baby steals my breath away.

I climb into the cold bed and pull the thin blanket up to my chin, tucking myself into a ball. This isn't right; I should be spending my first night as a Mother with my baby in my arms. I haven't even tried to breastfeed him yet. I ache to touch him, to hold him to my breast. As exhausted as I am, I know I won't be sleeping tonight. Instead, I stare through the open curtain at the white-faced wall clock until it tells me it is 5, then 6 and then 7 o'clock. I finally decide I can wait no longer. I really have to see my baby, so I hit the call buzzer attached to the metal-framed bed. Anxiety courses through me because I don't really know what the procedure is here.

A different nurse from the night before comes to my bedside, asking how she can help.

"Can I see my baby now please?" I ask her.

"Breakfast will be here soon," she assures me as if the food will solve my problem.

"I don't need breakfast; I NEED my baby." I start to cry, big irrational sobs. A few curtains are jerked open as my roommates check to see what's going on.

"You can visit your baby anytime you want, I just don't want you to miss breakfast. Do you know the way?"

"I don't know, I don't know anything, I just want to see my baby."

She rubs my arm, "It's OK, my lovely, let me show you how to get there."

I should never have left Liam and gone to the ward. The lack of sleep and anxiety of being separated from him has finally taken a toll on my body. By the time I make it to the NICU, I can barely move.

The nurse who lets me in immediately takes me under her wing. She settles me in the lazy boy next to his crib and gently lifts my baby into my arms.

I take note of how she must reposition the wires he is attached too.

"Would you like to try breastfeeding him?" she asks me.

"Can I?" I respond, unsure. I have no idea what I am doing.

"Of course, let me get a pillow."

The nurse is so helpful and patiently shows me how to get into position, but my breasts seem much larger than his head, and I'm not sure how we are going to figure this out. Rising panic starts to well up inside me as I try a few times to get him to latch onto my nipple, but with such a little mouth, it seems like an impossible task.

"Try not to worry Madeline breastfeeding is a learned skill. We can top him up with some formula through the feed tube if we need to."

I try to halt the panic that is threatening to overcome me, I know we can't afford to bottle to feed so I need to get this breastfeeding thing figured out as soon as possible.

But despite my fears about the future, sitting here with Liam in my arms is a soothing balm to my crippled soul.

For the next six days I have 'my' Mal back, the one I fell so completely in love with. The change in him is amazing, I feel like when the clouds break on a dark stormy day, and the sun pours through. He has been attentive and loving, and everything I imagined the father of my children should be.

He even brought me flowers, something he's never done before. But no matter how happy this is making me, I still can't stop crying. I've spent hours just sobbing with Liam pulled close to me. I think the midwives have put it down to baby blues, but I know better. I am just so grateful to my child for being the life that brought him back to us. Our tiny baby is his saviour.

Liam and I are transferred to the Maternity hospital after he is discharged from the NICU and then finally the rest of my family come to visit, we even get a visit from Phil and Elaine. The entire time Mal dotes on us and acts like the sun rises and sets with Liam and me.

My parents proudly present us with a Mountain Buggy complete with a bassinette. The relief I feel at our baby having somewhere to sleep when we get home is palpable. Aunt Jo and Uncle Geoff give us a nappy bag, a REAL one, and finally, I feel a little more confident we can do this parenting thing.

A week passes before I am allowed to go home, and I am full of mixed emotions about leaving the safety of the Midwives. Their care and attention, and of course the food they cook here is the opposite of what I can expect at home.

This place has cocooned us in false hopes for the future because like all things in life, they must come to an end. For my son and me, this happened brutally and without warning. One minute he is full of sweet loving sentiment and then the next hateful resentment.

Mal doesn't waste time or mince words after we get home, he immediately lets me know things aren't so changed after all. What do you do when your heart is so full of hurt you feel like it may break into a billion pieces? I was so worried about being a solo parent. I totally missed the fact that I am one already.

I try so hard to get him involved with Liam, but he barely holds him before he gets angry and yells at me to take him back, so I just give up trying. I am alone in this, and there is a big part of me that just wants him to go. I really do want him gone.

CHAPTER FORTY-THREE

With Mal directing my every move, all days' blend into one. Either he yells at me for hours on end or ignores me entirely. I'm still having trouble recovering from the fright I got the day he held Liam in his arms while shouting and bellowing at me. He ignored our infant's thin wails, and I was scared to death that he was going to hurt him.

Liam is so tiny and entirely dependent on me; I know I need to get us away, but I'm at a loss to understand how to do this. He makes sure to tell me daily how he could easily kill me and take my baby away.

Six weeks after the birth of our son Carla comes for our last home visit. Thankfully Mal is at work because I can't stop crying over the thought of losing her.

"If you don't start to feel less teary, you might want to consider visiting your doctor for some medication?" she suggests. "I am not going to forget you and this little troublemaker, gosh you both gave me such a scare!"

"I'm going to miss you, Carla," I tell her, and I really mean it.

I take Carla's advice, and I visit my doctor. Mal begrudgingly gives me cash to pay for my appointment.

"Daylight robbery!" he complains.

"I have to go," I tell him. "You keep saying yourself I have to sort out all my problems."

"It's about fucking time someone started to realise what I have to put up with."

Of course, he thinks it's my fault, I can't do anything right in his eyes. Half the time, I believe that myself.

The Doctor doesn't seem worried about prescribing me the same medication I have taken before for depression. She tells me it's normal to feel tearful after having a baby. I say nothing about my problems at home, and just like that, we have picked up my script, and I'm back at home staring at a familiar purple and green pill.

I stare at it for so long, my eyes blur, and I see double. The doctor has assured me that it will be safe for Liam, but there is a risk it might make my milk taste funny. I don't know if I want to risk interfering with my milk, the last thing I need is to have to convince Mal to buy formula. But the pill feels like something constructive I can do about my situation. I pop it in my mouth and chase it with water before I can second guess myself.

The medication takes the edge of my depression but doesn't do much for the high levels of anxiety I am living with. An antidepressant isn't exactly helpful for a person like me living with an oppressive force of nature that has lifted you up and swept you away in his tide of anger and abuse. However, they have given me a greater sense of being able to deal with the things that are within my control.

After receiving the final notice from Birth, Deaths and Marriages demanding that we register Liam's birth or face legal action, I know I must get Mal to sign it. Up to now, he has ignored my repeated questions about what I am supposed to do.

"We have to register him Mal otherwise we are going to end up in court." I really don't need all this extra stress in my life.

"I'm not legally, Malcolm! What do you expect me to do? There is *no way* I am putting Dominic on it; I changed my name because I didn't want my past following me for the rest of my life."

Exasperated I demand, "What could you have done that's so bad you can't sign your baby's birth certificate?"

He eyeballs me for a while, perhaps deciding if he can trust me with the truth. "I got in with a certain crowd, and we did some things that I ended up in prison for. I took the fall for these people, and they fucked me over."

"What did you do?" I ask him, amazed that he is answering my questions and not throwing a massive tantrum. Somehow, I am not surprised he has spent time in prison, but I am more determined than ever to find out what the hell he did.

"If you look hard enough online, you'll find it, why do you think I changed my name? It's not something I want following me," he punches the wall next to him. I cringe, keeping my mouth shut. "Either way, I'm not signing that paperwork, it's just another fucking way of the government tracking me."

I know I have no choice but to register it without Mal's details recorded. I feel wretched for my son, though, what might he think when he is older and sees 'not recorded' for his Fathers details? Will he blame me?

I send the paperwork off absent of Mal's details and every intention for no one to ever see that bit of paper.

"What we need is a fresh start," Mal tells me while gazing at our baby.

I look around the house he has wrecked. A fresh start sounds good, but I'm reluctant to move into another place just so he can destroy that too. The tenancy on this place is in my name, I wasn't sure why he was so insistent, he is not on it when we first moved in together. I guess the fact that Malcolm McPherson doesn't exist had a significant role to play in that. There are so many holes in the walls and doors from his fists, and stains on the carpet caused by his temper that I just don't know what I'm going to do.

"We'll probably have to fix the doors or something first," I say tentatively.

He gives me the 'how stupid can you be' look. "Give it a rest Madeline. I can just buy new ones off *Trademe*."

"Oh," I reply doubtfully, except the baby draws I've never seen him repair anything.

He spends days trawling the internet before settling on a newer house about 20 minutes from where we are currently. It's a lot easier finding a rental without Bessie, but he convinces me not to mention the cats on the application as he thinks we won't get it if we do.

I'm so worried he is just going to do the same thing to the new house, but right now I am helpless to stop it, just like every other aspect of my life I am swept along in his tide of self-riotous anger.

We pack up and move with no help from anyone. Dad and my brother offer but Mal declines and tells them he's getting a few boys from work to come. That was a bald-faced lie though because 15 weeks post-birth I am helping him haul couches, bed, and fridge down a flight stair and into a rented trailer.

Liam howls his displeasure at being so neglected; he's not used to his Mummy being anything but attentive. I do my best, but he spends most of the two days we are moving in his car seat.

"Can't you shut him up?" Mal asks several times throughout the move. I don't know what else he expects me to do. My back is sore, I am tired, and way past exhausted but I have no choice, so I keep moving.

I am shifting what feels like a never-ending pile of boxes from the lounge when I happen to glance down at the floor. A flash of pink and purple catches my eye. I look over my shoulder to make sure Mal is nowhere in sight as I bend down to investigate. Jammed under the TV cabinet is a $50 note. I speedily swoop up and stuff it in my pocket, feeling guilty even as I do so. I know that this will land me in deep shit if Mal catches me with it, but it's worth the risk for this small measure of independence.

All our stuff gets as far as the garage in the new place, and that's where it is apparently going to stay. The couches are stacked on top of each other in the lounge, meaning I have nowhere to sit to nurse the baby, he also doesn't bother putting the bed together, so we sleep on the mattress on the ground.

If I was under any delusion that things were going to get better at the new house, then I was very much mistaken.

"I can't believe how disgusting this house is, can you believe how dirty the shower is? You are going to have to call rental agent and tell them to send someone out to bloody well clean it." Mal moves around the house, making notes of all the fixtures that he believes aren't up to his satisfaction.

He hands the paper to me. "Call them and make sure they come and fix this, or I won't be paying them any bloody rent next week. This is totally unacceptable."

I look around the lounge, it seems clean and bright to me, and I'm not sure what he is so pedantic about. I can't help thinking of our other rental that is standing empty except for my cats, and the rubbish he deemed not worth taking. I'm sure that it won't take long for this house to be full of his fist holes too.

I feel ashamed to call the rental agent, but I do it, the alternative is to deal with Mal's anger with me for not doing what he wanted. I can expect a cleaner to come the following day. I wonder if they are second-guessing their decision to have us as tenants.

They come and clean the shower, but in my embarrassment, I forget to ask them to also clean on the top of the kitchen cupboards. Instead of having to explain to Mal why they hadn't done it or call them again, I haul myself up onto the kitchen benches and furiously wipe the accumulated dirt and grime away. I use spray and wipe with kitchen roll, and once I'm done, I dart out to the neighbour's bin to hide any evidence that I cleaned it myself.

Mal refuses to unpack anything apart from the basics, so we still have most of our kitchen stuff in boxes. He insists he will sort everything out in his own time so I should just leave it all to him, but after a week I finally get fed up with trotting to the garage to get milk and use what energy I can muster to push the fridge up the hallway to the kitchen. He hits the roof when he gets home, how dare I move something without his permission?

It's not enough that he has forced me to move everything by ourselves, without help while dealing with a four-month-old baby, he is also refusing to let me make any part of this new house a home for my child and me. Mal is fighting me every step of the way and life hasn't improved as I hoped.

"For God's sake Maddie, why can't you just let me sort this out at my own pace?" he tells me, as he pulls the couches apart and dumps one near the wall.

"I just need a place to feed Liam," I tell him defensively, which pulls him up short because it's something he can't possibly argue with. In response, Liam starts to squawk his hunger.

I quickly rearrange the couch cushions before lifting Liam from his bassinette. I latch him to my breast before his cries start to irritate his father.

Sundays always seem to drag on, mostly I suppose because Mal is home all day. It feels a lot like he is either ignoring me or watching me every move.

There is a new block of terrace housing being constructed over the street from us. Glancing out of the window, I survey the progress they have made in the short time we've been here.

"What are you looking at?" Mall inquires when he sees me watching out the window.

"I'm just looking at the new houses."

"You better not be eyeballing those cunts building over there," he warns me.

"It's Sunday," I point out. No one is working today.

"Stop being a bitch, I know what the fucking day is."

By the time Monday rolls around, I desperately need a break, even if that only means I can get out of the house for a few hours while Mal is at work. The moment I am sure he's gone I call one of the only people

I have left to call without Mal accusing me of being a slut, my Mum.

I look briefly around the lounge at the boxes wondering what Mum will make of this, but it's vastly better than having her come to the old house which was peppered with holes from his fist.

"Hey, Mum," I say after she answers the phone.

"Hello darling, it's lovely to hear from you. How are you settling into the new place?" I hear an unspoken question in her voice, different from the words she's just said.

"Yeah, it's OK. Unpacking feels like it's taking forever."

"Oh, I remember those days well darling, everything takes longer with a newborn in the house."

"What are you up to today?"

"I'm just heading into town for a haircut."

"Can I come?" I ask impulsively, thinking of the money I have hidden away. I can't remember the last time I had a haircut.

"Oh, I'd love for you and Liam to come, maybe we can get lunch too?"

For the first time in ages, I am quick to agree. "Sure Mum. I'd love that."

We arrange for her to come to pick us up in an hour. I send Mal a quick text telling him that Mum is coming to get me and that I am having lunch with her. He's not happy about it, but he is stuck at work, so it is very little he can do.

I feel a balance of trepidation and joy when I see her pull into our new driveway, but all the fear I have about how Mal will react dissipates as I see her sweep Liam into a hug. She adores him.

"Oh, you are just so squishable!" she exclaims. Liam stares up at her and smiles his brand-new gummy happiness. My heart swells to see him so content; I don't want anything to wipe that smile away. He deserves a happy life.

"Rosemary was going to meet us for lunch later, but I think she's gotten busy at work," Mum tells me as she coos over Liam.

"Oh, that's a shame, Mum. I've not seen her in ages."

"Well, you know she's been busy with that boy of hers! She may as well move in with the amount of time she spends there now."

I remain silent for a while, thinking about how she's probably only staying there so she can feed my cats.

"I'm guessing that Liam has been keeping you both busy," she says without making eye contact.

I mumble an agreement.

"If you need help getting the new place set up just let me know," she offers.

My heart quickens as I scramble to change the subject, "Where have you got your appointment? Do you think I could get a trim?"

Mum appraises my hair which is washed for a change. "It has gotten quite long, hasn't it? Penelope might have time, let's go early and see."

I take Liam from Mum and fasten him, and his car seat into the back of her car then hop into the passenger seat as Mum starts the engine. As she merges onto the road, my phone starts to ring silently in my bag. After glancing at it and seeing it's Mal, I hit ignore.

"Do you know," Mum says. "I think Jack might be thinking about moving in with Isobel."

"Isn't he a bit young?" I ask her.

"Well, there's no talking sense into any of you kids, is there," she says mildly.

There is no chance to ask her what she means because I see a blur of green hurtling towards us, blatantly ignoring a stop sign.

"WATCH OUT!" I shriek at Mum as a four-wheel-drive ploughs into the side of Mum's car, shunting us across the road and up onto the kerb.

The airbags deploy exploding in my face as the crunch of metal colliding fills my ears, and Liam starts to cry pitifully in the back. As I begin to panic, my first thought is for my son. In my haste to get to him, I can't make the seat belt release, so it takes me several failed attempts to get to Liam. I check him all over, and then check again before I realise that my Mother is stuck in the driver's seat, her door firmly jammed shut. I place Liam and his car seat in a safe spot and do my best to pull the door open.

I yank on the door, but it won't budge. "Mum, are you ok?" I ask, but she doesn't answer me.

I start to really worry about her as a passer-by helps me pull harder on the door. It finally flings open, and I pull her from the wreck, but in her shock, she backs out onto the road. "Mum, get off the road!" I yell at her, grabbing her arm to lead her to where I have left Liam.

"My car!" she mutters.

"It's ok, Mum," I tell her as a crowd of people start to form.

The lady from the four-wheel-drive descends upon us, yelling, "What were you thinking? You stupid cow!"

"You ran the stop sign!" I scream back

She shakes her head, pointing at Mum, "This was her fault!"

The man who helped me open the car door is still standing next to me and shakes his head, "I saw what happened lady. You missed that stop sign, this is your fault."

She clearly doesn't believe us as she pulls out her phone. The small crowd of spectators seem to have had the same idea, I look up, and everyone is on their phones.

"Look," points another onlooker to the signpost. "Stop sign."

Her face pales as she glances up at the sign, after which she climbs back into her car and pulls the door shut.

"I have to call Sam," Mum stutters while rummaging in her purse.

I pull it from her trembling fingers, but I'm not much better than she is. Shaking I try over and over to dial my Dad's number, something I've known by heart for years. By the time we manage to get through to him, the police have arrived.

Luckily for us, there is no shortage of witnesses to the accident, and it's obvious we aren't at fault. Mum's car doesn't look pretty though, and we aren't going to be getting our hair cut anytime soon. On top of that, I know I'm not going to be able to hide this from Mal. He's going to want to know in minute detail how this happened, and I'm sure he's going to find a way to turn this around to be my fault.

I clutch hard to my cell phone as I hear it ring on the other end.

"What's happened?" is his first response, like somehow instinctively he knew something bad had happened to us.

"Please don't panic, we're fine. But this woman ran a stop sign and crashed into Mums' car." I get it out as fast as possible, pulling my jacket closer as a gust of wind hits me.

"What the fuck? What happened?"

Patiently I explain again in a bit more detail. He pauses for a short time, and I hear him speak to one of his co-workers. "I'm on my way," he tells me. I don't know whether to feel relieved or panicked.

Dad and Mal arrive within 15 minutes of each other, and while Mal checks us over to reassure himself, we are all OK Dad calls a tow truck and the insurance company. The Police take some time collecting witness statements and then reassure Mum that she wasn't to blame.

"There's no way you'd have been able to stop in time, Mum," I try to comfort her. "I only had time to shout watch out before she hit us."

After hugging Mum and Dad goodbye, it's a quiet trip home. And after I am safely on the couch feeding Liam Mal rings his boss. I overhear him talking. "Yeah, it's was a bad accident, the car is totalled."

There is a pause while he listens to his boss.

"Yeah, I know. I don't know how much longer we will be in the hospital; Maddie has to get some x-rays done."

X-ray in the hospital? I have no idea what he is talking about.

"Yeah, OK, will do, I'll let you know how it goes, but I'll probably have to take few days off."

He hangs up the phone and looks at me for a long time. I hold my breath waiting for the lecture I know is coming. But instead, he sighs deeply and calls a different number taking the phone into the garage so I can't hear him.

CHAPTER FORTY-FOUR

Two days later, Mal still hasn't gone back to work. My phone buzzes again from where I have it wedged between the couch cushions and my leg.

Glancing in Mal's direction to make sure his back is turned, I gently shift Liam and slide it out.

It's Rosie, 'When r u coming 2 get ur cats? I can't keep coming out here 2 feed them.'

He still hasn't let me get them, despite repeatedly asking him. I need to fix this before my parents find out. I've told Mal over and over that we can't leave them there on their own, but it's like he can't hear me.

He just says, "I'll go get them when I'm ready." Just like that, case closed, and he will not tolerate any more conversation about it.

Anger simmers to the surface at all the injustice of my life, and I reply to Rosie before stopping to consider my words, 'AUGH Mal is being so difficult. He won't let me get them.'

'That man makes me SO mad!' her texts back immediately.

'Honestly, I just want to kick him in the balls.' I feel halfway guilty for texting this, but it also feels a bit good too.

'Yeah, with steel-capped boots ;-)'

I glance in Mal's direction before responding, 'Heh steel-capped boots WITH spikes!'

'Don't leave it 2 much longer, bcoz Dad will spit tacks if he knows I'm still feeding them.'

'I won't. Love you, xxx.'

'Love you too sis x.'

I stuff my phone back in my hidey-hole and gaze down at my sleeping baby. He looks so peaceful, totally unaware of how crazy his Mother's life is. He's so innocent. On our way to bed, I try to convince myself that tomorrow will be the day I stand up to Mal and tell him my cats have to come home. But for now, I follow him meekly to bed.

The next day is the third day Mal decides he would rather stay home, and watch Liam and I like a Hawk. It feels a lot like he doesn't trust me to be home alone anymore. Perhaps in case I go out and get into any more car accidents. It's way past 10 am, and we are still in bed, I know better than to try and get up before him. Instead, I spend the morning feeding Liam when he needs it and reading a paperback that my sister gave me a few months ago. I watch as he gets up and goes into the lounge, figuring it's OK to get up now I shift Liam to the mattress and sit up.

Before I make it out of bed, he returns, blocking the light from the doorway. "Where's your phone?" he growls.

My heart clenches and bile builds at the back of my throat. "In the lounge," I stammer, paralysed by fear. The texts I exchanged with Rosie flashing before my eyes. I've been so fastidious about deleting any and all texts that weren't from him. I can't believe I forgot to delete the ones from my sister! How stupid am I?

"What are you hiding from me now, slut," he demands menacingly.

I choke out a reply, "Nothing, I'm hiding nothing."

It's futile to lie to him as I'm sure he's already read them, but I am unable to tell him the truth.

He takes a step towards me throwing my phone at my head it collides with my left eye. As he stalks closer, I slide Liam further away.

"What is on the fucking phone cunt, tell me. You know I am going to find out, you can't hide anything from me." He punctuates each word with a jab of his forefinger, shifting forward until he is standing directly over me.

I glance nervously towards Liam, who is still sleeping soundly besides, "Nothing." The word tastes like ash in my mouth.

He lunges to snatch the phone back, his nails biting into my flesh. I try in vain to hold on to it, but he is stronger than me and easily twists it from my hands. He holds the offending phone out eyes wide in rage, nostrils flaring he snorts like an enraged bull. "Tell me what's on here, or I'll break it in two. Don't test me, Madeleine," he says with all the certainty in the world that I will obey.

Which I do, I fold just as he has trained me to do. "Just, just texts to my sister," I repent hoping he will forgive me. "I was just, I was angry. A little bit, about wanting to get my cats, and frustrated that we hadn't. I was just venting. I didn't mean it; I promise."

"You fucking slanderous hoe. How DARE you. Do you want to kick me in the balls? I dare you, just go ahead and try and I'll fucking kill you, and your fucking cunt sister."

His fist comes out of nowhere, and as it connects with my head, my world is plunged underwater. I don't have time to register how much the first blow hurts before the second one comes flying. His knuckles make a sickening crunch as they collide with my forehead. For a fraction of a second, I wonder if he's broken his fingers or my skull.

Again and again, punches reign down upon me, so many I lose count. I'm panicking, but with my baby so close I know I need to keep my wits about me and draw Mal away before Liam gets hurt. I slide off the mattress raising my arms trying to protect myself from any more blows to the head, but he pulls my arms down as I struggle against him and punches me again, this time, my left eye. I feel blood slide down the side of my face as another blow lands on my nose with an audible crack.

"I'm going to fucking kill you, you fucking cunt," he shouts as he backs away from me.

I lay half on the floor, half on the bed. Blood from my head wounds merge on my face and soak the pillow slip. I stare at Liam as he opens his bright blue eyes and starts to wail, long pitiful cries that tear at my soul. I want to move towards him, but I can't decide if I can move my body. I'm pretty sure I didn't lose consciousness and the numbness I felt while he was beating me is slowly being replaced with an intense throbbing matching of the cadence of my heart beating.

"Do you think I have done anything to you that hasn't already been done to me?" he yells and kicks me.

I instinctively pull myself into the foetal position as he kicks me again in the back. I can't die here; I must save my baby.

"You should be fucking glad I am holding back Madeleine. You should be glad that I am not wearing rings. If I were, you'd never see again, never see your precious baby."

He shifts his body towards Liam, spurring me to react. I move my battered body between him and our son. "Are you enjoying this?" I say, desperate to keep his attention on me.

"I want to get a knife and deal to your family. I want to rip their guts out and force you to watch." He grabs my hair and forces me to look at him. "Open your fucking eyes and look at me."

Then it starts again as he grabs my body and lines me up for another impact. He punches my milk swollen breasts, "please," I breathe out. "Please I need to feed Liam, please don't hit me there."

Instead, he hits my jaw. '*Oh god, he's going to kill me,*' I think to myself. There is so much blood everywhere. He's going to kill me, with my poor defenceless baby right next to me. What type of legacy are we giving this child?

Groaning I try to roll off the mattress again, I can't let him kill me and let Liam grow up without a mother.

Mal moves away from me again, but I think it's worse when he stops because it gives the pain a chance to set in because all the time he is hitting me I just feel immense pressure rather than registered pain. I always thought the full magnitude of a beating like this would be more painful, is that a weird thing to consider when someone is trying to kill you?

"You stay there, bitch," he warns me. "If you move, I'll kill you."

I believe him.

Blood is still pouring from my nose and mouth; my eyes are both swollen to slits, and my jaw feels weird. Every inch of my body is hurting, and the pain is making clear thinking impossible. It hurts now. Vaguely in the background, I hear Liam's angry cries soften to whimpers.

Fear vibrates my body, peaking every time he paces past me. I am beyond comprehending what he might do next, so I swallow any comment I might have made to placate him in the past.

Abruptly he stops to look at me before ducking into the en suite. I hear the faucet running, and then as he steps out, he tosses a damp flannel towards me. "Clean yourself up," he says indifferently.

I hold the cloth to my swollen face where tears and blood have started to dry. I look in his direction, my vision still blurred and as he leaves the room he flings over his shoulder, "This is nothing compared to the beatings I took as a kid, you should stop snivelling it could have been much worse."

I sink down on the mattress, awkwardly turning my body so I can see my baby. Liam has cried himself back to sleep. How can I let this be his future? I can't, I can't let him ever know this happened.

He comes back carrying a bag of frozen vegetables. He carefully wraps them in a tea towel before squatting next to me and applying them to my head. "Here, this should help."

I wince at the extra pain the pressure causes. My throat is dry and scratchy, but I manage to force out, "Thanks."

I'm so tired I can barely keep my eyes that are already mostly swollen shut, open. I vaguely remember something about not sleeping with a concussion, though, and since I am confident I that I have one I desperately fight the fatigue.

By mid-afternoon, I am still in bed, curled around my baby with a half-melted bag of frozen peas pressed against my face. I sneak glances at Mal who is lying next to us. He is staring directly at me, but I can't tell if he is feeling ashamed or admiring his handiwork.

Just when I think things couldn't get any worse, we hear a car pulling into our drive, followed by a knock on the front door.

CHAPTER FORTY-FIVE

My chest feels like a pinball machine as I hear my sister call my name.

"Maddie, are you in there?"

"What's she doing here?" Mal whispers.

"I don't know," I whisper back. "It's probably her day off."

"If she gets in here, she's dead."

I attempt to answer but Mal motions at me to keep my mouth shut as he creeps towards to door.

My cell phone that had remained inert all morning starts to ring. My fingers clumsily scramble to silence it. Finally, she gives up banging on the front door and as I hear her car drive away the mixture of fear and relief makes me sob.

"You better call your cunt family and tell them we want to spend the weekend alone. Do you understand?"

I nod silently, thinking that it's probably best they don't see me this way.

"Tell them we are going on a little holiday," he continues. "Actually, I think it might be a good idea if we move away."

"Move where?" I ask. I need to buy some time because he really has lost the plot if he thinks I am going to move further away from my family.

"Any-Fucking-Where that's not near your cunt of a sister!" he barks making Liam cry again.

He opens my phone and calls my sister's number before handing it to me. I juggle my whimpering baby and hold the phone to my ear.

God knows what he is thinking, but maybe he assumes he will be able to hide me until I heal.

"Erh, hi." I'm unsure what to say with Mal breathing down my neck.

"I was just at your place Sis, where are you?"

Thinking on my feet, I improvise. "We um, took Liam for a walk."

My focus is on keeping her away from Mal because I'm confident that if she sees me like this, he won't hesitate to hurt her too.

"How are you feeling? Mum thinks she has whiplash."

I take me a while to figure out she is talking about the accident, so I miss a few beats before replying, "I'm OK."

Mal motions towards his watch signally 'wrap it up' with his hand, then mouths 'HOLIDAY' at me.

Even to my ears, my voice sounds strained, but I dutifully do what I am told. "Can you let Mum and Dad know that we're going to head out of town for a few days? To umm, visit Mal's parents."

"What about the cats Maddie?" she asks, sounding a little ticked off, I don't blame her.

"Please, Rose, can you feed them for a few more days? I promise I'll figure something out."

"Jeez Maddie, I can't keep this up forever."

"I'm sorry, eh. I gotta go, Liam is waking up," I lie, glancing down at my now sleeping baby.

"Well, have a good trip. I'd love to know a bit more about Mal's family, I'm sure Mum and Dad would love to meet them too."

"Thank you … for everything." I bite my lip to stifle a sob.

"What's family for?" she reassures me.

I drop the phone from my fingers feeling like a traitor. Maybe I've just missed my opportunity to ask for help, to get away from him. But his descriptions of how he will hurt my family are too fresh in my mind.

I can't let him take us to away, I have no idea what is going on in his head, but I must get Liam away from him. I just need to figure out how to do it, how to get away.

Planning how to escape occupies my every thought. My mind keeps returning to the workmen across the street, they are tortuously close, but I can't decide if it's worth taking the risk trying to get out of the house to ask for help. I mean, would they even help me? My indecision is trapping me. I'm a complete wreck, but I can't do anything that might put Liam in further danger. Besides, I have no idea how I'd even get out of the front door while Mal is watching me like a hawk.

Hours later, after the sun goes down, he tells me he needs to go out for a bit. I spend the entire time trying to decide if I should call my Dad.

I just want to get away from him, but I don't want to risk Dad getting hurt, I'm too scared to try calling him. My phone mocks me from the floor beneath my feet. I am incapable of using it to call for help.

He's not gone long anyhow, barely fifteen minutes. Not long enough for me to grab enough supplies to escape. Has he to go back to work on Monday, right? If I can just last until Monday, I can call my Dad to come to get me, and we can escape.

The next day I feel even worse. It's like my head is literally going to explode, and I can barely breathe without pain racking my entire body.

"Fuck you're a mess," he calmly observes. "I need to take a little trip into town. You're coming with me.

I'm what? I think. I can hardly believe my ears. "I can't go anywhere looking like this," I tell him.

"You're right." He gets up and goes to the lounge, a few moments later he returns, holding out a pair of sunglasses. "Here you go, problem solved."

Oh yeah, problem solved. Hide the bruises that'll work. They may hide my black eyes by they don't do much to conceal the imprints of his fists on my forehead.

I look at myself in the en suite mirror, I really am a mess. I drag my hair across my face, but I doubt it will do much to hide the rest of the visible damage he has done to my body.

I follow him out to the Truck, sinking down low in the passenger seat in the hope I only have to last until Monday. About half an hour later, we pull into the parking lot of a large warehouse.

Mal gets out and then moves to the back seat to remove Liam. He looks at me, obviously trying to figure out what to do with me.

"Get out and follow me," he decides.

I ease myself out of the car and follow behind him slowly, carefully keeping my face averted. "This is my son," he tells a fair-skinned bald man who is just a little taller than him.

The man he has come to talk to looks at me for a few minutes longer than necessary. I weigh the risk of saying something to him, he is broad across the shoulders and looks like he would hold his own against Mal, but I don't know how well they know each other, for all I know their friends. I don't know him, and I certainly don't know if I can trust him. I desperately wish I could plead for help, to say anything at all, but Mal is holding Liam, and I'm petrified something might happen to him.

I've not been on my feet for this long since he beat me yesterday. I'm exhausted, I must waiver slight because Mal glances in my direction and says, "Take the baby back to the truck."

He passes Liam back to me, and I do what I'm told. *'He's so sure I won't run'* I think as I belt us back in. The keys are still in the ignition, I have my cell phone in my hand and my baby in the back seat. I have all the reason in the world to slide across to the driver's seat and drive away from him or to pick up my cell phone and call for help.

But I can't. I am so terrified that I am too scared to take my freedom when it's so blatantly dangled in front of me.

He doesn't drive me straight home after he talks with the man from the warehouse. Instead, he takes a long maundering route stopping at a food bar.

"Do you want anything?" he asks.

"I'm not hungry," I tell him. I don't have to lie; any appetite I might have had has fled.

"OK," he says, rolling his eyes. "Suit yourself."

I watch as he strolls into the takeaway. Tears start to fall as I realise; he has once again left the keys in the ignition. I pull the sunglasses from my face to wipe them, it got dark a while ago, but I still slide them back on. I look up to see a young boy; around twelve year's old sitting in the car next to us, watching me.

I turn my head, *'Oh god, how can I let people see me like this?'* I must get away from him, because next time, and I am sure there will be a 'next time', he will probably end up killing me.

CHAPTER FORTY-SIX

I spend another night in fear, replaying my plan of escape in my head. I've not slept much at all, and I'm barely holding on. The only thing keeping me sane is holding on the hope he will be going back to work on Monday.

By the morning, I know I am in serious trouble. I clamber over the toilet, throwing up until I am purged, then I continue to dry heave until all I can taste is acid. I don't understand much about concussions, but surely I should start to be feeling better?

I emerge into the lounge to find Mal lying on the lounge floor with a map of New Zealand spread out in front of him.

"If we go down via Hamilton, we can go to Waitomo caves," he tells me. I guess he is still planning our 'holiday'.

"Don't you have to go back to work on Monday?" I ask hesitantly.

Without responding to me, he grabs his cell phone from the where it's perched next to the TV and punches in some numbers. "Hey Darren," he says to his boss.

My empty stomach constricts.

He looks at me while he listens to his boss. "Yeah, Nah the baby is all good. I'm just a bit worried about Maddie.

There's another pause then, "She's got to go for some more X-rays." Pause, still looking at me. "Ha-ha yeah ok, maybe another week?"

My heart sinks, he's not going anywhere. How am I ever going to get away from him?

"OK mate, talk to you next week." He turns to me with a self-satisfied grin. "Now we can focus on our trip,"

I say nothing to him and try to keep my breathing regular. If we are going to get away, it needs to be soon, before he drags Liam and me across the country.

I wonder how much Lorazepam it would take to knock him out, that's probably the strongest drug we have in the medicine cabinet. I don't want to be the one who ends up being arrested, though, so immediately dismiss that idea.

There is only one logical choice, but I'm too scared to do it. I don't want him to hurt my family, but I have to call my Dad. I just need to wait for the right opportunity.

I play heavily on being unable to get off the couch, and by 6 pm, it becomes apparent I am unable to make dinner for him.

"What do you feel like? I'll get takeout," he asks me, being uncharacteristically attentive.

I'm so relieved he's suggested it and I didn't have too. I try to think of something that would take some time to cook. That rules out fast food like *MacDonald's* or *Burger King*. "Umm, a kebab would be nice." Not only is that restaurant quite far away, but they are usually swamped on a Sunday night.

"Sounds good to me," he agrees before grabbing the truck keys and his wallet. "I won't be long. Then we can plan the rest of our holiday."

"Yeah," I reply.

I ease myself from the couch to watch him drive down the street, and when I'm sure he's gone I grab my cell phone to call my Dad, I don't think I just dial. I don't want to give myself a chance to guess this second, and I'm silently thankful that Mal recently topped my phone up.

"Dad," I say timidly as he picks up.

"What's up?" he says, immediately on alert.

"Can you come and get Liam and me please?"

"What has he done?" he demands.

"He hit me." The words I've swallowed for months fly out of my mouth. "Please come and get me." I swipe at the tears stinging my battered face.

"Hold on babe, we're coming," he promises me.

"Please hurry," I beg him. "He won't be gone for long."

Dad hangs up and I suddenly I am treading water in an ocean far too deep and wide for me. In a panic, I fly around the house like a woman possessed, grabbing a bag for Liam and trying to shove as many of his things into it as possible. I don't worry about my stuff, at this point, I am prepared to walk out on everything I brought with me from my past.

I slide Liam into his car seat and pull my two meagre bags to the driveway. Pacing up and down a few times, I realise my Dad should have gotten here by now.

Frantically I call him back. "Where are you?"

"Please try not to panic; we're at the police station."

"WHAT!" I shriek. "He's coming back! Don't you get it? He's going to kill me."

I can't hold back the tears as I weep. "You're supposed to come and get me."

I know with certainty that if Mal comes home and finds me standing here in the drive, there would be no holding back his anger. He won't stop until I'm dead. Liam wails from the front door, so I do my best to pull myself together. I hang up on Dad without saying goodbye and dial 111.

I shriek into the phone as the dispatcher picks up and asks what my emergency is. "PLEASE! You have to send someone right now."

"Can you tell me what your emergency is?" she asks with practised patience.

"My partner, he's beaten me, you have to come. I called Dad, but he went to the police station instead, and he's going to be back any moment now. Please hurry."

"Can you tell me about yourself? What's your name?"

"I'm Maddie."

"OK Maddie, it's going to be alright, I just need to ask a few more questions. Can you tell me where the emergency is?"

I struggle for a moment to recall our new address, "24 Belleview Ave, Birkdale, in eh Auckland. Please hurry, Mal will be home any minute."

"Is that your partner's name?" she asks, unaware how much of a loaded question that is.

"It is," I answer slowly. "He goes by Mal, eh Malcolm McPherson, but that's just a name he uses. His actual name is Dominic Neill."

"Stay on the line with me Maddie, OK? All units are on call outs at the moment, but they aren't far away. A unit will be dispatched as soon as they become available."

"You don't understand," I tell her. "If he gets back and sees me standing here with my baby, he will kill me!"

"Can you go to your neighbour's house and wait there?"

"How can I do that? I can't bring his anger there; I don't even know them."

It has already felt like an eternity since calling Dad, and now Liam starts to cry in earnest. I don't have the headspace to deal with that right now, so instead, I pace up and down the driveway expecting to see

Malcolm pull up at any moment.

I jump as I hear a car approaching, straining my eyes in the darkness, my relief at seeing a police car heading my way is immeasurable.

He pulls up alongside me, and I run to the driver's side as he slides the window down without getting out of the car. "What happened to you?" he asks me.

"My partner, he hit me."

That's all I manage to get out because less than a moment later Mal himself pulls up behind the Police car.

He gets out of the truck and takes a few steps towards me, freaking out I back away from him.

"That, that's him," I stammer as Mal starts to walk around the police car. I move to keep the vehicle between Mal and me, but as I do, I realise I am moving further away from Liam. I'm torn between the complete terror at having to confront Mal and my maternal instincts.

"Are you alright?" Mal asks.

"I'm sorry," I sob. "I had too, I was so scared Mal, I'm so scared, I'm sick. I need to see a doctor."

"Where is Liam?" he asks me, looking around.

I try not to panic as I glance to the open front door, thankfully he's quietened down. "He's safe."

"Can I hold you?" he asks me.

I'm incredulous; did he really just ask me that? I look towards the policeman who has now gotten out of the car and placed himself between us.

"NO! Don't you come anywhere near me!" I shout, backing away from him. "I'm scared!" I tell the policeman, and I am. I take a few more steps back because I know in my heart that if he can reach me, he'll snap my neck and let the cards fall where they may.

He looks me with sad eyes, moisture glistening on his own cheeks, useless tears that now belong to him. "It's ok, Maddie, I understand."

"Come on," the policeman says to me. "I'll walk you inside." He looks at Mal, "You stay there."

I feel too relieved even to consider that Mal might run, I don't care, I just want my parents to get here and take me home.

"Will you be OK in here by yourself for a bit?" he asks me.

I glance down at my baby and then in the direction of the front door to see where Mal is standing in the darkness.

"I'll be fine," I assure him as exhaustion drags me to the floor. I release Liam from his car seat, and he lets out a shout of protest as I wake him.

I clutch him to my breast feeling somewhat numb. I don't think I really understand the full magnitude of what has just happened. Liam starts to fuss, so I rock back and forth, a motion that settles both of us, so I don't bother stopping once he stops crying.

"Hi, Maddie?" says a lady who enters the lounge.

I look up at her, confused. She's tall, with soft brown hair, wearing dress pants and a smart white shirt which is covered with a blazer. I'm taken aback when I notice a gun at her hip.

"Hi," I say meekly, worried about the sudden presence of firearms.

"I'm Detective Taylor," she says as she glances over her shoulder, "and this is Detective Smithson."

"Is it ok if we ask you a few questions about what happened?" Taylor asks as she motions towards my bruised face.

"We also need your permission to search the premises?" adds Smithson.

"That's OK, but why?" I ask, confused.

"We want to search for weapons," Smithson replies.

"Oh, OK. Sure." I respond like that's totally normal.

Smithson is about 7-foot-tall with a buzz cut and has a gun worn on his hip. I swallow back bile and continue to rock. I feel like this all moving too fast.

Smithson drags the other couch closer, arranging the pillows so they can sit down. They are both still wearing their boots, and for a crazy minute, I consider telling them they must take them off, but then I remember the guns and keep my mouth shut. I'm not sure why I even care about the shoes, but as they start to ask me questions, all I can think about it is everyone coming in wearing boots.

Because it is everyone, there is an army of police officers entering my house, swarming over everything. They must shake their heads in despair when they get to the garage. Mal hoards so much stuff he's just resorted to dumping it into barrels. Anything could be in those tubs.

I am still sitting on the couch, answering questions for the detectives when my parents arrive. Mum's eyes fill with tears when she sees me. The devastation about what has happened to me written clearly on both their faces.

"Oh, baby girl," says Dad as he crosses the room towards us. "I should have done more. I should have done more to save you from this."

To see both my parents look so helpless breaks the last shred of strength I have left. I start to cry, and I can't stop.

Mum sits on the couch next to me, wrapping her arms around both

Liam and me, tears steadily streaming down her face too.

"I'm going to kill that bastard," she spits venomously, shocking me as Mum never swears.

"He walked right past us!" Dad exclaims. "That bloody bastard walked right past us, acting like he didn't have a care in the world."

"It's not your fault," I tell them both, trying to protect them from the pain I know they must be feeling. They'd managed to keep us safe our entire lives, only to have something like this happen once we ventured out on our own.

Detective Taylor notices me stifling a yawn. "We can finish this in the next day or two; we've called an ambulance to take you to the hospital, its outside."

With all the flashing lights from the police cars, it was easy to miss the Ambulance that has pulled up too.

Two paramedics enter the lounge, and it doesn't take long for Liam, me and Mum to be driven back to the same hospital my baby was delivered in.

CHAPTER FORTY-SEVEN

The following days are a pendulum between sadness and elation. I feel like a great weight has been lifted off my chest, and I can finally breathe again, but I also feel an incredible melancholy. I can barely handle everyone being so patient and attentive like I'm some sort of fragile object that might shatter if they prod me too much. I suppose they may have a point because I feel that way also like I'm shattered glass held precariously together and the gentlest shake may disintegrate me.

I've taken to doing a lot of sitting on the single bed in my new room at my parents' house. Dad has already assembled the cot they have brought, and Liam is safely napping inside, peacefully unaware of how much our lives have changed course.

I grab my Mother's digital camera from where it sits on top of the chest of draws and snap a photo of him. Looking at my son calms me, centres me, and helps me remain focused on why I am doing this.

My thoughts are still very much all over the place, but Aunt Jo will be here soon and then along with Mum we are to make our way to the police station so I can make my formal statement. Mal is still being held in the cells there, and I'm not sure how I feel about being that close to him again.

I thought he was going to kill me, I very much thought after the beating he gave me I was going to die. The headache that I still have reminds me of the ferocity of his attack, and that if he pulled any of his punches, it wasn't because he cared if I lived or died.

His hateful words ricochet around in my head, he blinded me with his words so that I could no longer tell up from down. I know this with certainty, so why do I feel so conflicted?

I am equal measures of relief and confusion; I feel like one giant contradiction. I have to keep repeating to myself that he belongs there; he belongs in a jail cell. That he tried to crush my body and my soul and that he never stopped to consider Liam's safety at all.

Shaking my head, I rub my temples, trying to release some of the tension that is building up. If he belongs in prison, then why do I feel so wretched? I know I had to do it, leave him and end us, but why is leaving him so hard?

I am still sitting in the same position when I'm startled by a gentle knock on the door. "Can I come in?" I hear Aunt Jo say.

Getting up, I silently open the door to witness the horror that overcomes her the moment she lays eyes on me.

"Day three," I shrug. "The police told me that the bruises would start to pop."

Jo's eyes start to water, and I succumb to the urge to comfort her. "Well, the swelling is starting to go down; it's really not that bad."

She shakes her head at me. "Maddie my love, it is that bad. What he did to you …" She exhales loudly and shakes her head more firmly. "What he did was wrong, more than wrong. And you should *never ever* make excuses for his behaviour."

She pulls me towards her and embraces me, smoothing my hair. "Your Uncle Geoff has taken the day off work so He and your Dad can get a head start on packing up at your place. It's all going to be OK, Maddie; we've got your back."

Her words give me comfort and lend me strength. I give her a half-smile and scoop Liam from his slumber. He whimpers in protest but snuggled against my breast he soon settles.

"Come on, little man," I whisper. "Let's go do this thing."

CHAPTER FORTY-EIGHT

Aunt Jo sits in the waiting room with Liam, while Mum and I head into a small windowless room for me to give my report. The police officers are compassionate and help me sort through my statement step by step.

I rack my brain to try and tell them as much as possible, at times I see them looking at each other, probably deciding what else they can charge him with. They seem particularly interested in whether he held me captive at any point. I'm not sure I'm not sure about a lot of things. How can I say he kept me captive when he left me alone so many times? How can I call it rape, if I never said no? A huge part of me wonders how much I provoked him if I deserved the way he treated me.

Stupidly, despite everything he had done to me, I still love him, and I still miss him. But I've been missing him for a long time now, much longer than the few days it's been since I last saw him.

"Is he still here?" I finally ask the police officer interviewing me.

"Yes, he hasn't been transferred to Mt Eden yet."

"Bastard," Mum mutters under her breath.

"I still can't believe he just drove himself here," I say quietly. I was so sure that he'd go down 'guns blazing'.

"He's acting like a lot of men do in his situation. He still believes he can talk his self out of it."

"Lie his way out most likely." I agree.

After what feels like an eternity, I am ushered into another room where a photographer takes photos of the damage, he has done to me.

I have brought the hospital report listing the contusions, jaw dislocation, a nose fracture, and the photographer meticulously makes sure we have the images to support that.

I've already spent some hours staring at the imprint of his knuckles he left on my forehead and my blackened eyes. I'm not sure I'll ever forget the way I look right now, but I understand the need to have them taken.

I've swept along in a different kind of tide, one much gentler, but just as insistent. I am set up with a support lady from Women's Refuge and a person from Victim Support.

I've seen a Lawyer who makes sure we have an interim protection order and parenting order. I must wait for them both to be made permanent, but it's just a matter of time. It's just a flimsy piece of paper, but it does offer me a small measure of security for when he gets released. It looks likely he will be bailed back to his Mothers address. I briefly wonder what she will make of all this, somehow, I don't believe she will be shocked.

The police can't tell me why they turned up after his arrest with guns, but they indicate that there was reasonable cause for them to proceed with caution. The conversation I had with Mal about having been in prison before and his past being online remains in my head.

When we were still together, I spent a lot of time wondering what might have transpired, but without access to the internet, my amateur sleuthing was very limited.

I feel like it's imperative I find out what he went to prison for. I need to know not only for my own sanity but also our safety. It had to be bad if it meant he was willing to change his name to hide it. At least I know what his real name is, that's a good start.

It's been so long since I had the freedom to use the internet that a bubble of joy at this simple pleasure rises to the surface. I still can't get into my computer as Mal put a password on it, but Dad says he will have a friend look at it for me. Instead, I sit at my parent's computer, wondering how to go about finding out this information.

It takes a while and multiple combinations of google searches before I get a hit: Man found with stolen weapons. His name is emblazoned in the first paragraph, which leaves me with no doubt that it's him. I skim the article until I arrive at the last paragraph; the Judge is concerned there was something sinister to be read into his behaviour and ordered him to undertake a psychiatric assessment. Fuck. Maybe everything he told me about killing people was true? I don't know what to believe anymore. I back away from the computer like it to has attacked me.

He had broken into a weapons storage facility and stolen rifles and ammunition. They found that along with substantial army gear at his house. My family and I aren't sure what to do with this information, so I save a copy to give to my Lawyer.

I am surer than ever that I won't go back to him. I've already been told the statistics that it takes on average seven times for women to leave their abuser. I count on my hands at least that many times and more that I desperately longed to leave him.

I have always been resilient, but although I am determined to be a success story, extreme anxiety plagues me. I compulsively check and recheck that doors and windows are closed and locked. I don't take anyone's word for gospel that it's already been done. Jack, who has spent a lot more time at home now we are living here, he follows me dutifully, keeping me company and letting me know that it's ok to feel like this. It's reassuring because I can't stop swallowing and making a clicking noise in the back of my throat.

I'm referred to a counsellor; she tells me I am suffering from post-traumatic stress disorder. I feel like I'll never get away from him, I've left him, but the abuse he subjected me to will follow me for the rest of my life.

The phone rings during dinner one week later and my sister answers. "Maddie, it's for you," she says worriedly, passing it to me.

"Hello?" I answer timidly, wondering who on earth could be calling me at my parent's house.

"Hello, is this Madeline?" asks a voice I am unfamiliar with.

"Yes, who is this?" Every single pair of eyes in my house is staring at me. Dad inches closer to where I am standing, gingerly holding the phone.

"I'm a pastor Mt Eden Corrections Facility, and I am calling on behalf of Malcolm."

"What?" I almost yell at him *what the fuck is happening*.

"He asked me to contact you and tell you how sorry he is. That he didn't mean to hurt you and that he loves you and Liam. He asks for your forgiveness."

"He loves me?" I scoff. "Did he love me as he forced me to have sex with him? Did he love me as he punched me in the head over and over until my blood was all over the walls, and on our son? Did he love me as he fractured my nose? Did he love me as dislocated my jaw? I think not! I don't think he knows the meaning of that word. Why the hell are you even calling me? I have a protection order; he's not supposed to contact me at all. You tell him to go to hell!"

I've become hysterical; I know that, but it doesn't mean I can stop myself from shouting at this man who claims to be a Chaplin, and it doesn't mean I want to stop. It feels good to purge this, and I hope somehow Mal hears every single word. "I HATE HIM!" I scream as my Dad takes the phone from me.

Rosie puts her arms around me as I start to sob uncontrollably, and I vaguely hear my Dad telling whoever that man was exactly what will happen to him if Malcolm ever tries to contact me again.

"I hate him; I hate him so much, so why do I love him?" I cry to my family.

Mum puts her arms around me, my family closing rank to protect me. "You can't help who you love Madeline. It will fade in time, I promise."

I really hope she's right; it would be easier just to hate him.

CHAPTER FORTY-NINE

Months pass and finally I hear from Julia, my lawyer that we have a date for the Deposition.

I'm livid that he's still maintaining that he's 'not guilty'. I'm not sure how he thinks he is going to prove that he didn't beat the shit out of me or abuse me for the last year and a half, but he's undoubtedly arrogant enough to try it.

Danielle, my support person from Women's refuge, tells me that this is a tactic a lot of abusive men use. They hope if they drag it out long enough the victim will change her mind and no longer want to testify against them. The sad thing is this is precisely how it does work in many cases. The abused woman does change her mind and take her ex-partner back, and so the cycle continues.

The court system is really doing us a disservice when there is such a long time between the criminal act and the 'justice'. Not that I'm sure what sort of justice can be served here, I'm already broken.

I don't know how I am going to cope with going to court and seeing him again. I feel sick about it. I lay awake for hours at night running through everything I feel I need to say. I feel like this is just another way he is being allowed to abuse me because the deposition isn't going to be the end of it, this is just to prove to the court that he has a case to answer. I need to PROVE that he hurt me enough for us even to have it tried in a proper court.

I'm frustrated by everything, and on top of my grief that I had to give up on him, I also don't know what to do with my anger. Reading Malcolm's affidavits have made me furious. How can he tell so many lies and get away with it? He is trying to say to the judge that the reason he lost his temper with me was that I was cheating on him with TWO OTHER MEN! I have no idea how he assumes I fitted this in a while dealing with his mania and a newborn baby. That's just the tip of the ice burg with all the fabrications he has created.

I even had the police call me a few weeks ago to question me about the things I had been selling. He was accusing me of stealing his belongings when he knows full well that Dad managed to contact his Mother while he was still in prison. She along with his sister came to pick all his stuff up; otherwise, my parents were going to have the Salvation Army pick it all up.

I was very careful to explain to the officer who called me that the only things I kept were items he purchased with money he had stolen from me. I had to recoup costs somewhere to pay off the loan for the truck. There was no way the sale of it was going to cover all the debt he had left me with.

The police officer lets me know that it wasn't a criminal issue, and Mal would have to take me to civil court. He's made plenty of reference to me stealing his stuff in his affidavits, but I've not heard anything else about it, so perhaps he realised he was fighting a losing battle on that one.

Before I've had a chance to prepare for seeing him again, I am ensconced in a tiny room with my parents, Danielle, and Julia.

"It's going to be OK, Maddie," Dad reassures me. "We're going to be right there with you."

I don't respond. I'm glad they're going to be here, but it doesn't stop the acid burning in my chest or prevent this feeling of suffocation.

"Let's go through this one last time before we go in Maddie. Stick to the facts and try not to talk too fast because the court reporter will be recording everything that's being said."

I nod, still unable to speak. I don't know how I am going to do this.

"It's time to go," Julia tells me, way before I am ready. I inhale, fortifying myself for what's to come.

The courtroom already has a few people sitting in the gallery. Detective Taylor and Smithson are seated in the front row, and both stands to greet us as we take our places.

I hold my breath long enough to feel faint as Malcolm walks in with his own Lawyer, a tall and intimidating man in his forties. I stare at him, I can't help it, but he looks resolutely away from us. If he feels any guilt for what he's done to me, he's not showing it.

He's wearing clothing I don't recognise dark jeans and a grey turtleneck jumper. I notice that his hair has grown out in the months since I last saw him, and grey is now peppering his jet-black hair, making him appear much older than I remember.

Nervously I start to spin the ring I am now wearing my right hand as the summary of facts is read and we are both sworn to in 'tell the truth'. I have done a bit of research on how the court system works, so I know enough to believe that I am being tested by the defence.

I've been prepared to expect many intrusive questions that will make me out to be the party responsible. It makes me so mad that I can be put in this position after everything I have been through already, but I know I am strong enough to survive this. This might be the only trial I get, so I intend on having my say.

Mal's lawyer does not disappoint my expectations and cross-examines every word I say. I monitor them both closely, so I see Mal lean across to mention some other factious event he's conjured up.

"No," I repeat again. "I was not cheating on him. No, there were no other men. No, I did not provoke him."

I'm told over and over to slow down, which is hard because I am desperate for everyone to hear my side of what happened. I feel like the defence is trying to make out that I am just bitter, but this isn't about him being punished. I just want him to take ownership of what he did to me. He's a serial abuser; I can't take a back seat and pretend it didn't happen. I must at least try to prevent this from happening to someone else. This is what keeps me in the courtroom, keeps me talking instead of sobbing and running out of here and away from him.

Eventually, they are finished with my testimony, and I'm told that I can either stay to hear his or go home. I'm still breastfeeding Liam, so an entire morning without my baby means my breasts feel like they might explode. I'm emotionally drained anyhow, so it doesn't take much urging from my parents for me to agree to leave. There's nothing he can say that will make a difference to me anyhow. I've read his court documents, so I know most of it will be fictitious.

CHAPTER FIFTY

Four months later and I am preparing myself to see him again. I've worked hard on my testimony with Julia, but I can't shake the nagging feeling that I'm going to vomit. The thought of having to see him again tears at my insides.

As I countdown to the final days, Julia calls to let me know that Mal entered a plea of no contest.

"What does that mean?" I ask her, confused.

"It means you won't have to go back to court Maddie. That he will be sentenced, and you can move on with your life."

"I don't understand; why did he wait until the last minute to change his mind?"

"The court sees a lot of cases like yours. They try to drag it out as long as possible in the hope that victim changes their mind. It's just a strategy."

"It's stupid." I spit, I'm angry. "How can the court let this happen? I've agonised for months over this, and now it's not going to happen. Please don't tell me that the judge will go easy on him because he changed his plea."

"I'm sorry Maddie I can't say for sure, but maybe. I'll let you know when they set a date for sentencing. In the meantime, you might like to think about if you want to say something then or submit a written statement to be read by the judge."

I hang my head and rub the space between my eyes. I have a headache coming on. "Thanks, Julia, I'll write something."

In the months since we separated, I've done a lot of soul-searching, but I still feel like what happened was my fault, that somehow, I caused him to hate me. I feel like I deserved that treatment after all the mistakes I've made, but then I look at Liam and remember why I am doing this. At nine months old, he is truly the light of my life. When he giggles delightedly and wraps his chubby baby arms around me, I'm reminded that he deserves every single good thing to happen to him. He needs a Mother with the ability to provide him with it.

Liam is the promise to fulfil every ounce of potential Mal ever had, and because he won't be saddled with a legacy of violence and abuse, despite not having a father in his life, he will grow up happy and secure. I'm going to make sure of it.

I sit down at my computer, jiggling the mouse to wake up the screen. I stare at the blinking cursor for a bit trying to think what I need to tell the Judge sentencing Mal. I know I need to write something because I'm not sure I will be able to verbalise how I feel on the day.

I know how to start, and that's to stop calling him by his own chosen name and label him with the name he tainted with his own bad decisions. It takes a while, but eventually, it starts to flow:

There just aren't enough words to express how hurt and humiliated my association with Dominic Neill, the man I knew as Malcolm McPherson has left me, not only physically but also emotionally. It's not spite that compels me to write this, but a genuine concern for the public and any other vulnerable women Dominic may prey on in the future.

He is a serial abuser and in desperate need of professional help. I believe that without intervention, he will continue this cycle of abuse with a new victim. He needs to be held accountable for what he has done to me, but more importantly, he needs to learn how wrong he has behaved.

From my association with Dominic, I find it unlikely that he feels remorse. I am sure he feels like he is the victim and that he was completely justified in hurting me all those times, but no one has the right to physically and psychologically abuse another person.

My dreams are now plagued with terrors, I often wake and fearful, in pools of sweat. I constantly imagine his face at the window, I have to check and recheck, making sure curtains and latches are closed tight.

I find it hard to believe he has just walked away, and I live in constant fear of him coming to find me.

I startle at every thud and bump; all the usual noises of a home terrify me. I cower in fear if someone gets too close to me or makes a sudden movement. I can't help it, and I am told that this is a symptom of Post-

Traumatic Stress Disorder. PTSD has taken over my life, and even working with a counsellor is difficult for me.

All I did was try to love the man I thought he was, that I believed he wanted to be, my only mistake was placing my trust in him. I understand that Dominic had a terrible childhood, but he is now 29 years old, and its way past time he started taking responsibility for his own actions. He blames everyone else but never points the finger at himself.

My life has been impacted forever; I have a son with this man. I can't just walk away and pretend this didn't happen to me. Please treat Dominic like an unexploded bomb, because it's only a matter of time before he is set off again.

I knew that it was only a matter of time before he would hit Liam, our son. I am relieved that my baby will not remember what happened. Liam was laying right next to me on the bed when he punched me repeatedly in the head and body. Liam was barely four months old at the time, in his frenzy, he might have missed me and hit him. This could have easily resulted in both of our deaths.

I feel I am an intelligent woman, but I don't understand how this could have happened to me, but I will recover. I refuse to continue to be a victim. However, this does not lessen the impact of what Dominic has done to me, or how much this will impact my son in the future, and in fact, my entire family.

I fear that if he is not stopped now, this will happen a fourth time, and the next time she may not survive to tell a court what he made her live through.

I feel like he pushed the court case out for as long as he could in the hopes, I would change my mind, and that he only plead guilty to get leniency on his sentence.

I know that there are no guarantees in life, but I am hopeful that there is some way of putting Dominic on the path to rehabilitation. I am entrusting the law and the judge to make the best decision on how he is best held accountable, not just for my own broken heart, but for my son who will never know his father.

. . . .

It's almost Christmas, and the change in my life is profound. I feel stronger than I have in a long time, so I know that I can go to the sentencing and hear what the Judge has to say to Dominic.

I arrange for Rosie and Tom to look after Liam, and I carefully plan what I'm going to wear. Mum and Dad refuse to go with me, even though I asked several times for their support. Instead, they tried to talk me out of going and told me no good would come of reliving it.

"I have to," I say, but I can tell they don't understand.

I think they just want to move on and pretend it never happened. They can't grasp how I carry this around with me every minute of every day. It's OK, though because I understand the need to write a different story for ourselves. I did it daily when I was still with him; it was the key to my survival.

I park my car quite a distance from the Courthouse and slowly make my way on foot. I know I am early enough that I can find a secluded spot to wait for his case to be heard and that hopefully, he won't spot me.

I had every intention of attending the sentencing. Of facing him down, but even from my spot hidden behind a pillar, I don't feel safe. Tears spring unbidden from my eyes as I run in a panic, surprising many people standing around. But I don't think he sees me, I hope he doesn't see me as I escape, and don't stop running until I fling myself into the driver's seat of my car.

My heart beats wildly in my chest, and I wonder if I'll ever face him without fear.

I don't know if it would have made a difference if I had been there, but after hearing the sentence, I don't feel like justice has been served, not that anything would ever be enough. I wonder what he will learn during his 150 hours' community service, or during his mandatory living without violence program, or what his probation officer will make of him over the next 12 months.

Sometimes I think about how long it will take him to find his next victim, or if he feels guilty for what he did to me. I wonder if he thinks of our son and regrets his choices. Mostly I just hope he stays away as I slowly rebuild my life. I don't know what my future holds, but I am looking forward to watching my baby grow, and I am hopeful that one day I can live without fear and learn to trust, maybe even fall in love again.

EPILOGUE

Someone once asked me how long it took me to get over what happened and in all honesty, I couldn't give them an answer. More than a decade has passed since this man reached into my life and did his best to destroy me, and although I have gotten much better at living with PTSD and can handle these memories without having an episode, there is still so much I carry with me.

Learning to trust again was a slow process, and I made many attempts before finally meeting the man I was to marry. Every day I recognise something in me that helps build on making better decisions for my future, I can't say I always get it right, but I am still trying.

Since having the courage to pick up the phone and call for help, so much has changed, and changed for the good, but I still carry so much with me. On the surface, I have a great life: a loving husband and three beautiful children. My husband opened his life, and heart to all of us, cats, and my dog, who finally moved back in with us, and my son, who he has made his own.

Our son, on the cusp of turning 14, has always known of 'another Daddy' he doesn't see. He was two when we moved in together and became a family. Our son has a good memory, he remembers living with my parents, remembers a time before his Dad was in his life. Sometimes I wonder and worry that what I lived through while I was pregnant with him, what happened to me while he lay beneath me, has had some lasting impact on him, some inherited trauma. In my irrational moments, I worry and blame myself for any harm that could have befallen him.

I carry it with me, and although there are longer spaces of time in which I don't think of it, it's still there. Some days I am still on the floor, under his fist. Some days getting up feels impossible. Resilient is a word I hear a lot from people who I share my story with, and I am. I was never meant for a life of abuse and violence, the home my children live in is happy and safe, and they wake up and go to bed feeling loved, best of all so do I.

In the wake of the me-too movement, I had plenty to say. I have been using social media to comment on intimate partner abuse every November for White Ribbon day. Silence does hide violence, and after being silenced so completely, I rally against any feeling that I am being oppressed.

I wasn't my abuser's first victim; I wasn't even his second. I was the third women he had emotionally, physically, financially, and psychologically abused. I was the third woman he had gotten pregnant; I was the third woman he had beaten, the third woman to have a life scarred by his treatment. Because anyone who suffers from PTSD will tell you, it doesn't just go away, you can't just therapy or medicate that out of you.

My abuser, the man who tried to tear me apart. The man who is the reason my son exists, he is still out there, still in the community, still playing out his cycle of abuse on other women, still fathering children.

He was arrested, charged, and sentenced for the last beating he gave me. I have a protection order that offers a measure of comfort to me, my son and my family. And he is gone.

You might think that this ended it, that maybe the court process had taught him something, I certainly hoped that it might have. But I was wrong. He moved on to another victim, creating and then destroying another family. This woman has found the courage to leave him, and not just that, but found the strength to reach out and ask me for help.

Maybe that is the part that's hardest to accept. I wasn't the first, and I'm not the last, and he's learned nothing. He continues as always play the victim, and the thing that scares me the most is that that he has convinced himself that his made-up version is the truth of what happened. His victims will always be to blame, and he will always be the injured party.

In a world where one in three women will experience domestic violence in her lifetime, my abuser is responsible for at least five, and the chances of him creating another victim seem predetermined by his past actions.

Something unexpected has come from this, though, other than my beautiful son who is truly a light in my life. This man who has caused me and others so much pain has also been the catalyst bringing three other women and me together, amazing, strong and inspiring women who are providing their children with loving stable homes that they would never have found with our common abuser. Linked by our children, I consider them my family now and stand beside them in solidarity.

To quote words I have heard many times, "Not All Men" commit domestic violence against women. However, just because this statement may be true, doesn't do anything to tackle the ever-presence violence in our communities. Not all men abuse woman, but with the same sentiment, most women who suffer from domestic violence do so at the hands of man. So, where does the buck stop? How do we find a solution? The sad truth is that this is as complicated as the reason's women do not leave their abusers.

I feel we can all be part of the solution; we can all be where the buck stops. With me, and you and everyone you know. So, I say 'no' I will not tolerate violence in any form. I will not tolerate emotional, financial or physical abuse to myself or for anyone around me. I will not remain silent; I will not condone it, and I certainly won't commit it.

We can't tolerate it in our homes, our extended families, our friends, or neighbours. The statistics tell us that one in three women will experience domestic violence at some point in their lifetime, which means all us must know a person who has been abused, and know person who is an abuser.

This violence and abuse often happens behind closed doors. She is too beaten down to speak up and ask for help, he obviously feels like he is untouchable. But it never happens in a vacuum. People notice, people hear things. So, I challenge you all too simply not tolerate it.

Do not tolerate it from your Fathers, sons, brothers, cousins, friends, neighbours, or the stranger in the street. And let those victims know you do not tolerate it. Tell those Mothers, daughters, sisters, cousins, friends, neighbours and strangers that you don't tolerate abuse and violence, and that each and every one of us has the right to live without fear of the person who is supposed to love us the best.

Love is not controlling and manipulative. Love does not hit you, or push you, or hurt you. Love lets you be angry with each other without fear of punishment. Love does not prevent you from spending your own money, or from forming friendships outside the relationship. Love lets you speak your mind, and keeps you warm at night. When tended love endures, and ensures that there will always be someone in your life who will have your back.

ABOUT THE AUTHOR

I lost Bessie to heart failure just before her 13th birthday. I miss her every day, she has left a space in my heart that can never be filled.

This book took me over a decade to write, then several more years before I felt able to share it with the public. Within these pages are a life time of experience, that in reality spanned two short years.

While writing this book I have kept myself busy, I got married, had twins, completed my undergrad in Design, and I am now teaching my passion to a new generation while completing my Master's Degree.

Some say everyone has at least one good book in them, if that is true, then this is mine. If you made it this far, thank you for reading my story. If I can help even one person understand domestic violence a little better, then I will feel like this book has fulfilled its purpose.

Thank you.

243